The Burial of the Urban Poor in Italy in the Late Roman Republic and Early Empire

Emma-Jayne Graham

BAR International Series 1565
2006

Published in 2016 by
BAR Publishing, Oxford

BAR International Series 1565

The Burial of the Urban Poor in Italy in the Late Roman Republic and Early Empire

ISBN 978 1 84171 995 5

BAR Publishing is the trading name of British Archaeological Reports (Oxford) Ltd.
British Archaeological Reports was first incorporated in 1974 to publish the BAR
Series, International and British. In 1992 Hadrian Books Ltd became part of the BAR
group. This volume was originally published by Archaeopress in conjunction with
British Archaeological Reports (Oxford) Ltd / Hadrian Books Ltd, the Series principal
publisher, in 2006. This present volume is published by BAR Publishing, 2016.

Printed in England

BAR
PUBLISHING

BAR titles are available from:

BAR Publishing
122 Banbury Rd, Oxford, OX2 7BP, UK
EMAIL   info@barpublishing.com
PHONE   +44 (0)1865 310431
FAX   +44 (0)1865 316916
www.barpublishing.com

CONTENTS

LIST OF FIGURES

LIST OF TABLES

PREFACE

The horror of the *puticuli*, and their traditional association with the poor, has often led to this socio-economic group being viewed as somehow 'different' to the rest of the ancient urban community; this is a theory that I find difficult to accept. Why should this part of the community care so little about the disposal of the dead when other members of society were devoting huge amounts of time and money to ensuring that the deceased received not only burial, but also lasting commemoration? The original thesis, on which this volume is based, emerged from a growing sense of unease at the way in which the urban poor of Rome seemed to be forgotten about, not only in discussions of burial practice, but also general societal trends. It stemmed from a wish to try to identify and re-humanise these often neglected people, as well as to use this information to more comprehensively assess the disposal practices of the ancient city dweller. Hopefully the text presented here goes some way to beginning this process. Much of the world of the ancient urban poor remains still to be explored, and this study does not claim to be comprehensive in any way, but I hope that it will re-insert the poor inhabitants of Rome into the consciousness of scholars of the ancient world and contribute towards the development of new and exciting dialogues that take account of the attitudes and activities all the varied members of ancient society.

* * * * *

This volume began as a doctoral thesis that was completed at the University of Sheffield in 2005. The original PhD could not have been conducted without the generous financial support of the University of Sheffield. A Petrie Watson research travel grant, awarded by the University of Sheffield, also made it possible for me to travel to Rome in order to conduct essential research and to visit several of the sites that are central to the project.

I could not have completed the original research without the assistance and support of several other individuals and institutions, although, of course, all errors remain my own.

Firstly, I wish to express my extreme gratitude to Maureen Carroll who acted as supervisor for the duration of the research and who provided a constant source of support, assistance, encouragement, inspiration and friendship. She also very kindly shared with me the manuscript of her new publication, spent a considerable amount of her own time translating German articles, and provided me with an excellent opportunity to spend quality time in Pompeii. Without her genuine interest in the project, unerring support, and extensive knowledge of

the subject as a whole, the research would not have gone as smoothly as it did. Thank you.

I also wish to thank my advisor Andrew Chamberlain who expressed great interest in the research and was always willing to read anything with which he was presented. His comments, particularly on the subject of mass graves and patterns of mass mortality, have greatly enhanced the text. I am also particularly grateful to Valerie Hope and Mike Parker-Pearson for their comments on the original text, and particularly the continued support and assistance that has been generously offered by Valerie. Thanks must also go to other members of staff in the Department of Archaeology at the University of Sheffield, including Peter Day, John Barrett, and Dawn Hadley. I would also like to thank John Drinkwater for expressing an interest in the research and for introducing me to one of his own research students working in a similar area. I very much appreciate his ongoing support. Thanks also to Kathryn Goldsack and Anne Callinswood in the Archaeology Department offices. I was at times heavily reliant on the Inter Library Loan system and I wish to thank the staff of the Main University Library for their assistance with this. Thanks must also be extended to Charlotte Tupman at the University of Southampton who kindly allowed me to read her MA Dissertation on the subject of the *columbaria*.

Thanks must of course also go to all those who have provided a continuous source of emotional and intellectual encouragement over the last few years. In particular, I wish to thank Nat Husk for agreeing to visit every ancient cemetery in Rome and wait whilst I took photos of every single tomb; Richard Queripel for assisting with French translations and biscuits; and Claire Richardson for appearing genuinely interested. I also wish to thank Cat Howarth, Sally Smith and Eileen Ko for many stimulating discussions, and especially for patiently explaining some of the more complex aspects of archaeological theory. The opinions and broad knowledge of all three have contributed greatly to the text. Thanks to you all.

The text was partly revised and re-written during a Fellowship at the British School at Rome, where I had the opportunity to explore many of the sites discussed in the text in greater detail. Thanks must go to Colonel Mike Montagu of the British Embassy in Rome who kindly invited me into his home and allowed me to explore the *columbarium* in the garden of the Embassy; to John Bodel for a stimulating seminar at the American Academy and for expressing an interest in my work; and to the staff of the Museo Nazionale Romano at the Baths of Diocletian. My thanks go especially to the staff of the

British School, particularly Valerie Scott, Beatrice Gelosa and the other library staff; Maria Pia Malvezzi, without whom I would not have been able to visit so many of the great hidden sites of Rome; Robert Coates-Stephens; Geraldine Wellington and, of course, Sue Russell for her constant encouragement and cups of English tea. Thanks must also go to my fellow residents for their insightful comments on various aspects of this and other research. This includes especially, Janet Huskinson, Angela Kalinowski, Ian Wood, Michele George, and Carlos Machado. Kate Litherland dragged herself away from the 20th century to explore the ancient world, Keith Roberts was amazed by everything, and Peter Keegan, who has a pun for every occasion, provided an enormous amount of support, knowledge and assistance.

Sue, thank you for everything.

Finally, I must express my extreme gratitude to my family who have been unwavering in their support during my time in Sheffield, Rome and afterwards. I can not thank you all enough.

INTRODUCTION

THE HIDDEN VOICES OF THE ANCIENT COMMUNITY

Mass graves and the poor: introducing the problem

Towards the end of the nineteenth century, the eminent Italian archaeologist Rodolfo Lanciani uncovered a series of vast pits on the Esquiline at Rome. Describing the contents of each as "reduced to a uniform mass of black, viscid, pestilent, unctuous matter," and composed of "men, beasts, bodies and carcasses" (Lanciani, 1891: 64), he proposed that they represented the last resting place of the urban poor of ancient Rome. Varro's reference, in *De Lingua Latina* (V.25), to "burial pits" outside Roman towns that were known as *puticuli*, provided Lanciani with a name and an explanation for his discoveries and he went on to suggest that these features were used by the lower classes on a regular basis for the unceremonious dumping of corpses; a process that continued until the area was eventually buried beneath the *Horti Maecenati* during the Augustan period (Lanciani, 1891: 64 – 65; see also Lanciani 1874, 1892 and 1897).

Lanciani's conclusions concerning his remarkable discoveries were undoubtedly instinctive for an archaeologist working in the nineteenth century when similar features could be found in the urban cemeteries of large cities. Disposal of the dead represented a considerable problem for the increasingly overcrowded and dirty cities of the early modern world, with a lack of adequate hygiene and squalid living conditions producing large numbers of corpses each month.[1] Cemeteries of the age were frequently unable to cope with the demand, and recently buried corpses were often disinterred after only a few months in order to provide space for new burials. As we shall see below, the solution to these demands often lay in the creation of mass graves, and contemporary sources speak of large pits left open to the sky and packed with layers of corpses "piled like bacon" (Aries, 1981: 56-57) in the major urban centres of England, France and Germany. No doubt Rome faced similar difficulties as it underwent a radical urban expansion during the eighteenth and nineteenth centuries. During this period, society was also greatly concerned with ensuring that individuals received a decent Christian burial, and clubs or associations consequently emerged in order to allow individuals with limited financial resources to save money for their eventual burial (Harrison, 1990: 136). The very poor, according to Cannon (1989: 438), often lived in more extreme conditions than necessary in order

to make sure that they could eventually afford the inevitable funeral expenses related to a decent burial. Furthermore, and again with remarkable similarity to the ancient city, burial was not always enough, and funerals of the period were often elaborate affairs (for examples in Hamburg see Whaley, 1981: 91) and lasting commemoration with a suitable monument was highly desirable. Those who could not afford such burial may have often found their way into the communal pauper's graves of urban cemeteries, but, as we have already seen, this does not mean that they remained immune to the pressures and demands posed by the death of a family member – they were eager to provide a decent burial, as far as their economic position would allow. It is unsurprising, given the parallels that can be drawn between the funerary and disposal practices of the nineteenth century and those of ancient Rome, that Lanciani interpreted the Esquiline pits as mass graves for the ancient poor.

The validity of these conclusions, however, has very rarely been called into question since Lanciani first published his findings, and the *puticuli* continue to be interpreted simply as communal graves in which the corpses of the urban poor were left to rot (see for example Jongman, 2003: 107). Consequently, the funerary practices of the urban poor are frequently disregarded in discussions of Roman burial activities. Sweeping statements are made about the corpses of the lower classes finding their way into the anonymous pits of the Esquiline[2] and the attitudes and activities of this section of ancient society are, as a result, often considered to have been very different from those of other members of the community who were interred within or beneath large elaborate tombs or monuments. Amongst the lower classes particularly, functional or practical considerations are often perceived to have overridden those of a more ideological or social nature. It was a sense of dissatisfaction with these opinions that led to the study which follows. Are we really to believe that the poor, despite living in the same society and being subjected to the same religious and social forces, believed radically different things to the wealthy? The majority (although not all) of modern studies of ancient Roman burial practice tend to focus on wealthier members of society and the architecture of the elaborate tombs, funerary processions and inscriptions that they produced (for example, Bodel, 1999; Eck, 2001; Flower, 1996;

---

[1] Indeed, Lord Amulree (1973) in *Medical History* has directly compared the unhygienic conditions of ancient Rome with those of 'modern' London

[2] See Chapter 4 for a fuller discussion of these statements and related assumptions.

Koortbojian, 1996; Walker, 1985; and, although very comprehensive in its coverage of the subject, Toynbee, 1971). Much attention has also been paid to the burial activities of the freedman classes, and the attempts of these former slaves to negotiate for themselves a superior or legitimate social position through the manipulation of the material culture of funerals (for example, Hope, 1998; Saller and Shaw, 1984; Woolf, 1996). These approaches and investigations are all perfectly valid and absolutely essential to understanding Roman funerary practices and their role and significance to wider social processes. However, if we wish to comprehensively understand ancient funerary customs, it is also necessary to examine the activities of those who did not leave evidence for their existence in the form of permanent funerary monuments.

It is, of course, relatively unsurprising that the funerary practices of the lower classes of Rome have received little attention from modern scholars given the paucity of evidence for their burial activities. Oliver (2000: 11) has observed that "burial of some sort may have been expected for all people, but the quality and nature of burial was almost certainly affected by wealth and status " This observation is particularly pertinent to this study - large elaborate mausolea such as those of Augustus and Hadrian or the great pyramid built for the remains of Gaius Cestius outside the Porta Ostiensis at Rome, evidently lay far beyond the economic resources of the majority of the urban population. The *physical* manifestations of burial practices certainly varied in accordance with wealth and status, but did vast differences also exist between the attitudes of the rich and poor towards these activities and their related social processes? How valid is it to assume that simply because an individual could not afford to celebrate or memorialise their life, or that of a loved one, with an elaborate structure, that they were unconcerned and unaffected by the forces that led people with access to the necessary resources to do just that? The appalling conditions of the *puticuli* and the grandeur of the pyramid of Cestius certainly seem to imply, at first glance, that those buried in each held radically different attitudes towards the disposal of their remains and the commemoration of their memory, but was socio-economic status influential enough to create different funerary practices, beliefs and attitudes or were the expressions of these simply different because of economic factors?

The *puticuli* are largely without parallel in the funerary sphere of the Roman world[3] and their unique presence at Rome has been interpreted as evidence for an absence of concern for the dead and 'traditional' Roman ideals of burial and the preservation of memory amongst a vast lower class population faced with unsanitary living, high rates of mortality and an absence of recognised social or political status, which led to an immunity to the pressures of a competitive society. The widespread absence of other substantial evidence for the burial practices of this socio-

economic group has also contributed towards the association of the *puticuli* with the poor, compounded further by a lack of any detailed study of the *puticuli* and their contents since their initial discovery in the 1870s and the unquestioning perpetuation of Lanciani's conclusions.

The 'other' communities of ancient Rome

In recent years scholars of both archaeology and ancient history have embarked upon a new attempt to give a voice to the lives (and, most often, deaths) of marginal, or invisible groups within the Roman urban community. The social and legal position, beliefs and activities of slaves, women, children, the elderly, and foreigners have all been focused on within recent dialogues on the ancient city, in an attempt to more comprehensively understand the varied perspectives that these can contribute to our knowledge of ancient urban living.[4] Much of this discourse has focused on the funerary behaviour (particularly the commemorative habits) of these underprivileged, marginalized or overlooked groups – perhaps largely a consequence of the scarcity of other substantial evidence for their activities. As Joshel (1992: 5-6) has observed: "while law and literature allow us to write a history of Roman society in the early empire, this is a narrative based on exclusion. For however much legal and literary texts describe social reality, they do not truly represent the nonprivileged groups who lived and worked in the city of Rome because, quite simply, these texts were not written by those they describe." We shall return to the specific issue of identifying the lower classes in the literature of antiquity and its significant impact on the way in which this socio-economic group was perceived (and often still is) in Chapter 3.

Although literature and legal texts may hamper attempts to reach these underprivileged groups, funerary practices and burial activities provide one route by which to trace these individuals and groups. Every member of society eventually died and their remains were disposed of in some way, sometimes leaving physical traces in the form of a tomb, grave marker, epitaph or grave, other times

---

[3] Except, perhaps, for mass graves which were dug on the battlefield which were, however, considered an essential measure rather than a decent means of burial.

[4] Much of this literature has focused initially on attempts to identify and comprehend the structure and relationships that made up the Roman family. These naturally include, or lead on to, discussions of the role of women, both within the confines of the family and their role in commemorative practice (in most cases their involvement in the creation of memorials to deceased members of their family), but also as independent social actors. Attitudes towards children also feature heavily within these discussions, again focused largely on how and by whom they were commemorated. See for example, Bradley 1991; Dixon 1992; Rawson 1992; Rawson and Weaver 1997, and individual articles by Dixon 2001; Flower 2002; George 2005; King 2000; Kleiner 1987; McWilliam 2001; Weaver 2001. Amongst others, Hasegawa (2005) has recently investigated the relationships between slaves interred within family *columbaria* at Rome. Finlay (1991) and Harlow and Laurence (2002) have thrown considerable light on the place of the elderly in the ancient community, again drawing heavily on funerary inscriptions as a profitable source; and Vlahogiannis (1998) has spotlighted attitudes towards disability and the disabled – another no doubt significant but difficult to trace, sector of society. Finally, Noy (2000a) has examined the place of foreigners within the urban community of Rome.

without. Critical examination of these sources of information have allowed insights, for example, into the relationships between the slaves and former slaves of a household (Hasegawa, 2005); attitudes towards the children of lower-class families (McWilliams, 2001); and the make-up of 'lower class' (in its broadest sense) families (Weaver, 2001). Death provided a chance for those without the opportunity to make permanent expressions about themselves during their day-to-day lives, to make statements about their personal relationships, about their beliefs (social, religious or even political), about their successes (both economic and familial), their identities, their lives, their loved ones.[5] This did not necessarily always take the form of a lasting public statement in the shape of a tomb or epitaph, indeed as we shall see, only a small percentage of the many hundreds of thousands of inhabitants of Republican and early Imperial Rome left explicit statements about their lives in this way. The provision of a decent burial and the observance of ongoing commemorative rituals could also give expression to these attitudes, beliefs and relationships. In order to find the lost voices of the urban poor (who should be included amongst the other groups listed above) we must therefore listen to the spaces between the large monumental tombs that crowded the urban cemeteries of Roman Italy, and explore new approaches that might allow us to understand their attitudes towards life, death, immortality and memory. This study belongs in the context of those already mentioned which strive to identify, understand, and give voice to the overlooked, and often difficult to find, members of the urban society of Rome. In this case it aims to investigate the beliefs and behaviour of what Dixon (2001: 7) has referred to as "those most mysterious ancient denizens, the free poor."

Studies of Roman burial and commemorative customs have long been closely associated with discussions of social structure, display, status negotiation and identity creation within urban communities. The place of the free lower classes within these process, their attitudes towards them and their role in shaping the environment of the urban cemetery in which many of these social negotiations took place, are frequently ignored within these dialogues. It is essential however, that this vast section of the urban community (for indeed, we are dealing here with the great majority of the urban population) be taken into account within these discussions in order to better understand ancient urban society. The aims of this study are therefore to re-examine the funerary activities of the urban lower classes, particularly in terms of the methods employed for the disposal of the body and subsequent commemorative activities, in order to increase our understanding of:

- the urban lower classes as a whole, including the way in which they should be defined, their place within wider society and the manner in which

they established, maintained and promoted their status and identity;
- society-wide attitudes towards burial and commemoration, but particularly the impact of common religious, legal, emotional and social demands, customs and norms, on the funerary activities of the lower classes;
- the attitudes and responses of this socio-economic group towards the proper religious disposal of the body in comparison with those of wealthier members of the community;
- the *puticuli* and their place within urban disposal practices and funerary activities.

Identifying the urban poor: slave or free?

Before embarking on a study of the burial practices of the urban poor, it is essential to first establish exactly which members of the community this definition encompasses. Chapter 3 addresses more comprehensively the issue of providing a useful definition of 'the poor', but here it is necessary to make a key distinction between different groups that comprised the lower classes of Rome and to identify some of the problems that can arise if this is not established. The main problem that must be addressed is that most definitions of the Roman 'lower classes' tend to group freeborn, freedmen and freedwomen and slaves into a single category, making little, if any, differentiation between them when discussing the impact of particular social issues and pressures on this section of the community (for example, Rawson, 1966: 71). As will become evident, this rather wide definition is largely rooted in ancient attitudes towards poverty whereby slaves and free individuals, seen to be working alongside one another, were considered equally contemptuous. This has, however, created a false sense of homogeneity which is particularly unhelpful for an in-depth examination of the burial practices of the urban poor that aims to provide an insight into the activities of a specific group of people and the forces that influenced them.

It is actually not difficult to make a theoretical distinction between free individuals and slaves, both in social and economic terms. Each group held a distinctly different legal position and role within society, in addition to experiencing different economic conditions and pressures. This is a particularly significant distinction to make in the context of this study given the well-established influence of both of these factors on burial and commemorative behaviour (see Oliver, quoted above). Social status and identity - the ways in which individuals were viewed by themselves and others - undoubtedly influenced attitudes towards funerary activities, particularly when it came to issues of identity display or negotiation for status or social recognition. A slave's identity would have been formulated on the basis of very different elements to that of a freeborn, or even to an extent, a freed individual.

---

[5] See Chapter 1 for a fuller discussion of the role commemoration played in the life of the urban community at Rome.

Slaves and free individuals were also distinguishable in economic terms. For members of the free poor survival depended upon securing employment and thus an income to support themselves and their families. As will be demonstrated below, regular employment was vital for the free members of the community, but expenditure often outstripped income and prevented these individuals or families from saving money for inevitable funerary expenses. Slaves, on the other hand, were largely free of these concerns (although they were, obviously, subjected to many other demands, pressures, fears and limitations). The payment of rent, purchase of food and the unreliability of temporary employment had little effect on the economic position of a slave and it has been pointed out (Jones, 1968 4) that slaves were often fed and clothed by their owner. For slaves there were greater opportunities for putting money aside for the future, with Hopkins (1978: 126) noting that "there is evidence that masters paid some of their slaves a regular monthly wage. Slaves could save out of their earnings." This money may have been used for securing manumission in later years but if the slave died before this occurred his *peculium* could be used to cover funerary expenses. Moreover, the slave may have had the opportunity to join a domestic burial club, a *collegium domesticum*, and if they then died during service the disposal of their remains became the responsibility of their master or fellow slaves. Hasegawa (2005: 85) has recently speculated that the *familia* may have been obliged (one may guess on moral and practical grounds) to provide burial for a slave who died without family or savings.

The slave therefore had potential access to a stable support network which would ensure that, under normal circumstances, they received some form of burial. From the first century AD especially, slaves were increasingly provided with burial space within the family mausolea of their owners and consequently received not only decent burial but also continued commemorative activities essential for providing peace in the afterlife (see Heinzelmann, 2001). Similarly, once they had received their freedom, many former slaves retained close ties with their former masters, and no doubt the relationships formed with their fellow slaves also remained important to them. The result of the former may have been the award of burial space within the family tomb, as attested by the common inclusion of the formula *libertis libertabusque posterisque eorum* in tomb inscriptions.

It must be stressed, of course, that these opportunities were not necessarily available to all enslaved individuals, or indeed former slaves. We should not begin to imagine that every slave was treated so well. A great many slaves were probably disposed of as economically as possible, especially those belonging to smaller, perhaps less wealthy, households, and those which lacked access to domestic *collegia*. Nevertheless, it is fair to say that these opportunities did represent reality for more slaves than the free poor and, for the purposes of this study, it is essential to acknowledge these differences.

The support network outlined above, although certainly absent in some cases, was not available in any form for members of the free poor who depended entirely upon themselves, their family and their own unreliable income for everyday survival and, eventually, for burial and commemoration. For these individuals there was little prospect of being provided with a space in a family tomb. The economic position of the free poor was inherently more unstable than that of slaves, and, although their social and legal status may have been marginally elevated, the prospect of a decent burial was far less likely. The funerary activities and attitudes, customs and beliefs of these groups would therefore have been formed as a consequence of these differences and the varied demands they posed. As a result, they properly form two separate areas of study, each requiring detailed examination and investigation within their appropriate legal, social and economic context. This study focuses on the *free* members of the urban lower class population of Roman Italy: those who have been most often associated with the *puticuli*.

The 'free lower classes' also encompassed a large number of former slaves who had bought, won or been given their freedom. Although these freedmen and freedwomen often became very wealthy and commercially successful after their manumission,[6] this was not true in all cases and many, once they had joined the masses of the free community, faced the same socio-economic demands, pressures and fears as their freeborn counterparts. It is therefore very difficult to separate these less successful former slaves from the bulk of the free community without specific statements concerning their legal status – something that is often absent in the humble funerary material that does survive (see Chapter 5). Where suitable evidence does exist these groups can be separated in other ways; inscriptions provide biographical information, for example. But the key issue here is that these people were fundamentally affected by the same economic pressures as freeborn individuals once they had left the household of their master. The desire to display their new status as free individuals certainly effected the desire of these *liberti* to be commemorated, but in economic terms they were largely indistinguishable. Any definition of 'the poor' is, by its very nature, an economic rather than purely social definition, and therefore both free and freed have been included within the scope of this study. It is, of course, not possible to completely ignore the presence of slaves in the archaeological record, and many of the anonymous burials examined in Chapter 5 may belong to such people. Without epigraphic evidence it is almost impossible to distinguish between the anonymous graves of slaves and free individuals, but where possible attempts should be made to do so. They formed two separate socio-economic groups and consequently their funerary activities of each deserve to be studied in their proper context. Unfortunately, this is beyond the capacity of this study.

---

[6] As exemplified by the fictional character of Trimalchio in Petronius' *Satyricon*, but also witnessed on many tomb monuments from Rome, including the famous *panarium* tomb of the baker Eurysaces outside Porta Maggiore (see Chapter 1).

Investigating the burial of the urban poor in Italy

In order to understand both the *puticuli*, their role in urban disposal practices and the funerary activities of the urban poor it is essential to place any discussion within its appropriate and relevant context: in this case the wider place of burial and commemorative activities with Roman society as a whole. Chapters 1 and 2 therefore set out to examine these practices in detail, highlighting their social, legal and religious significance and the ways in which their physical manifestations were manipulated in order to satisfy particular social and religious demands made by both the living and the dead. It has been noted here that the 'lower classes' comprised individuals of differing socio-economic status, but in order to examine the responses of these individuals to demands for burial and remembrance, it is necessary to establish a less ambiguous definition of 'the poor'. Chapter 3 reviews ancient and modern attitudes towards the Roman poor and poverty and examines the economic resources of these individuals in order to propose a more precise definition of this significant sector of the population that is directly applicable to a discussion of funerary activities. On the basis of this definition, and in the context of Roman funerary activities as a whole, Chapter 4 critically re-examines the archaeological and textual evidence for the *puticuli* in order to gain a more detailed understanding of their function and involvement in urban disposal activities. Evidence for other modest burial activities within the ancient urban cemeteries of Italy forms the focus of Chapter 5, where a brief summary of the relevant archaeological evidence is presented and examined before some concluding remarks are made.

CHAPTER ONE

MEMORY AND COMMEMORATION

For neither the costly pyramids soaring to the skies,
nor the temple of Jove at Elis that mimics heaven,
nor the sumptuous magnificence of the tomb of Mausolus
are exempt from the ultimate decree of death.
Either fire or rain will steal away their glory,
or they will collapse under the weight of the silent years.
But the fame my genius has won shall not perish with
time: genius claims a glory that knows no death.

(Propertius, *Elegies* III. 2. 19 – 26)

Propertius believed that the written word guaranteed him eternal fame and recognition. Literary creations, he argued, were more robust than the most expensive and majestic monuments of the world. As a result, his name and achievements would live forever, and his future reputation could be compared to that of Homer: "I, too, will be praised by late generations of Rome: I myself predict that after I am ashes such a day will come" (*Elegies*, III. 1. 35 – 36). These sentiments are echoed by the *Odes* of Propertius' contemporary, Horace, who also suggested that poetry was more enduring than the grandest of monuments:

"I have finished a monument more lasting than bronze and loftier than the Pyramids' royal pile, one that no wasting rain, no furious north wind can destroy, or the countless chain of years and the ages' flight. I shall not altogether die, but a mighty part of me shall escape the death-goddess. On and on shall I grow, ever fresh with the glory of after time."

(Horace, *Odes* III. 10. 1 – 8)

Both writers believed that their names and achievements would be remembered for all time. To an extent, their belief in the longevity of their works has been borne out by the fact that, two thousand years later, these works are still widely read, whereas many of the built structures of the ancient world, both elaborate and simple, have long since succumbed to the ravages of time. However, despite their faith in the durability of their words it is unlikely that either man was buried without some form of material memorial to commemorate his existence. Several times Propertius refers directly to his gravestone, writing: "When, therefore, fate claims back from me my life, and I become a brief name on a tiny marble slab" (*Elegies* II. 1. 71 – 72) and:

Then, when the fire beneath has turned me into

ash, let a little jar receive my ghost, and above, over a tiny tomb, let a laurel be planted to cast its shade over the site of the burned-out pyre, and add a line or so to say 'Who now is buried here as gruesome dust, once was the slave of a single love.'

(*Elegies* II. 13. 31 – 36)

Although the poet emphasises the modest nature of his future tomb, the assumption is made in both these, and other, instances that he will eventually be commemorated with a permanent monument inscribed with an epitaph. Having compared his fame to that of Homer, Propertius states that "Not neglected shall be the grave where the tombstone marks my bones: so decrees the Lycian god, who approves my prayer" (*Elegies* III. 1. 37- 38), indicating that despite the immortality of his poetry, he would, in addition, have the extra insurance of a more conventional memorial.

The words of Propertius and Horace on the subject of everlasting fame and memorials to their existence and achievements reflect a wider desire within Roman society for recognition and remembrance. Monumental arches, building dedications and personal statues, to mention just a handful of the ways in which an individual could advertise their existence, indicate that it was considered particularly important for members of Roman society to assert, through images or the written word, their place and status within it. As Keppie (1991: 55) observes, "prominent local families had the most opportunity, reason and funds to ensure that their names received permanent commemoration. The visitor to an ancient town could quickly learn who the important families were." The sponsoring of games, building of fountains and aqueducts, public buildings or distributions of food or money by prominent members of the community acted to promote the social position of these individuals and were lent greater force when details of these generous acts were permanently recorded in inscribed form. These texts were placed in a public place as evidence of their generosity and to ensure that both their contemporaries and future generations remembered their good deeds and, consequently, the individuals themselves. This practice was frequently carried out by magistrates and other office-holders and is illustrated particularly well by a sundial in the temple-precinct of Apollo at Pompeii which bears the following inscription:

L(ucius) Sepunius (Luci) f(ilius) / Sandilianus / M(arcus) Herennius A(uli) f(ilius) / Epidiarus / duovir(i) i(ure) d(icundo) / d(e) s(ua) p(ecunia) f(aciundum) c(uraverunt).

'Lucius Sepunius Sandilianus, son of Lucius, (and) Marcus Herennius Epidianus, son of Aulus, joint magistrates with power to dispense justice, had (this) made at their own expense.'

(CIL X 802, cited in Keppie, 1991: 53).

Many other examples of such public displays of wealth, status and beneficence, can be found amongst the epigraphy of the Roman world, including that naming a former military tribune who, upon retirement and election to *duovir* of the colony of Luceria, built an amphitheatre "on his own private property with a boundary wall round it, in honour of the emperor Caesar Augustus and of the Colony" (*EJ* 236, cited in Keppie, 1991: 57). Such action not only enhanced his position within the contemporary community but also ensured that he and his family were remembered by future citizens who used the amphitheatre he had so generously provided.

The desire for self-promotion and display appears to have begun during the Republic, but gathered pace under the rule of the Emperors in response to social change and increased opportunities for social mobility. The ultimate example of personal advertisement, in terms of the accomplishments recorded and the widespread influence of the text, can be found in the *Res Gestae* of Augustus. Composed in order to record and celebrate his achievements in expanding Roman rule and culture, it was inscribed on huge bronze pillars raised outside his mausoleum in Rome and copies were cut on walls elsewhere in the Roman world, including the Temple of Roma and Augusta at Ankara (Brilliant, 1974: 86). Publicising his achievements in written form and then subsequently disseminating it to other areas of his Empire, allowed Augustus to ensure that they, and by implication he, would never be forgotten. These displays presented individuals at the apogee of their social status and therefore how they wished to be remembered for eternity (Elsner, 1998: 95). Pliny the Elder (*Nat. Hist.* 34. 17) regarded this practice as vulgar, but although his nephew quotes Frontinus' words arguing that artificial means of memory promotion were unnecessary if a man was truly great, he himself concedes that "In my opinion, every man who has acted a great and memorable part, deserves not only to be excused but extolled, if he

pursues that glorious immortality of fame he has merited and endeavours to perpetuate an everlasting remembrance of himself, even by an epitaph" (Pliny the Younger, *Ep.* 9. 19). The persistence of such activity further attests to its widespread popularity.

Displays of political success and civic generosity also often took the form of honorific statues. Flower (1996: 70-71) observes that statues celebrating great leaders increased in importance from the end of the fourth century BC, although "the right to erect a statue in a public place in the city was carefully controlled because of its political influence." Although the original purpose of erecting honorific statues was closely associated with political power and influence, she notes (*ibid.*: 71) that these statues also became "memorials serving the glory of that man's family rather than his personal political ambitions. As a result, Roman citizens were often reminded of ancestors by public buildings, statues, and monuments throughout the city." The impact of these displays was increased by their location in public places, which Elsner (1998: 44) describes as fluid and "dynamic space[s] where images had their greatest power in antiquity ... where an individual's self-identity met with the images, views and representations of others." Here images were capable of negotiating status and identity. As emperor, Augustus was able to take full advantage of the opportunities offered by the public spaces of the Roman world and his *Res Gestae* was disseminated to all areas of the Empire. Other members of society were unable to promote themselves so freely over such a wide geographical area but took advantage of the public spaces of their own towns and cities to advertise their achievements and heighten their status in the eyes of the community. Ordinary members of society were equally eager to ensure that their accomplishments were advertised to their fellow citizens during their lifetime, as well as to subsequent generations.

However, despite the number of public building dedications and individual statues that lined the colonnaded walkways of city forums, individuals who were commemorated in this way during their lifetime formed the minority. Most members of society never contributed to the construction of public amenities, due largely to lack of opportunity or financial means, and were thus unable to publicly promote their identity (Hope, 2001: 90). Often the only opportunity for these individuals to register their existence in the memories of their contemporaries and future generations came after their death.

Commemoration in the funerary sphere

Given the inherent diversity of the Roman world, it is unsurprising to find that its sepulchral monuments are equally varied, ranging from the simple to the complex, the large to the small, and the cheap to the expensive. In the context of the present study it is not possible to discuss this assortment of monument types in its entirety,

Figure 1. *Columbarium* of the Vigna Codini, Rome (photo: author)

but it is essential to briefly examine the most common forms of tomb and monument found at Rome (and surrounding urban areas) during the late Republic and early Imperial period in order to understand the ways in which urban commemorative practices operated.

The Etruscans and other early Italian peoples dug elaborate chamber tombs but such matters were apparently of relatively little concern to Romans until at least the mid-Republic.[7] However, excavation has revealed early cemeteries in the vicinity of the Forum Romanum and the Esquiline, with the latter providing the bulk of information concerning early burial at Rome. Included amongst this evidence are simple burials in tufa-lined trenches, a chamber tomb dated to the sixth century BC, fourth century trenches (*fossae*) protected by stone slabs, a single monolithic sarcophagus and twelve chamber tombs (Davies, 1977: 16). It was also in this area that the so-called *puticuli* were dug, possibly during the second and third centuries BC. Purcell (1987: 27) observes a shift, after the fourth century BC, away from modest and functional burial practices which simply

satisfied the need to ritually cover the remains of the deceased with at least a symbolic covering of earth (Cicero, *de Leg*. II. 22. 57; see Chapter 2 for a fuller discussion), and cites the tomb of the Scipiones on the Via Appia as the first of the true Roman monumental tombs, designed to attract the attention of passers-by and to glorify the memory and name of the family.[8] By the end of the second century BC it had started to become very common to erect large monuments that served both to commemorate the departed and protect their remains.

From the mid-Republic to the early Imperial period, a variety of established tomb forms developed. For example, the emergence of the *columbarium*, a partly or wholly subterranean 'dovecot' with rows of niches designed to hold cremation urns or chests, has been dated to this period. Well-preserved examples of such are found at Rome, including the three large 'Colombari di Vigna Codini' on the Via Appia, which housed the cremated remains of many hundred Julio-Claudian freedmen[9] (**Fig. 1**). Smaller *columbaria* are also found at Rome, including

---

[7] Davies (1977: 16) describes Rome as "a cultural backwater" even until the first century BC.

[8] For descriptions and discussion of the tomb of the Scipios see Mancioli (1997) and Spera and Mineo (2004).
[9] See Braun (1852) and Astolfi (1998).

Figure 2. *Columbarium* of Pomponius Hylas, Rome (photo: author)

the famous tomb of Pomponius Hylas, on the Via Latina (**Fig. 2**). This tomb, built in the early Imperial period was elaborately decorated with frescoes and provided a last resting place for several freedmen.[10] A variation on the large *columbaria* of Rome can be found in the cemeteries of Ostia where above-ground barrel-vaulted structures are found with a decorative frieze around their exterior (*ibid.*: 116). The Ostian cemeteries also include a type of tomb described as "a rectangular roofless enclosure, with plain reticulum walls some metres high and no entrance, ladders being the only possible means of access" (Toynbee, 1971: 115 – 116). The ashes of the dead were buried in urns sunk into the ground along the walls.

The so-called Street of the Tombs outside the Herculaneum Gate at Pompeii provides an almost unparalleled opportunity to examine the various types of monuments and tombs erected during the late-Republican and early Imperial period.[11] Toynbee (*ibid.*: 119 – 126) lists some of the common forms found along this street including simple unroofed enclosures, such as that of Titus Terentius Felix, an early Imperial aedile; a more elaborate sepulchral *triclinium* with painted walls built by the freedman Callistus for his patron Gnaeus Vibius Saturninus; and several other unroofed enclosures with individual burials marked by small stylised busts, known as *columellae*. In addition, the niche or *exedra* tomb,

consisting of a large monument with a niche containing a bench can be found in this cemetery, and Toynbee (*ibid.*: 123) describes a cylindrical drum to the east of the Villa of Diomedes within which a sepulchral chamber contained three niches. Finally, Toynbee (*ibid.*: 123 – 124) describes the "most homogenous group" of sepulchral monuments at Pompeii – the monumental altars. Surrounded by low enclosure walls, these were placed on a base of varying height, with the ashes of the deceased deposited in the earth below the monument. This very brief summary of some of the common Pompeian tomb types illustrates only a handful of sepulchral monuments but gives some idea of the range of types that were built. It is important to note that although many shared the same basic form each was then elaborated upon in accordance with the wishes of those involved in their creation, and that different types appear to have been in use contemporaneously.

The city of Rome has also produced evidence for tomb structures of this period, specifically late-Republican *cella*-type tombs such as those uncovered during the late nineteenth century along the Via Caelimontana. These simple structures were cut into the rising ground with facades constructed of tufa blocks and were covered by simple vaults. Significantly, the façades of two of the four structures bear relief portrait busts. Toynbee (*ibid.*: 118) has suggested that "in view of this evidence it would seem to be extremely probable that most of the numerous stone or marble late-republican portrait-busts worked in relief on square or horizontal slabs were originally set in the facades of tombs, similar to those of the group here

---

[10] For the tomb of Pomponius Hylas see, Ashby (1910) and Pavia (1996).
[11] See Kockel (1983) for a more comprehensive treatment of these structures.

Figure 3. Family portrait relief from the façade of a
Republican tomb. Villa Wolkonsky, Rome
(photo: author).

described" (**Figs. 3** and **4**). The large number of extant
portraits of this type suggests that this was a particularly
popular design during this period.[12]

Tombs came to play an increasingly important role in
Roman society during the late-Republic and consequently
became more elaborate. The simple stone-lined *fossa* of
earlier periods was no longer relevant to the needs of an
increasingly status-conscious society. Heightened
concern with the architecture of tombs and monuments is
best illustrated by a tomb which Davies (1977: 18)
described as belonging to "the lunatic fringe," although is
probably better viewed as the result of an individual's
wish to commemorate himself with a strikingly unique
tomb. Located near the Porta Ostiensis and constructed
during the late first century BC, the tomb of Gaius Cestius
(*septemvir*, praetor and tribune of the people) takes the
form of a giant marble-covered pyramid 36.40 metres
high (**Fig. 5**). Inscriptions on the sides of the structure
provide details about Cestius and the offices he held, in
addition to the circumstances of the construction of the
tomb. Vout (2003: 181) has observed that "pyramids
were commonly associated with royal power and
enduring fame," and Cestius evidently wished to
associate himself with these qualities and make a specific
statement about his position within society. Monuments
on such a scale were relatively rare, even at Rome, but
this example vividly illustrates the increasing elaboration,
of Republican funerary structures.[13] This trend was
further influenced by the construction of Augustus' large
mausoleum in the Campus Martius in 28 BC. The great
circular mausoleum affected the design of tombs that
were constructed by wealthy members of society, with
other large structures of similar form emerging at this
time, including the 'Casal Rotondo' and the tomb of
Caecilia Metella, both on the Via Appia (**Fig. 6**).

---

[12] See Zanker (1975) for a full discussion. For the immense importance
of this form of funerary portraiture to the freedman classes of ancient
Rome see Kleiner (1977) and Kockel (1993).
[13] Although, at one stage, there were at least 2 other pyramid tombs at
Rome, in the vicinity of the modern Piazza del Popolo and on the other
side of the Tiber near the Vatican. The pyramid of Cestius, however,
remains the only extant example.

Figure 4. Tomb of the Rabirii on the Via Appia, Rome
(photo: author).

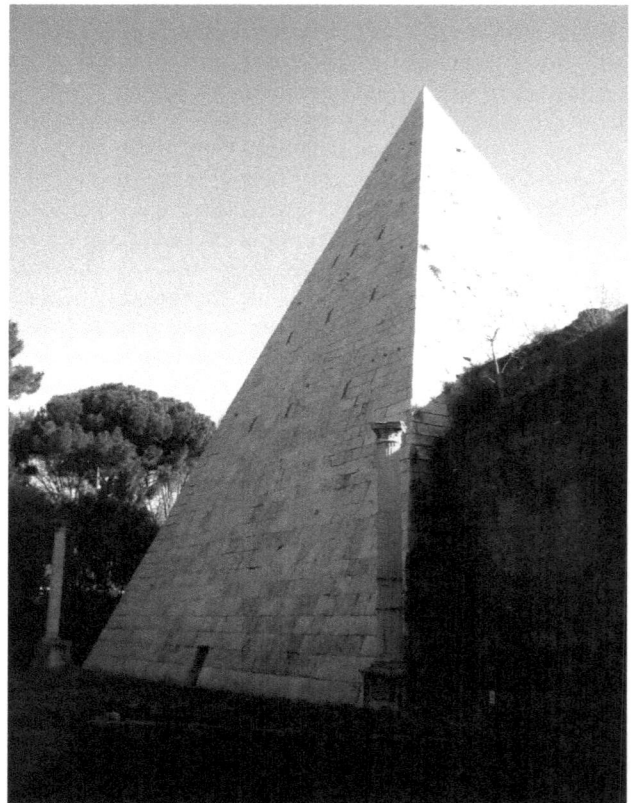

Figure 5. Pyramid tomb of Gaius Cestius, Rome
(photo: author)

The desire for increasingly elaborate tombs was a major force during the late Republic but did not remain so. Patterson (2000a: 266 – 267) observes that "in general, tombs of the empire tended to be more restrained in their exterior appearance and more lavishly decorated inside than their late-republican predecessors; and often they were located away from major roads, suggesting that visibility was less of a priority than in former times." Heinzelmann (2001: 183 – 186) has linked this change to a new wish to create tombs designed to accommodate and commemorate the entire *familia*, rather than just the individual. Commemoration, he argues, no longer focused only on visual imagery but the emphasis had now shifted to group activities that allowed the dead to be remembered. The shift which accompanied this is illustrated by the so-called house tombs which began to emerge during the second century AD at Rome and in the surrounding urban areas. Those located at the third milestone of the Via Latina, for example, "date from the second century AD and take the form of large rectangular houses, normally with a subterranean burial-chamber and, originally, two storeys above ground containing rooms for funerary cult and family or club reunions" (Toynbee, 1971: 132). Similar brick-built house tombs are located under the Basilica of San Sebastiano on the Via Appia. Constructed in the remains of a collapsed quarry in the middle of the second century AD, these three tombs also have subterranean chambers with elaborately decorated interior walls, whilst the tomb exteriors bear inscribed panels. House tombs such as these generally contained niches to hold cremation urns, although several also have larger arched recesses (*arcosolia*) cut into the walls in order to accommodate inhumations. A group of similar house tombs was discovered under St. Peter's Basilica on the Vatican. Dating also to the second and third centuries AD, the interiors are decorated to a particularly high standard (Zander, 2003). The Vatican house tombs share their design and construction methods with those of the Isola Sacra cemetery near Ostia and Portus (**Fig. 7**). These single-storey tombs, dating to 100 – 250 AD, are probably the most well-preserved examples of their type to remain in the open air. They are built of brick and *opus reticulatum* masonry. The door is placed at the centre of the façade and above the travertine frame and sill a decorated inscription panel (usually of marble) provides the names and titles of the tomb owner and his family (see Hope, 1997: 75). The tomb façade is usually completed with a cornice and triangular pediment.[14] The tombs of Isola Sacra and the Vatican clearly illustrate the shift from external display to elaborate internal decoration.

Smaller gravestones, or stelae, were also sometimes raised at the site of burial or, in the case of a *cenotaph*, to honour those buried elsewhere. Stelae are most commonly found in the provinces of the Empire, but

examples have been recovered at Rome.[15] Toynbee (1971: 245) identifies three types of free-standing stelae, the first and commonest of which she describes as "two-dimensional vertical stones, normally taller than they are wide, erected on the ground above the burial. They may have flat, rounded, or gabled tops. Sometimes they carry only an inscription, filling nearly all the field, or an inscription that is accompanied by carved or incised non-figured decorative motifs" (*ibid.*: 246 – 247). Included within this category are the first century AD tombstones of the Praetorian Guard and *Germani corporis custodes* (Bellen, 1981) which consist of a framed inscription panel and an incised wreath flanked by two rosettes (**Fig. 8**). There also existed more elaborate forms of tombstone, in which "the text is confined to a die or panel specifically reserved for it, while the field or fields above or below it, or both above and below, are occupied by figure scenes" (Toynbee, 1971: 247). The gravestone of Publius Sulpicius Peregrinus, in the Museo Nazionale Romano, provides an example of this type, with the figure of an equestrian depicted within the pediment and ornamented with rosettes. The marble stele dates to the late first or early second century AD.

The second group comprises those with relief portraits of the deceased which may take the form of simple busts or full length figures. Such stelae have been recovered from Rome, for example in the Via Triumphalis necropolis on the Vatican, where during the Neronian period a stone bearing portraits was dedicated by *Nunnius, Neronis Clau(di) Caes(aris) ser(vus) saltuaris* to himself, his wife and their son (Steinby, 1987: 93). These are perhaps similar in design to the funerary altars with reliefs, examined by Kleiner (1987a and 1987b). The final form of free-standing stelae, described by Toynbee (1971: 250), are large four-sided square or rectangular blocks "richly carved with figure scenes on at least one side, often on three sides, and sometimes described as funerary 'pillars.'" Although these monuments are found in a simple form at Aquileia, they are more commonly known in the western provinces (*ibid.*: 250). Free-standing stelae are uncommon at Rome, but examples, often associated with slaves, freedmen and the military have been recovered.

Text and Images

Two elements which feature significantly in the design of sepulchral monuments deserve closer attention: inscriptions and images. One of the most important elements of the funerary monument, large or small, was the inscription. This was essential for identifying the structure as a funerary monument, but also for imparting

---

[14] See Baldassarre (1996) for a detailed description of each tomb and Chapter 5 of this volume for discussion of the cemetery of Isola Sacra as a whole.

[15] As well as local tradition, issues of survival in the archaeological record must also be taken into account when assessing the extent of this type of memorial. Slabs of cut stone may have been particularly attractive to people looking for ready-made building material, consequently leading to their re-use elsewhere. A clear example of the latter can be found at Ostia where tombstones were re-used as seats for a public toilet (Meiggs, 1973: 143).

(a)

(b)

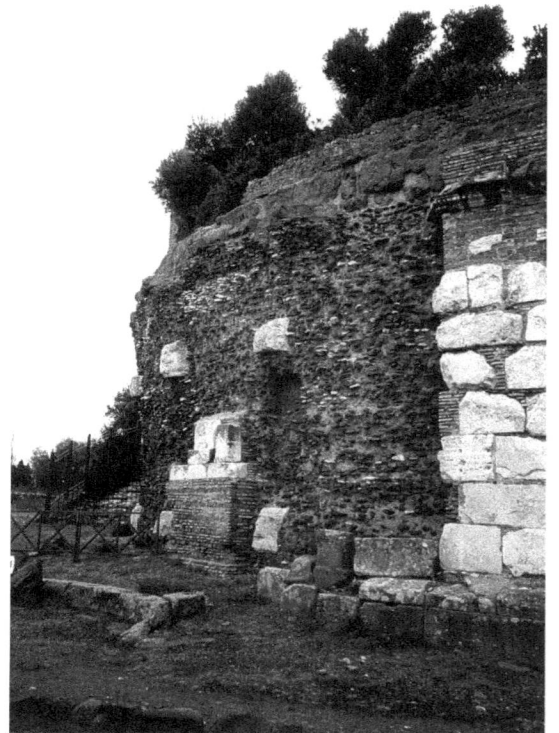

(c)

Figure 6. Circular monuments of the early Imperial period:
(a) Mausoleum of Augustus (b) Tomb of Caecilia Metella, Via Appia (c) Casal Rotondo, Via Appia
(photos: author).

Figure 7. House tombs of the second century AD at Isola Sacra, near Ostia
(photo: author).

Figure 8. Tombstone of a praetorian guard, Rome
(photo: author).

specific information about the deceased. In its most basic form the epitaph included information about the deceased, usually their name and that of the person who dedicated the monument. Occasionally these details included the age of the deceased and their occupation in life, whereas other epitaphs took a more elaborate form, sometimes in verse, and gave additional information about the family of the deceased, their civic or military rank, a description of their virtues and personality, and other biographical information. The written word recorded these details for posterity and communicated them to anyone who read the epitaph, for as long as it remained visible. However, although writing was found in all aspects of urban life, on shop signs, public notices and graffiti, Hanson (1991: 159 – 160) observes that, "literates made up only a small proportion of Graeco-Roman populations at most times and in most places," and Koortbojian (1996: 218 – 19) has suggested that most members of Roman society were incapable of reading the texts. Despite this, the formulaic nature of funerary inscriptions may have allowed even those with minimal education to understand the nature of their content and their significance. This was assisted by the location of the inscription in a cemetery environment, which would have shaped the reader's understanding of the text, and as Woolf (1996: 28) notes, "formulaic elements were developed, like the ligatures that represented groups of letters with a single symbol, or abbreviations like DM, HSE, VSLM, or LDDD, which may in time have been read quasi-pictographically as symbols in themselves, just as we read R.I.P or Q.E.D." If this was the case, it is clear that the potential audience for memorials was very large, with the reader able to understand the inscription in relation to its context, the familiar formulae and their own experience.

Inscriptions were often supplemented with images, indeed Hope (2003: 118) has suggested that "remembering the dead was a visual feast." Portrait busts, either accurate representations prepared in advance of death or sculptures considered representative of the deceased, have been mentioned above. These often took the form of family groups, as illustrated by those seen in **Figures 3** and **4** (see also Bonanno, 1983: 92). One of the commonest forms of monument commissioned by members of the Roman military in the provinces, portrayed the deceased standing full-length or on horseback (the latter most commonly associated with non-citizen auxiliary soldiers) with the insignia of their rank and military decorations clearly displayed.

Regardless of the many complex reasons for self-portrayal (see below) the simplest understanding of these monuments focuses on the identification of the deceased as a soldier or veteran, a message that is transmitted directly by the image and could be understood even by the illiterate.

was that images were the most direct means of communicating information. They were capable of operating on various levels, from the identification of the profession of the deceased to a complex assertion of their identity and status.

One final example of the way in which images directly communicated information about the deceased can be found in the tomb of a baker located outside the Porta Maggiore at Rome (**Fig. 10**). Built in the second half of the first century BC by the freedman Marcus Virgileus Eurysaces, the tomb bears a frieze depicting various stages of bread making, including weighing grain, kneading dough and baking loaves in the oven (Friggeri, 2001: 63). If it was not evident from this frieze that the owner of the tomb was a baker (*pistor*), this fact was asserted further by the design of the monument itself, which takes the form of a grain silo, described in the inscription as a *panarium*, a bread container (*ibid.*: 63). The entire monument unequivocally displays the occupation (and evident success) of its owner.[16]

Figure 9. Occupational relief (modern copy) showing a blacksmith, mounted on Tomb 29, Isola Sacra (photo: author).

In a similar manner, funerary reliefs depicting the deceased at work provided easily accessible information about that individual. The facades of tombs at Isola Sacra provide examples of so-called occupation reliefs. Tomb 29 (built 160 – 180 AD) exhibits two terracotta reliefs depicting blacksmiths, surrounded by tools and equipment including scissors, knives, scythes and anvils. On the basis of these images it is believed that the owners probably produced and sold iron tools (Baldassarre, *et al.* 1996: 139 – 141) (**Fig. 9**). The neighbouring tomb (Tomb 30) also bears a terracotta relief depicting a waterseller (*aquatarius*) surrounded by amphorae (*ibid.*: 142 – 143). On a shelf behind the figure can be seen a large amphora above two jugs hanging from a shelf and two further reliefs depicting amphorae flank the tomb's inscription. The inclusion of these images was probably motivated by several factors, but perhaps amongst the most important

Figure 10. The *panarium* tomb of the baker Marcus Virgileus Eurysaces, Rome (photo: author).

[16] See Brandt (1993) for a concise description of the tomb and a summary of the issues surrounding its identification and date. For the context of Porta Maggiore and other tombs belonging to bakers in the area, see Coates-Stephens (2004).

Imagines and eulogies

Funerary monuments were not the only means available to those wishing to perpetuate their own memory or that of a deceased relative or friend, and may actually have emerged as a popular response to the traditional commemorative practices of the Republican aristocracy. Two aspects of aristocratic funeral ritual illustrate this point: the eulogy (*laudatio funebris*) and the practice of carrying ancestor images (*imagines*) during the funeral procession.

In a comprehensive study of the history and use of *imagines* in aristocratic Roman culture, Flower (1996) assesses the literary evidence for *imagines*. The earliest author to mention their use is Plautus, probably during the 190s BC, but later writers, such as Livy and Sallust, suggest they originated before the third century BC (*ibid.*: 46). The *imagines* comprised life-like wax masks of deceased ancestors, probably made whilst the individual was alive. They were the sole preserve of male office-holders who had achieved the office of *aedile*, and therefore had an intimate association with the politics of the state (*ibid.*: 2). Customarily kept in wooden cupboards (*armaria*) in the *atria* of aristocratic houses, the *imagines* were actively used during funerals, when actors wore the masks and dressed in clothing appropriate for the rank of the ancestor. Polybius (6.53.6 – 9) describes the scene:

> "And whenever a leading member of the family dies, they introduce them into the funeral procession, putting them on men who seem most like them in height and as regards the rest of their general appearance. These men assume their costume in addition, if the person was a consul or praetor, a toga with a purple border, if a censor, the all-purple toga, but if someone had celebrated a triumph or done something like that, a gold embroidered toga. These men now ride on wagons, and the rods and axes and the other customary equipment of those in power accompanies them according to the dignity befitting the rank and station achieved by each man in politics during his lifetime. And when they reach the rostra, they all sit in order on ivory stools. It is not easy for an ambitious and high minded young man to see a finer spectacle than this."

The practice of parading the *imagines* had obvious political significance, and Flower (1996: 120) suggests that they "emerged as the ultimate means for representing a family's past achievements and consequently also their present claims to pre-eminence." Focus on the illustrious ancestors of the deceased allowed a family to justify its social position and provided opportunities for advancing this status: "the more previously held offices were associated with a family's name, the more easily its members might expect to obtain future election victories" (*ibid.*: 63). However, although the *imagines* played a political role

in legitimising the status of an office-holding family, they also visibly perpetuated the memory of the deceased. Bodel (1999: 260) suggests that "their role was to make the ancestors come to life again at the funeral, so that "always whenever someone dies his whole family, anyone who had ever existed, was there on hand" (Plin. *HN*. 35. 2. 6)." Not only did the life-like quality of the masks remind family members of the appearance, rank and achievements of their ancestors but their active participation in the procession brought them temporarily to life once more. Flower does not specifically refer to this, but she does acknowledge that the *imagines* were "more than simple markers of rank. They were used as devices to recall individual lives and specific qualities. They promised a glorious and undying memory to those who served the state" (1996: 11). The revival of the long-dead as active participants in the funeral procession was witnessed by both relatives and onlookers gathered to see these great aristocratic spectacles; a process that can perhaps be compared with the stranger encountering a monument and absorbing the information it presented. The actors wearing the *imagines* also created an impression of the deceased in the minds of the viewers, thus facilitating their temporary revival in the consciousness of others.

There are evident similarities between this practice and the use of the sepulchral monument to facilitate the revival of the deceased in the minds of the living, albeit temporarily, and it is conceivable that the popularity of the funerary monument developed as a response to this aristocratic practice – as a more effective and lasting means of enabling the same process. The *imagines* allowed the dead to appear physically before an audience, but this appearance was fleeting and could only occur in public on the death of another family member. The funerary monument, on the other hand, was permanent and could be seen by members of the public every day, allowing the memory of the deceased to be brought to life on a regular basis and to have a wider impact.

Dupont (1992: 23) disagrees that the *imagines* were a successful form of commemoration, stating that "if these masks were shut away it was because they constituted only a trace of the deceased and not a monument to his memory, as did, for example, an inscription. A waxen face only disclosed those trivial peculiarities that distinguished one man from the next." Although her observation that "the honour of a man could not be read in his lifeless face, since his honour was not linked to his facial features" (*ibid.*: 23) is perhaps valid, the mask still stood as a representation of an individual who had once existed and whose honour and identity continued to exist in the memories of his family. It formed a physical reminder in the same way that a funerary monument acted as an "aid to memory" (Hope, 1998: 179). The fact that they were not constantly on display did not diminish their significance as a form of commemoration. Even when they were shut away and invisible to view, they continued to exist and people continued to be aware of this existence. Similarly, a funerary monument continued to exist when there was nobody there to see it. This did not detract from the power of these monuments to perpetuate the memory of the individual to which they were dedicated.

Polybius (6. 53. 1 – 3) also provides an insight into the *laudatio funebris*, the eulogy, the origins of which appear to have been as ancient as the *imagines*:

> "For whenever one of the leading men amongst them dies, when the funeral has been arranged the body is brought with the rest of the adornment to the place called the ship's prows (rostra) in the Forum where it is usually propped up for all to see, but rarely it is laid out. If a grown-up son is left behind and happens to be present, he mounts the rostra with all the people standing around. But if not, then another family member who is available delivers a speech about the virtues of the dead man and his achievements, during his lifetime. As a result of this the people remember what happened and picture it before their eyes, not only those who shared in the deeds, but also those who did not. Both share the same feelings to such an extent that the misfortune does not appear as the private concern of the family, but as a public matter for the people."

This practice was again primarily reserved for the aristocracy, since permission was required to address the crowd gathered in the Forum from the *rostrum*. However, although the *laudatio*, like *imagines*, appears to have been restricted to the male elite, a fragmentary inscription from Rome provides the text of an oration pronounced at the funeral of an aristocratic *woman*, often identified as Turia, wife of Quintus Lucretius Vespillo (Friggeri, 2001: 65; CIL VI 41062). Inscribed around 8 – 2 BC, the text of the eulogy tells of the brave and noble actions taken by Turia in order to ensure the safety of her husband, in addition to listing her virtues and proclaiming her husband's grief. This inscription, although reporting unusual circumstances, may be representative of other eulogies and indicates that, at least on occasion, these orations were permanently recorded in inscribed form. Eulogies were probably commonly pronounced at the graveside during the funerals of other members of society, with a relative or friend saying a few words about the departed loved one, but the extra prestige obtained by doing so from the *rostrum* was immense. From this prominent position the family directly addressed the community of the city and praised the achievements of the deceased and the line of illustrious ancestors from whom he was descended. Flower (1996: 128) describes the eulogy as the "high point of the public part of the funeral ceremonies. It also offered a commentary on the procession of *imagines* and enabled the family to present the career of its newly deceased member in the context of the achievements of his ancestors." The *laudatio* and the *imagines* therefore operated together in order to advertise and promote the political ambitions and successes of important families in front of the wider community.

The impact of aristocratic funeral processions and eulogies upon other members of society can be seen in the fact that the only extant pictorial evidence for these practices derives from the funerary art of freedmen. Flower (*ibid*: 98) specifically highlights a relief from Amiternun, dating to the late Republic, depicting a procession without *imagines*. She proposes that these images were not a regular part of Roman iconography and that the art of freedmen "is consistently alluding to elements of much grander funerals" (*ibid*.: 98). The customs of the upper-classes were clearly recognised as a successful means of self-promotion and to depict such an image on one's tomb associated that individual with aristocratic practices and implied that such activity had occurred for the deceased.

In addition to the political nature of the *laudatio funebris*, it also perpetuated the memory of the dead, reviving them in the consciousness of those listening by recounting details of their life and achievements. As Polybius (6.53.3) noted, "the people remember what happened and picture it before their eyes, not only those who shared in the deeds, but also those who did not." These achievements may well have been exaggerated, but the funerary monument could be equally selective in the image it portrayed. Dupont (1992: 24) suggests that this practice "served to commemorate the glory of the ancestors and to afford them immortality by fixing them in the Romans' collective memory – for there was little point in striving for glory if it was to expire with the last witnesses to the deeds that have given rise to it." Not all members of society had the opportunity to do this, and although their ancestors undoubtedly remained important to their sense of identity, they may not have been entitled to an *imago*. However, the funerary monument acted in a similar manner to the *laudatio*, fulfilling "the same human needs" (Kampen, 1981: 49) and inserting aspects of their lives into the collective consciousness of society, even if only temporarily.

Why commemorate?

The primary function of a sepulchral monument is to mark the location of human remains (Hope, 2001: 3). In addition, monuments, in theory, prevent disturbance or re-use of the ground and provide a focal point to which relatives can return at specific times. However, funerary monuments also function in a variety of other complex ways.

Memory preservation

The word 'monument' derives from the Latin verb *monere*, "to remind" (Varro, *L.L.* VI. 49) and the *Digest* (11.7.2.6 (Ulpian)) states specifically that a monument is "something which exists to preserve a memory." The funerary monument therefore acted not only to remind the family where relatives were buried, but also to ensure that the deceased remained alive in the memories of people encountering the memorial, whether they were relatives, friends or strangers. Biographical details provided by the inscribed epitaph, occupational reliefs or images of tools and equipment associated with everyday life, as well as sculpted portraits of the deceased, allowed people who had known the deceased to recall precisely who they were, what they were like and what they did, thus keeping their memory alive. Equally, they conveyed key aspects of the identity of the deceased to strangers - a process that brought them temporarily to life in their memory too. Creating a 'memory' of the deceased, either real or artificial, in the minds of relatives and strangers allowed individuals to proclaim their existence. As Keppie (1991: 98) states, "Romans, like most other societies in ancient and modern times, were much concerned with the permanent recording of the life and achievements of an individual on his death," and funerary monuments were vital to this process. They confirmed that an individual had lived, worked, loved, and died – essentially that they had existed. This existence may have been humble and short and may not have involved deeds comparable with those of Augustus and other great individuals of the period, but a funerary monument allowed an individual to show that they had made an impact on the world simply through their existence. Indeed, the desire to register this may have been greater if they had no specific claims to greatness or anything in particular to distinguish them from the masses.

This practice also satisfied a religious need. It is apparent from Cicero's *Tusculan Disputations* that popular belief concerning the immortality of the soul varied and many, including Cicero himself, were undecided on the matter.[17] Lattimore's study of *Themes in Greek and Latin Epitaphs* (1942) examined a wide range of texts and assessed popular ancient attitudes towards the nature and immortality of the soul. He sums up the thinking of Cicero and many of his contemporaries thus: "Cicero inclines to believe, and wishes to believe, in immortality; so the Platonic arguments are rehearsed, together with reasoning from customs and the practice of famous men. Such arguments seem to prove, if they prove anything, only that many of Cicero's contemporaries, like himself, hoped for an immortality the reality of which they could not demonstrate, even to themselves" (*ibid.*: 48). This lack of conviction concerning immortality contributed to the significance of funerary monuments as a method of memory preservation. Many individuals undoubtedly had firm beliefs about life after death, but there was no common consensus or official doctrine concerning the immortality of the soul and whether it passed to a better (or worse) place after death.[18] Widespread uncertainty about existence after death led to a greater desire to continue to exist amongst the living, seen in the wish for immortality expressed by Horace and Propertius. Being remembered by the living allowed the name and identity of an individual to remain alive. As Lattimore (*ibid.*: 126) suggests, funerary monuments were "designed to attract the attention of the wayfarer, to make him at least read the name on the stone, to have some value attached to

that name alive in his consciousness for a while. This is a tacit acknowledgement of the finality of death." This process was aided by the fact that inscriptions were intended to be read aloud (Ireland, 1983: 221). Walker (1985: 62) explains how "in so doing, we are to speak for the dead: 'Be aware, traveller, that your voice is really mine' (CIL XIV 356, a marble tablet found at Ostia)." Monuments thus allowed the dead to come alive and speak directly to the living. This probably provided a degree of comfort for both the individual contemplating death and those left behind. Mourners could be comforted by the knowledge that, if the soul was mortal, their loved ones remained alive in their minds and those of strangers who encountered their memorial (Lattimore, 1942: 234). Strangers were particularly integral to this process, partly because there remained the possibility that the family would die out or move away and thus be unable to play an active part in perpetuating the memory of their ancestors. Strangers also expanded the sphere in which the deceased could live as a memory. The location of sepulchral monuments along major roads, contributed to this system considerably by introducing the memory of the deceased into the consciousness of travellers from distant locations.

Funerary monuments were clearly considered essential to guaranteeing that individuals did not face oblivion after death and as such they represented the last link between the dead and the surviving mourners. The importance of this link, and the fear of annihilation, is further illuminated by its occasional use as a punishment, in the form of *damnatio memoriae*. This official decree "condemning an individual to historical oblivion as well as to public disgrace" (Brilliant, 1974: 86) through the complete removal of their name, titles and images from monuments, was unlikely to often, if ever, affect the sepulchral monuments of ordinary members of society, and was usually inflicted upon disgraced emperors, usurpers, traitors and military or political leaders. Although Hope (2003: 115) points out that "the damned became infamous rather than completely forgotten; a damned memory was still a memory," it was still considered a particularly fearful punishment. The mere erasing of a person's name damned that individual to obscurity and total annihilation, and provided an insight into the perceived effectiveness of the inscribed word and significance of memory preservation.[19]

Self-promotion, identity and status change

It was not only essential to perpetuate the memory of the deceased but in addition it was important to *promote* it in order to enhance their status in the eyes of the living. The desire for self-promotion and display permeated all social levels, and during the late Republic and early Empire social mobility became a particularly influential force. Woolf (1996: 33) highlights the uncertainty experienced

---

[17] See Jackson Knight (1970).
[18] The impact of religious beliefs concerning the fate of the soul on Roman burial practices is examined in Chapter 2.

[19] As Cooley (2000: 2) has pointed out, this practice also shows that "inscriptions continued to attract people's attention." Ironically, however, the erasure of an individual's name and image from a monument may have attracted *more* attention.

by members of society in a period which was "characterised by a loosening of the bonds of society together with a concomitant rise in individualism. Mobility brought fears as well as hopes, since not all change was chosen or desirable." Under circumstances in which one's social status could decrease as rapidly as it could be enhanced, the need for a sense of stability was great. As Woolf (*ibid.*: 34) continues, "the desire to fix the past in stone for posterity was an understandable response to the uncertainty of the present." In this context it is possible to further examine the motives behind funerary commemoration, including the confirmation of an individual's place in society in order to minimise challenges that might be made against it, and an attempt to further promote status through the selective use of words and images. Individuals from all social levels and backgrounds were vulnerable to status change, but monuments could be employed either to cement the status of an individual fearing that it may subsequently be lost, or one who wished to express a recently acquired higher status. The pyramid tomb of Gaius Cestius, for example, made a specific statement about the individual responsible for its construction; its dimensions and the organisation required for its construction indicated that Cestius was an important, wealthy man.[20] Encountering such a monument would leave little doubt about the importance of the man it commemorated and the monument ensured that this was the impression that survived for eternity.

As already noted, all members of society were vulnerable to status change but it was to those who had recently experienced an improvement in status that the funerary monument was most important. Those who most commonly found themselves in this situation were freedmen and freedwomen who, released from the bonds of slavery, experienced a sudden improvement in their legal status (through the award of citizenship) and their position in the wider community. A great many extant funerary monuments record freedmen, a fact that might be explained by pride in their new status, as Ross Taylor (1961: 129) explains: "unlike the average man in the freeborn population, they had something to record, something in which they felt as much pride as the men who shared the space along the major roads and in the cemeteries, senators, knights, and soldiers, felt in their titles and honours." Former slaves were unable to compete with senators and other elevated members of society in many ways, but were nevertheless eager to demonstrate that they were citizens of the same society. This could be achieved in a variety of ways, including the direct statement of citizenship conveyed by the *tria*

nomina. Treggiari (1969: 6 – 7) throws further light on the significance of this, observing:

> "*Libertini* in fact stand out among the *plebs* because they possess a *cognomen*, since the name by which they had been known as slaves remained as surname when, on manumission, they took the *nomen gentile* and (usually) *praenomen* of their patron. *Cognomina*, except for the aristocracy, were of comparatively recent introduction, and although for the upper classes they were regular by the first century BC ... the lower classes seem to have been slow to follow the fashion: among their inscriptions mention of a third name is the exception."

The name not only asserted the new-found status of the deceased but also that of their family and subsequent generations. Parker Pearson's cross-cultural studies of burial and commemorative customs (1999: 193) have allowed him (amongst others) to observe that "the living can also profit as well as they may from both the death itself and from the opportunities presented by holding a funeral." That it was considered important to advertise citizenship is emphasised by the observation of Ross Taylor (1961: 122) that over time the "decline of the use of *libertus* in the freedman's name is undoubtedly a reflection of the freedman's unwillingness to declare his inferior status and his dependence on and obligation to his patron." The funerary monument displayed *selected* information, thus allowing freedmen to assert their status within it whilst concealing their slave origins. The decline of the use of *libertus* does, however, make it difficult to identify these individuals as former slaves. Nevertheless, there may be certain other clues hidden within the name of the individual (for example a cognomen of Greek origin) that might reveal their history. By the later Imperial period ex-slaves may have wished to assert different aspects of their identity and status in light of increasing numbers of freedmen and freedwomen within the urban community and the decreasing value of citizenship. During the Republic and early Imperial period however, ex-slaves were generally proud of their status as citizens and wished to display it. Pride in newfound citizenship was also demonstrated by increased emphasis on the family, to whom their status would be passed. The image of the ideal citizen family advertised the success of freed slaves and their hopes for the future.[21] The example of the sculpted family portrait of Quintus [ ]aelius, a herald and assignor of seats, illustrates this practice. Not only did the couple flaunt their "superior economic condition with the construction of a pretentious tomb" (Friggeri, 2001: 59) and emphasize their status by depicting the man dressed in a toga, but, in addition, they also showed their family. The stone is damaged but a third figure was originally included and probably represented their son or daughter

---

[20] His knowledge of the culture of the wider world was also demonstrated by his emulation of the pyramids of Egypt - apparently unaware of the warnings of Horace and Propertius that these structures would not stand the test of time! Perhaps, by specifically mentioning "pyramids", the poets were actually passing judgement on the arrogance of people like Cestius (or perhaps even the man himself) rather than referring directly to those of Egypt. See Vout (2003) for a detailed examination of the role of Egyptian symbolism in Roman society, particularly its association with the afterlife and funerary imagery.

[21] See Hope (1998: 191) and studies by Kleiner (1987) and D'Ambra (2002). George (2005: 39) points out that "the family provided protection, economic and emotional support, and was the institution through which wealth and property was protected and transmitted."

(*ibid.*: 59). The couple were not only economically successful but were also the proud progenitors of a family of free individuals who would stand as living monuments to their parents and their success.[22] Meyer (1990: 83, n. 46) points out that it was also possible "to make status claims through a child's epitaph – if he or she had a citizen name, for example, or special status, titles, literary achievements, etc." The increased frequency of lower class funerary inscriptions commemorating children has also been attributed to "the desire of freedmen to advertise their newly-gained status as Roman citizens" (King 2000: 122).

The monument not only commemorated the deceased but provided an opportunity to advertise the identity of the dedicator, and it has been suggested (Meyer, 1990: 75) that the name of the commemorator was included in approximately 80 per cent of funerary inscriptions from the Western empire. This is illustrated by the *panarium* tomb of Eurysaces. The tomb was erected by Marcus Vergilius Eurysaces for his wife Atistia, but as Kleiner (1987b: 546) observes, it is Eurysaces and his occupation as a baker that takes precedence on the monument: "Atistia is not represented alone in the portrait relief placed above the epitaph plaque on the front of the tomb, but in a group portrait with her husband. And it is Eurysaces alone who is honoured in the larger inscriptions and in the baking frieze that decorates three sides of the structure." Kleiner uses this to illustrate the status of women on family monuments but it can also be seen as an example of the way in which funerary monuments displayed the status and identity of the living commemorator.[23] Advertising the identity of the deceased was evidently essential for ensuring their immortality in the consciousness of the living, but those dedicating the monuments also accrued certain benefits. Their status within the community could also be heightened as they reaped the rewards of ostentatious display and honourable piety to the deceased. As Kleiner (*ibid.*: 546) concludes: "Eurysaces has ostensibly erected a tomb in honour of his wife, but, in truth it is his name, his profession, his achievements, and his facial features that he hopes will be preserved for posterity."

Economic status was also significant, particularly in the commemorative practices of ex-slaves. Many former slaves used the skills acquired during slavery to become successful in commerce and manufacture, often aided by the financial support of a patron (Garnsey and Saller, 1987: 124). Funerary reliefs portraying the deceased at work record these successes and tombs such as that of Eurysaces illustrate the great wealth that it was possible for these 'new men' to achieve. The levels of prosperity that resulted from a successful professional career after manumission undoubtedly varied but often enabled these

individuals to afford a commemorative monument upon their death. Their economic status thus provided the means by which to advertise it and assert their position within society as successful individuals. As shall be demonstrated in Chapter 3, other members of the lower classes are unlikely to have been unable to afford such an expense. Furthermore, Dyson (1992: 202) notes that "occupations also served as a means of personal identity for those individuals who lacked real family traditions and compensated for the lack of other family identities," and Joshel's (1992) study of occupational titles has shown how important this part of their identity was to members of the 'lower classes.'

Finally, the funerary monument displayed and celebrated the new status of freedmen through reference to their heir. As Meyer (1990: 77) observes, unless specifically assigned elsewhere, the task of burial was the responsibility of the heir. This legal relationship appears frequently on funerary monuments because "it was a moral duty which the heir or the person responsible for the burial wished to indicate had been discharged" (*ibid.*: 78). However, it also signalled the legal status of the deceased since only those in possession of citizenship had the right to make a valid will and it therefore served as a means by which to demonstrate that the deceased was a legitimate member of society. Occasionally this was taken further, with the text of the will, either complete or in part, being inscribed on the monument itself. The inscription mounted on the façade of Tomb A in the Vatican necropolis, for example, begins:

> Into the hands of the gods. From the three testamentary codicils of Popilius Heracla. Caius Popilius Heracla salutes his heirs. To you, my heirs, I ask, order and give you mandate, in the name of your faith, to erect for me a monument on the Vatican, near the circus, near the monument to Ulpius Narcissus, for a value of six thousand sesterces.

> (Zander, 2003: 23)

Meyer (1990: 81 - 83) has examined the significance of such displays of citizenship within provincial contexts, emphasising the desire of individuals to advertise their legal status in a particularly Roman manner, concluding, "[t]estamentary privilege, in short, is a documentable and desired consequence of the acquisition of Roman citizenship, if not a verifiably major factor in its pursuit, at a time when citizenship was increasingly sought and acquired." These concerns were also found amongst the freedmen of Rome, many of whom were probably of foreign extraction, and influenced the frequency with which heirs were alluded to on funerary monuments.

To contemporary observers there were various other signs that indicated the legal and social status of the deceased freedman and allowed him to assert for posterity that he was a citizen. In addition, other elements highlighted his involvement with Roman traditions and customs;

[22] This was particularly the case with sons who bore the same name as their father. The surviving family was as essential to the perpetuation of memory as the funerary monument for it was through them that the status of the deceased was significant in the long term.
[23] Eurysaces probably commissioned the tomb with a view to his own burial there at a later date but the tomb was officially dedicated to Atistia.

Figure 11. The tombstones of the *Germani corporis custodes*, Rome
(photo: author).

something which was considered particularly important if he was of foreign origin. Amongst these were the use of portraiture and images of the deceased partaking in traditional Roman activities or as they believed a "Roman" should appear. The latter commonly took the form of an image of the stern and serious Roman of the Republic, dressed in a toga as a further declaration of citizenship which represented how "they thought old Romans ought to look" (Ross Taylor, 1961: 132; see also Zanker, 1975; Kleiner, 1987a; George, 2005). The immediate visual indicator of legal status that was provided by the image of the toga (only legal for citizen men) and the *palla* and tunic (the traditional clothing of the Roman matron) served to cement their place within society as citizens and allowed them to celebrate it in public. This desire of ex-slaves to advertise their new status may have been further influenced by previous contact with elite culture. As slaves, they directly witnessed (and possibly took an active role in) the customs of the elite, in addition to observing the dynamic and unstable nature of society which they would eventually experience themselves, through manumission. Woolf (1996: 36) suggests that this experience "must have heightened their sensitivity to the mutable nature of their social identities. The fact that such mobility was upward, predisposed them to personal monumentalization." Freedmen received citizenship but this did not release them from the pressures of society and was not a guarantee against further changes in status. The freedman's desire to hide their slave origins reveals that citizenship involved several complex status levels and that it was preferable to be a freeborn citizen than one

with a past rooted in slavery. Hope (1998: 180) suggests that "for certain groups enduring persistent inconsistencies in their social or legal status, and thus occupying liminal positions, the Roman tombstone had a particular significance as a symbol of legitimisation." Freedmen must be included amongst these groups and they especially used the funerary monument to assert their legal and respectable position within society.

Sepulchral monuments not only displayed identity and status but also actively created these identities. In his study of cycles of commemorative behaviour, Cannon (1989: 438) describes death as "an opportunity for social advancement" and funerary monuments were central to this process. Monuments could create identities either by making claims to a status or identity that was not grounded in reality, or by attempting to gain recognition for the existence of an individual or family in a society in which they held an undefined or particularly low status. The first of these has been illustrated by examples of freedmen advertising their citizenship and obscuring their slave origins and can also be seen in reliefs depicting ordinary individuals partaking in upper class activities, such as formal dining. However, freedmen were not the only 'liminal' group within the urban community who wished to legitimise their identity. Hope (1998, 2000a, and 2001) has examined the ways in which funerary monuments contributed to the creation of individual and collective identities, stating that "the cemetery became the ideal display ground for the aspirations of those who struggled for acceptance" (Hope, 2001: 90). In one example, she draws upon the case of a group of gladiators at Nîmes to illustrate how the practice and characteristics of commemoration allowed men with virtually no recognised position in society to integrate themselves into the community and gain legitimacy. The shared appearance and standardized epitaphs of their funerary monuments facilitated the expression of "group affiliation in death" (Hope, 1998: 183), which in turn gave the gladiators a sense of legitimacy in the face of social isolation.

Identity was also particularly significant for foreigners or newcomers to the city of Rome. The early emperors, from Augustus to Galba, surrounded themselves with a personal bodyguard of mounted Germans known as the *Germani corporis custodes*. This small group of men (between 500 – 1000 in number) were recruited from the Lower Rhineland, specifically amongst the Batavi and Ubii, between the ages of 17 and 18 to serve in Rome for approximately sixteen years (Bellen, 1981: 78). Whilst resident at Rome, the *custodes* appear to have retained many of their Germanic traits. Whether this was a conscious decision on the part of the guards themselves or enforced as a means to prevent corruption is unclear, but it is evident that the *custodes* remained distanced from the wider community, apparently not forming relationships with members of the public or actively participating in social activities. The extant funerary monuments of the *custodes* illustrate that the identity shared by these Germanic individuals was based on several aspects of their lives, specifically their occupation, and was affirmed by the monuments themselves. These take the same form (stelae with rounded gables depicting a wreath and two rosettes) and include the following information always presented in the same order: their name, the name of the emperor, the title of the unit (*corporis custos*), the title of their *decuria*, their origin (for example *natione Bataus*), age at death, *hic situs est*, the dedicator of the monument and that the *collegium Germanorum* was to act as heir. For example, one epitaph reads:

> *Paetinus / Ti(beri) Claud(i) / Caisar(is) Aug(usti)*
> */ corp(oris) cust(os) / dec(uria) Pacati / nat(ione)*
> *Bataus / vix(it) ann(os) XX / h(ic) s(itus) e(st) /*
> *pos(uit) Virus dec(uria) Pacati / h(eres) eius ex*
> *col(legio) Germa[n(orum)].*

(CIL VI 8807)

The use of a specific formula stating basic facts about the deceased is reminiscent of the gladiators discussed by Hope (1998) and can be viewed as a statement of group identity. There were many aspects of the lives of the *custodes* that may have contributed to their sense of collective identity, including their shared origins and experiences, their military organisation and their ambiguous status within Roman society, but it is significant that they expressed this through the medium of the funerary monument. Stone funerary monuments were not traditionally erected amongst the Germanic tribes of the provinces (see Carroll, 2001), and the fact that the guards were commemorated in this way indicates a desire for acceptance and recognition within the

community in which they lived but were not really considered to be members. Their lack of contact with the population of Rome provided few opportunities for this to occur during life, but death made it possible for them to negotiate a place for themselves within that society. They did this, however, not as individuals but as a tight-knit group with standardised monuments and inscriptions. The audience for these monuments not only consisted of the wider Roman community, but the guards themselves and the tombstones served to reaffirm to the unit their shared identity. This can perhaps also be compared with the tombstones of auxiliary soldiers erected in the Roman provinces. These commonly depicted the deceased in full military dress on horseback and will have served to create, assert and advertise their shared identities as soldiers of Rome.

Commemoration and the poor

So far this discussion has illustrated the ways in which commemorative monuments were used by diverse groups of Roman urban society to publicise, promote, create and preserve aspects of their lives and identities. However, although this encompassed all levels of society, substantial funerary monuments were not erected by all members of the community. Ross Taylor (1961: 131), discussing the lack of "permanent" memorials dedicated to freeborn members of the "lower population" of the city, suggests that "it would appear that they were little interested in having their names survive," and that "the social and economic condition of the freeborn is at least partly responsible for this seeming lack of interest" (*ibid.*: 131). The significance of these statements lies in the fact that they suggest not only that the lives of the lower classes were unworthy of commemoration, but also that these people were uninterested in self-promotion, identity display or immortality. However, although these individuals may have been unable to afford the expense of elaborate tombs this should not be used as evidence of apathy, especially in light of the extreme importance of commemorative processes outlined already. A useful insight into the likely responses of the urban lower classes to these pressures and demands can be gained by briefly examining the situation in Victorian Britain, discussed by Cannon (1989). British urban society of the nineteenth century bore many similarities to that of early Imperial Rome. Society was highly structured and position within it was vital to personal identity. More specifically, according to Cannon (1989: 438), it was a period of "unprecedented ostentation in funeral pageantry that was the equal concern, if not obsession, of the highest and the lowest extremes of the social spectrum." This situation was undoubtedly linked to the fact that "increasing affluence and social disruption created an atmosphere of status uncertainty in which increased efforts were required to establish, maintain, and improve status through material display" (*ibid.*: 444). Competitive display in the funerary sphere was as essential to processes of identity creation and self-promotion during the nineteenth century in Britain as it was in ancient Rome. The apparent similarities between these two societies, make it possible to productively compare the situation more closely in terms of the desire of the lower classes to compete for recognition and status within a dynamic society. Cannon (*ibid.*: 438) makes the following observation:

"At the time of an 1843 parliamentary report on burial practices and funeral expense, it could be said that the desire to secure respectful interment was the strongest and most widely diffused feeling among labouring people (Chadwick, 1843: 55) and would cause them to neglect their well-being and that of their families in order to ensure provision of sufficient funds for a "proper" funeral. Absolute levels of funeral expenditure varied with social and economic status, but the important consideration of the time was the pervasive desire for funeral display among all classes and the relative hardship this entailed for the poor and even the middle classes (Chadwick, 1843: 197)."

The extent to which we can (and should) draw conclusions from this statement and apply them directly to Roman society is, of course, limited. However, it provides an opportunity for us to see that in other competitive societies, the lower classes strove to emulate the practices of the aristocracy. It is very possible that the same occurred in ancient Rome. Cannon examines other societies in which funerary display was directly associated with competitive status and identity display, all of which include the lower class aspiring to emulate the upper class in order to obtain recognition. It is therefore not possible to concur with Ross Taylor's dismissive view that the poor had no desire to commemorate or preserve the memory of their existence.

Why monuments?

As we have seen, the only opportunity available to many members of Roman society for lasting personal displays and self-promotion lay within the funerary sphere. However, the popularity of the medium suggests that there were more complex reasons for its adoption as the most significant form of self-display in Roman society. So, what were the fundamental characteristics of funerary monuments that made them such an effective means of display?

Both Propertius and Horace implied that monuments were less permanent than literary works, and as late as the fourth century AD, Ausonius (*Epitaphs* 32) expressed doubts about the permanency of stone: "Are we to be surprised that men are forgotten? The stones decay, and death comes to the stones and the names on them." However, it is the very durability of stone that modern scholars have asserted as the primary characteristic which made it attractive to people wishing to erect a memorial. The survival of so many Roman funerary monuments, although clearly only a small percentage of the original number, illustrates the suitability of stone as a medium for lasting

commemoration. However, the permanency that was offered by stone monuments extended beyond the physical characteristics of the material. Woolf (1996: 30) suggests that the *knowledge* that stone was robust contributed to the ability of the monument and its text to assert a particular message, especially if that message was vulnerable to challenges from others, stating that "it is the capacity of monuments to resist time that makes them suitable as vehicles for representing the contingent as permanent and the contestable as fixed." Once something had been inscribed in stone it became difficult to deny its existence or argue against its fundamental truth, the process of inscribing being one in which questionable information or statements could be made fact. This would have appealed particularly to those members of society who wished to be portrayed in the best possible light, and to those who wanted to see their new-found social or legal status cemented.

The power of the funerary monument to present information as unchallengeable may have been further emphasised by the legal context in which it was erected. The final regulation of Table X of the XII Tables reads: "A fore-court or *bustum* is to be *religiosus*" (cited in Crawford, 1996: 583). This applies specifically to the *bustum*[24] but this was also commonly the place where the memorial was set up. Being a *locus religious* meant that the site became "subject to divine law and therefore not susceptible of human ownership or possession or alienation of any kind (by sale or gift or legacy or anything else). It is *res nullius*" (Crook, 1967: 133). The legal and religious status of every burial site would have lent extra weight to the statements made on the monument. The words, by virtue of their location, also became *religiosus* and thus virtually incontestable. This authority was enhanced even further by the "monumentality of the text" (Woolf, 1996: 28). The use of inscribed text to assert the authority of Roman rulers and to convey political and civic information in a formal context lent a significant amount of weight to the practice. For the ordinary, possibly (semi-)illiterate, member of the urban community, the presence of inscriptions in the city signalled the power of the city authorities. Funerary epigraphy claimed association with this authority through the presence of the inscribed word, drawing on implications of superiority and power to add further weight to their message.

Woolf (*ibid.*: 28) suggests that "both the format and location of an inscription might be said to constitute a claim to authority by association, and an assertion of conformity with the accepted norms," hinting at a further two points that can help to explain the desirability of memorials. Firstly, the location of sepulchral monuments allowed for superior levels of communication with the living. Roman cemeteries were public places which often lined major highways, and they were regularly frequented by members of the public (Graham, 2005b). In fact, they were so public that Martial (*Epigrams*, I. 34. 8; III. 93.

---

[24] The place where a body was burned and/or buried (Berger, 1953: 377), see also Chapter 2 of this volume.

15) describes how tramps, beggars and prostitutes took up residence in abandoned tombs. The grave site was also the location for post-funeral ceremonies, including festivals such as the *Parentalia* and celebrations of the anniversary of the birth and death of the deceased. Given the public nature of these areas, they can be compared with the fluid and dynamic public spaces within the city and thus as a suitable environment for highly visible display. However, the cemetery differed from other civic spaces in that the ordinary person was not excluded from the events that took place there. D'Ambra (1993: 3), for example, states that "the forum and other civic spaces in Rome provided backdrops for spectacles in which the elite made appearances and maintained the high visibility that designated privilege. Others – the citizens and masses at the bottom of the social hierarchy – took part in these events as spectators rather than players." The cemetery, where there was little competition from civic statues, elaborate temples, inscribed governmental decrees and similar displays found in other public spaces, provided an ideal environment for personal display and the communication of status and identity ideals. Here the funerary monument competed only with other funerary structures and the high public visibility that the location offered was exploited solely by the dead. Woolf also refers to "conformity with the accepted norms," and, as we have already seen, for an individual of non-Roman origin, a stone memorial stressed their conformity with traditional *Roman* customs, thereby making substantial claims about their allegiances and identity. This is illustrated particularly well by the tombstones of the *Germani corporis custodes* who chose a Roman form of funerary commemoration despite clinging to their German sense of identity.

There were several options available to those who intended to create a sepulchral monument. Not only could the structure take many forms, but there were also text and images to consider. Undoubtedly financial factors were a major consideration but, theoretically, the funerary monument was a clean slate and could be used to express, display and promote a wide variety of issues in multiple ways. These operated either separately or together to create the desired image of the deceased. Conventions were nevertheless closely observed. The words *hic situs est* (he/she lies here) are commonly found at the end of funerary inscriptions dated to the first century BC and first century AD, and from the middle of the first century AD it also became customary for the epitaph to begin with *Dis Manibus* ('To the Underworld Gods or Spirits of the Departed'). Keppie (1991: 107) notes that this was originally written in full but eventually became abbreviated to *Dis Man* and finally DM. That these became standard elements of funerary inscriptions is demonstrated by the continuity of their use within later Christian epitaphs. For example, the epitaph of a third-century AD funerary stele found near the Vatican necropolis and commemorating Licinia Amias, a Christian, includes both the abbreviation DM and the Christian expression Ἰχθὺς ζώντων, 'fish of the living' (see Friggeri, 2001: 164). *Dis Manibus*, with its pagan connotations, has no religious meaning in this

context but its use shows that it still remained an essential element of proper commemorative practice and was also a means of signalling to the illiterate that the inscription was related to the funerary sphere. However, beyond economic and traditional constraints, the funerary monument could be as complex or simple as was desired. As Hope (2000b: 155) observes, *everything* about these objects communicated with the living – size, décor, text and location were all used to express various things. The ways in which these elements were manipulated and elaborated (or simplified) were, theoretically, limitless. The fictional example of Trimalchio and the description he provides of his future tomb (Petronius, *Satyricon* 71) demonstrates the almost limitless manipulation of funerary monuments:

> "I strongly beseech you to put my puppy dog round the feet of my statue and some wreaths and perfume jars and all the fights of Petraites so that by your skill I shall live on after death. I want the monument to have a frontage of 100 feet and a depth of 200 feet. For I should like to have all kinds of fruit growing round my ashes and a profusion of vines. Most of all I want it stated that "This monument is not to descend to my heir." It will certainly be my concern in my will to provide against any injury being done to me when I am dead. I am making one of my freedmen guardian of the tomb to prevent folk running up and shitting on it. I beg you to put ships too, in full sail, on the monument, and me sitting in my official robes on the official seat, wearing five gold rings and distributing money to the populace from a little purse. For, as you know, I gave them a meal costing two denarii each."

Although this is a work of fiction and greatly exaggerated in order to demonstrate the vulgarity of Trimalchio's tastes, it illustrates that the individual or group erecting a sepulchral monument could theoretically include *any* aspect of their life, real or created, through the use of text and images. It is highly unlikely that a tomb such as that described by Trimalchio represented the norm, and Petronius undoubtedly wished to illustrate the vulgarness of such ostentatious displays of wealth by "new men." Convention probably exerted a considerable influence over the design of sepulchral monuments. Although people wished to stand out and make bold statements about themselves through unique and eye-catching structures, at the same time they undoubtedly also wished to blend in, and not appear to be unfashionable or to betray their lack of knowledge concerning Roman styles. Equally, the skills, experience and opinions of the stonecutter or architect may also have played a significant part in the creation of a tomb or monument. Nevertheless, the tomb of Trimalchio demonstrates the way in which funerary monuments were capable of being moulded to suit the needs and desires of those involved in their commission, even though concerns for taste and decency probably prevented the common occurrence of particularly vulgar displays such as this.

Despite the almost infinite forms that sepulchral monuments could take, they remained a selective form of communication. This is discussed at length by Hope who states that "the funerary monument was a selective medium ... what was said or left unsaid was part of a deliberate shaping process in the presentation of the deceased" (Hope, 2001: 24).[25] In this way it was possible for the commemorator to promote certain aspects of their lives and to overlook others, thus shaping the image that was portrayed. Hope (1998: 193) has also suggested that the Roman funerary monument represented "a limited form of communication;" intimating that it was incapable of displaying the vast quantities of information that other communicative structures could. However, as we have seen, these monuments took various forms and information was transmitted in diverse ways, on different levels that could be understood by the various groups that comprised society. Beyond the fact that an extended epitaph, something comparable in length to the *Res Gestae* for example, was in reality unlikely to be read, and that shorter texts and interesting reliefs or statuary were more attractive to the traveller passing through the cemetery, the funerary monument was not limited in terms of the options that it made available for display. That the majority *chose* to be limited in their communication is, however, significant. Overlooking or ignoring information and aspects of the identity of the deceased, their personality, lifestyle, occupation or family was a conscious choice made by the dedicators of the monument and not imposed by the nature of the medium. Indeed, Hope (2000b: 155 – 56) also recognises that it was the very variety of memorial forms that allowed the inherent diversity of Roman society to be displayed. The images portrayed may not have reflected reality but they were given a sense of legitimacy by the finality of their existence in stone form.

Commemoration and emotion

Social competition was undoubtedly a crucial factor in the creation of monuments, but it is equally essential to recognise the emotional context in which they were set up; as Hopkins (1983: 204) explains, "Romans had feelings, and it seems reasonable to ask what they were." In her study of *Bereavement and Commemoration* (1999) Tarlow acknowledges the difficulties of attempting to identify the influence and expression of emotion in the archaeological record.[26] However, she repeatedly emphasises the importance of doing so in order to fully understand the material culture of the past, stating that "if archaeologists are unwilling to consider the minds of people in the past, they are powerless to approach areas such as motivation, without which the narratives they produce are two-dimensional and dehumanising" (1999: 26). Tarlow does not consider emotion "a part of some universal and essential humanity" (*ibid.*: 35) and observes that emotions and their expression can of course be socially constructed. However, she considers these forces

vital to a study of death and burial: "how can we consider burial (death) without considering grief, fear and other emotions, which inform and structure funerary practices?" (*ibid.*: 30). Although Tarlow notes that individual responses to "emotional" situations vary, an inability to identify the specific feelings of individuals does not render the attempt to search for their manifestation in the material record less legitimate. Indeed, despite a rejection of the universalism of emotion, Tarlow proposes that "feelings" were central to increasing levels of commemoration in Orkney between the late eighteenth and twentieth centuries. Hopkins (1983: 223) has also highlighted the problems inherent in identifying "a single, constant, cross-cultural human nature," and, most importantly, has recognised that "we should not take for granted that our modern patterns and habits of reasoning necessarily linked Roman motives with Roman actions. Their rationality was probably different from ours" (*ibid.*: 204 – 205). Finley (1981: 159), discussing attitudes towards the elderly in antiquity, agrees, and suggests that in a society in which early death was routine, "the intensity and duration of the emotional responses were unlike modern reactions." Nevertheless, Hopkins (1983: 222) firmly states that "grief cannot be evaded; it is part of the human condition," and, despite the difficulties of identifying a universal human nature, "there are some constant human elements or drives" (*ibid.*: 223). Rawson (1966: 80) concurs, asserting that "the desire to care for one's own dead – both at burial and in commemorative rites at future times – is a primitive and basically human one and is not imposed by law or nationality." In order to discuss funerary practices in their fullest context, therefore, it is clearly essential that we be aware of the emotional forces of grief, sadness and loss, and we must investigate their material expression and impact on the actions of the living.

In simple terms, "to erect a monument is a way of showing how much an individual has meant to you, and showing that to the rest of the community" (Hopkins, 1983: 131). The funerary monument stood as a memorial to a specific relationship, and its ability to display and forge personal bonds has been illustrated here by examples such as that of the *Germani corporis custodes*. However, families were also closely involved in the dedication of monuments. Expressions of emotion are not uncommon on Imperial period tombstones, and personal relationships are often signalled through the recognition of the virtues of the deceased. Friggeri (2001: 161 – 162) observes that these "can be found even in the most concise funerary inscriptions, although only a single adjective may have been used: *pientissimus*, *benemerens* (often abbreviated BM), *dulcissimus* (generally referring to young children) or a sign of affection for that person: *amatissimus*, *carissimus*, which emphasized the sadness felt upon the death of dear ones." Questions can, and have been, raised with regards to the authenticity of these direct expressions and the widespread use of standardised formulae has been used to argue that sentimentality played little part in the process of epitaph composition. King (2000: 129) proposes that "the influence of

---

[2] See also Hope 1998 and 2000b.
[2*] Tarlow (2000) also examines these issues in considerable detail.

tradition implies that the sentiments recorded in stone cannot be genuine," before suggesting that the stonemason probably played a more significant role in the choice of monument and epitaph. However, she later observes (*ibid*.: 132) that "the expression of emotions, whether verbally or in written form, always follows a standard, formulaic pattern." Hopkins (1983: 220) also suggests that "the very act of transforming feelings into words automatically channels them along conventional lines. Language is a set of conventions." This is supported further by Tarlow's (1999: 131) proposal that "the significance of the stone was personal and emotional, and the fact that it was publicly visible should not make us cynical about the feelings of bereavement experienced by those who erected them." What is more, the creation of a memorial provided a formal and standardised outlet for the expression of grief and a response to the uncertainty caused by death. Cannon (1989: 446) notes that "death's disruption of social and personal bonds creates a powerful medium for expressive response, and this response can take any number of forms, all tied to the emotional and social effects of death's created loss." The act of memorialising was therefore directly influenced by the need of the mourners to cope with a highly emotional situation within the limits of convention. It therefore also provided an ideal context in which to make statements about a relationship or loved one that under other circumstances may have remained private.

In order to understand the impact of the emotional desire to commemorate, particularly amongst the poor, it is necessary to examine the form and extent of relationships experienced during life, particularly those of a familial nature. According to Brunt (1987a: 139 – 140), "craftsmen and landless labourers were unlikely to marry if they had little prospect of being able to provide for a wife and family." High mortality rates that may have rendered lasting relationships impossible or reduced the emotional investment individuals were prepared to make, have been cited in support of this proposal. Economic factors are also considered integral, Brunt (*ibid*.: 139) for example, suggesting that "there must be a level below which a man cannot afford to take a wife."[27] However, poverty and emotion are not mutually exclusive and it is important that we acknowledge the existence of human relationships. Dixon (1992: 3) has argued that, the family "is a universal human institution, and the Romans were human." Furthermore, without the existence of real personal relationships and families, the lower class population would have declined dramatically. The importance of personal relationships and family structures to members of the freedman class in particular, have been stressed above and can be seen in the emphasis they placed on the family on their funerary monuments. These families were probably small at both ends of the social scale, Patterson (2000a: 270) proposing that "many Roman families must have been of the nuclear type (i.e. husband, wife and children), largely because the effects of high mortality rates and consequent low level of life

expectancy at Rome would have meant that few families would have had more than two generations living at the same time." Indeed, during the Empire the state attempted to encourage birth rates by awarding status benefits to families who produced three or more children (Stambaugh, 1988: 158). At the lower end of the social and economic scale especially, the nuclear family unit probably consisted of between two and five people, and acted as a means of both emotional and economic support for the individual (Dixon, 1992: 162 – 163). It is unlikely that larger families could have been maintained on an unreliable wage.[28]

The need for economic support was also a feature of family life that was of particular importance to poorer members of society who looked to their offspring for support in old age and, eventually, burial. However, a need for material support, much stressed by scholars wishing to demonstrate a lack of emotional investment in family and personal relationships, does not necessarily lessen the significance of emotional relationships. Dixon (1991: 113) has argued that there was a strong sentimental ideal of the family, at least amongst the elite, during the late Republic and early Empire and there is strong evidence to suggest that emotion played a central role in upper class family life despite the arrangement of marriages on social or political grounds. Lucretius (3.894 – 6), for example, describes the happy home in which, "sweet children race to win the first kisses, and thrill your heart to its depths with sweetness." It is therefore unlikely that emotion was absent in the lives of poorer classes, especially since "there was no consideration of family interests to prevent [them] marrying for love" (Wilkinson, 1975: 129). Moreover, for those sharing small apartments, constant contact with other individuals and families probably resulted in the creation of extended family networks based not on genetic links but co-habitation. Bradley (1991: 92), discussing the terms "*tata*" and "*mamma*", suggests they were used by lower-class children as affectionate titles for unrelated individuals who formed part of their "extended family," possibly "their parents' co residents, co-workers and neighbours – who at times came to play within their lives a quasi-parental role, even though unrelated." The family (nuclear or extended) is therefore likely to have provided a significant means of support for members of the poverty stricken classes on the basis that "it seems to satisfy certain constant human needs, especially the need for material aid and the sense of belonging and mutual emotional support" (Dixon, 1992: 162).

Golden (1988: 155) has proposed that between 30 and 40 percent of children died in the first year of life. The frequency of infant death has led to suggestions that parents limited emotional investment in children, at least until they reached an age at which they were likely to survive to maturity, a conviction that is shared by

---

[27] These economic constraints are set out in more detail in Chapter 3.

[28] For a more detailed discussion of these relationships and the composition of the Roman family see Rawson (1992), Nielsen (1997) and Saller (1997). See Chapter 3 for discussion of the unreliability of employment.

scholars of other historical periods. Hopkins has examined the work of Stone (1979) on sixteenth and seventeenth century England. He argued that, "when mortality was high, frequent death and the expectation that death might at any time rupture close relationships prevented people from investing huge amounts of emotion in loving attachments or intimacy: 'to preserve their mental stability, parents were obliged to limit the degree of their psychological involvement with their infant children'" (Hopkins, 1983: 222, citing Stone, 1979: 57). Similar attitudes can perhaps be seen in evidence for infant exposure at Rome, particularly amongst the lower classes. However, as Harris (1994: 113) explains, the commonest reason for exposure was an inability to feed an extra mouth, *not* an absence of attachment to the child. Moreover, exposure was often carried out "in such a way as to make it as likely as possible that the child would be found and rescued, mainly by leaving it in a conventional place for exposure" (*ibid.*: 9).

Literature and epigraphy provide additional evidence for emotional attachments and even the use of stock terms can indicate "the strength of ideals of marital harmony, affection for young children, and regret for "children" of all ages who died before their parents" (Dixon, 1992:30). According to Bradley (1991: 117), Plutarch, in the *Moralia* (493 – 497), argued that "human affection for children is a natural emotional response and (contrary to Epicurus) that human procreation is not dictated by hope of material return." Rates of infant mortality were high and parents presumably experienced the death of children on a regular basis but they were not necessarily immune to that loss. Indeed, Golden (1988: 154) notes that, under such circumstances, feelings of attachment may be *greater* rather than less. Thus, "far from being indifferent, members of cultures in which children are at risk often make sure that their infants are in almost constant contact with a care-giver, quickly see to them when they cry, and feed them whenever they suspect they are hungry – precisely because they know the danger that they will die if they are not attended to" (*ibid.*: 155). Although children may have been a substantial financial burden for the lower classes, parents eventually came to depend on the support of their children. It thus made sense to invest in them both financially *and* emotionally in order to ensure their own comfort and survival later in life. Golden (*ibid.*: 157) concludes that "the argument that adults in high-mortality populations did not care when their children died fails to convince," and Hopkins (1983: 218) observes that the prohibitions of the XII Tables (X.4) concerning excessive mourning, and later writings advising men and women against "grieving too loudly, too much or too long … surely imply that uncontrolled or 'unseemly' mourning was widespread." Mourners were hired to accompany aristocratic funerals, indicating that public expressions of grief were acceptable, and perhaps even expected. Economic factors may have prevented the purchase of a substantial memorial for a family member but this did not necessarily signal any diminished sense of loss at their death, and there is no reason to suggest that the desire to express their bereavement in a permanent form was reduced. Saller and Shaw (1984: 130) point out that in

urban centres, such as Carthage and Ostia, the largest single category of inscriptions comprises dedications to children under the age of ten and, "in Rome, from the Republic to the Principate and from the lower classes to the senatorial aristocracy, a strong urge was felt to perpetuate the memory of the family relationship between the commemorator and the deceased (72 to 78 per cent of commemorators being from the nuclear family)" (*ibid.*: 134).[29] Poorer members of society formed personal, intimate relationships with one another, which they undoubtedly wished to commemorate as much as wealthier members of the same community.

Every member of the Roman urban community had personal experience of death and their responses to funerary monuments was further conditioned by these experiences. As Elsner (1998: 145) observes, "the marking of a death is perhaps the moment at which human beings especially reflect upon the vanished life they are mourning and their own mortality." Funerary monuments were not only expressive in terms of information, but they also conveyed and constructed the emotions of those involved. This not only affected the form of the monument but also the ways in which it was perceived by the onlookers and strangers who were enticed to pay closer attention to monuments with which they perhaps felt they had more in common than the statues of civic patrons and public building dedications. As Horace wrote:

"Whether thou be rich and sprung from ancient Inachus, or dwell beneath the canopy of heaven poor and of lowly birth, it makes no difference: thou art pitiless Orcus' victim.

We are all being gathered to one and the same fold. The lot of everyone of us is tossing about in the urn, destined sooner or later, to come forth and place us in Charon's skiff for everlasting exile."

(*Odes*, II. 3. 21 – 28)

The common fate of all men, regardless of wealth or age, is a common theme within the *Odes* of Horace[30] and, despite his apparent need to remind his audience repeatedly of this fact, it is likely that the population of Rome was intently aware of the proximity of death. Their responses to funerary monuments were conditioned by this knowledge and their personal emotional experiences.

Sepulchral monuments were evidently, therefore, an ideal means for the ordinary Roman (or non-Roman) to make public statements about themselves and their loved ones in an accepted and conventional manner. For many individuals there were few opportunities for lasting self-promotion and display and the funerary monument

---

[29] Their definition of "the lower classes" is, however, rather broad, comprising "those below the curial order" (Saller and Shaw, 1984: 127).
[30] See for example *Odes*, I. 4. 13 – 17; I. 28. 15 – 20; II. 3. 4 – 8; II. 14. 1 – 12; II. 18. 29 – 40 and III. 24. 1 – 8

allowed individuals to assert aspects of their lives, emotions and relationships in a publicly accessible format. The truth of these statements was emphasised by the context in which they were made, even if the reality they presented was actually a created ideal.

Conclusions: incorporating the lower classes

Before leaving this discussion of memory preservation and commemoration, it is essential that we briefly examine other forms of commemoration that might have taken place in the ancient world.

As Williams (2003:7) has pointed out, "monumentality is certainly not a pre-requisite for remembrance and societies can construct complex ways of negotiating the dangers and the advantages of remembering without creating enduring cemeteries or graves." This is a particularly significant observation in the context of a study that aims to elucidate the funerary practices of the urban poor – a section of the community for whom even the most modest of monuments often lay out of reach. The importance of remembrance and commemorative practices at Rome during the late Republic and early Imperial period has been emphasised throughout this chapter and it has become very evident that *all* members of the ancient urban community were concerned with the perpetuation of their memory and the public display of their lives, identities, successes and relationships, for a complex variety of reasons. These concerns were certainly not restricted to the elite of the city. However, for those who did not have access to the required economic resources were there other options available with which they could commemorate the dead and promote their identities?

Connerton's study of *How Societies Remember* (1989) provides a particularly useful insight into the ways in which the urban poor may have responded to the demands and pressures that led other members of the urban community to create lasting funerary monuments. Connerton (*ibid.*: 72 – 73) has distinguished between 'inscribing practices', which involve the creation of a device (in this case a sepulchral monument) that "traps and hold information long after the human organism has stopped informing," and 'incorporating practices' taking the form of active participation in commemorative activities, ceremonies and bodily practices. Connerton's in-depth analysis of these different forms of commemorative practice allows us to suggest alternatives to the funerary monument: repeated ritual practices that involved individuals and groups who wished to remember and celebrate the departed.

The group under the spotlight in this study, the urban poor, were probably excluded on economic grounds from the competitive world of the funerary monument, but they remained, at the same time, subject to the same pressures, demands, fears and desires as the rest of the community. Connerton's model provides a means by which to identify and the explore the burial and commemorative activities of the lower classes of Rome. It allows us to move away from the search for purely material expressions of remembrance and enter the realm of ritual and bodily practice. If we are to understand these processes we must examine in more detail the funerary practices of the Roman urban community and identify the situations and activities that may have provided the lower classes with opportunities to join the rest of the community in practices of lasting commemoration.

27

CHAPTER TWO

FUNERALS AND BURIAL PRACTICE

"Though thou art eager to be going, 'tis a brief delay I ask. Only three handfuls of earth! Then thou mayst speed upon thy course."

(Horace, *Odes*, I. 28(2). 15 – 16)

The acts of commemoration seen in the previous chapter formed only one part of the ancient funerary process and before such activities could occur the remains of the deceased had first to be disposed of in accordance with the appropriate rites. This process was in some ways even more important than commemoration and was similarly influenced by a multitude of complex factors. Although disposal was essentially a practical necessity, it was also entangled with issues of religion, real and ritual pollution, the law, duty and, perhaps inevitably, competition amongst the living for recognition, status and identity.

The Roman funeral

The ritual of the funeral began immediately after death. Modern reconstructions of these activities are based largely on extant literary accounts which recall the actions of the wealthier classes of the urban community. It is therefore difficult to establish with any degree of certainty the extent to which poorer members of Roman society observed the same practices and rituals. As we shall see, however, the impact of religious beliefs concerning the fate of the soul and the afterlife on all levels of society indicates that similar rituals were probably performed by the less wealthy, albeit on a less extravagant scale.

Before examining these processes and activities, however, it is essential to acknowledge the very patchy nature of the evidence. The descriptions of the funeral and the rites that were performed immediately after death that are presented here are based on secondary sources that draw together all of the evidence for these activities from a variety of sources from different periods of time. Although this provides a useful insight into the types of activities that occurred, it must not be forgotten that these run the risk of creating an inaccurate composite picture with very little chronological specificity. It is possible that some, or all, of these practices changed either their form or meaning over time, or were abandoned all together. Some families may have specifically chosen to leave out certain activities, whilst others may have assumed a particular importance. Nevertheless, these descriptions allow us to create a basic impression of the types of activities that occurred at the deathbed and during the funeral and it is with these that this discussion must begin.

Toynbee (1971: 43 – 44) provides a comprehensive description of the death of a family member that it is worth quoting in full:

> "When death was imminent relations and close friends gathered round the dying person's bed, to comfort and support him or her and to give vent to their own grief. The nearest relative present gave the last kiss, to catch the soul, which, so it was believed, left the body with the final breath. The same relative then closed the departed's eyes (*oculos premere*, etc), after which all the near relatives called upon the dead by name (*conclamare*) and lamented him or her, a process that continued at intervals until the body was disposed of by cremation or inhumation. The next act was to take the body from the bed, to set it on the ground (*deponere*), and to wash it and anoint it. Then followed the dressing of the corpse – in a toga, in the case of a male Roman citizen, the laying of a wreath on its head, particularly in the case of a person who had earned one in life, and the placing of a coin in the mouth to pay the deceased's fare in Charon's barque. All was now ready for the body's exposition or lying-in-state (*collocare* = προτιθέναι) on a grand bed (*lectus funebris*), if the family was well-to-do, with the feet towards the house-door."

Paoli (1963: 128) has additionally observed that burning lamps and candles were placed around the corpse, which was itself strewn with flowers, wreaths and garlands, and that the fire on the hearth was extinguished as a sign of mourning. The body then lay in state for up to seven days, during which the funeral was arranged. Family members were closely involved in the rites that took place immediately after the death of a loved one, but funeral professionals also seem to have been entrusted with funeral arrangements and other activities such as preparing the body and bearing the bier to the place of burial. Although often grouped under the title *libitinarii* (undertakers) these workers were more specialised than the term implies. Bodel (2000: 136) defines the *libitinarii* as "funeral contractors and suppliers of workmen rather than tradesmen themselves," with the latter becoming less commonly referred to by their specialist titles during the middle and late imperial period and more often simply as *funerarii*.

An examination of the specialised roles played by members of the funerary trade provides a useful insight into funerary activities and emphasises the considerable importance that was attached to the burial ritual. Amongst the funerary specialists can be found *pollinctores*, referred to by Plautus as "morticians, who took their name from the practice of covering the face of the corpse with powder (*pollen*) in order to conceal the discolouration of death" (*ibid*.: 138; Plautus *Poen.* 63). Those responsible for carrying the corpses of the poor were known as *vespillones*, and reference is made to grave-diggers (*fossores*) and corpse-burners (*ustores*), in addition to horn players (*siticines*, *tubicines*), flautists (*tibicines*) and mimes and dancers who were all involved in the funerary procession itself. Responsibility for organising the cortège fell to the *dissignator*, the funeral director. Bodel (*ibid*.: 139) suggests that the *dissignator* had a higher status than the other workers, possibly due to his lack of physical contact with the corpse, and that the title was often associated with that of *praeco* (herald or auctioneer). Perhaps the "herald and assignor of seats" (CIL 22997a) whose tomb relief commemorated himself and his family with portraits, discussed in Chapter 1, was one such individual.[31] An indication of the cost of hiring *libitinarii* can perhaps be gained from a legal text from Puteoli, the *lex Puteolana* (*AE* 1971, 88), in which it is stated that they were also responsible for executions and other punishments. The total cost of such activity was reportedly no more than 50 – 60 sesterces (Saller and Shaw, 1984: 128, n. 23).[32] Although, as will become clear in the following chapter, for the poor this remained a considerable, and probably unaffordable, amount.

The emergence of funerary specialists during the Republic can perhaps be explained in several ways. Firstly, it is evident from the events immediately surrounding death that the corpse was considered to be polluted and that certain activities had to be performed in order to ritually cleanse it. This spiritual pollution extended beyond the corpse itself and rendered the entire family unclean until the ninth day after the burial. Various measures were taken, including the placing of a cypress branch outside the door of the house, in order to warn people of the presence of a dead body within. Anyone attending a funeral was forbidden from bathing before they did so, and everyone had to undergo cleansing with water and fire (*suffitio*) afterwards.[33] As Hope and Marshall (2000: 6) have suggested, until it was

correctly disposed of, the corpse lay "halfway between the world of the living and the world of the dead; an ambivalence and uncertainty which could affect all of those who came into contact with it." This was especially true for magistrates and high priests, who must avoid spiritual contamination at all costs (Bodel, 2000: 142).[34] Since the corpse was considered spiritually polluted, certain members of the family may have wished to minimise the physical contact they were required to have with it, especially upper class office holders. The skills of funerary specialists, who by virtue of their occupation were already unclean, were therefore required to perform the necessary activities. Bodel (*ibid*.: 143) suggests that perceptions of the individuals who handled corpses directly as polluted led to increasing segregation, citing an example at Puteoli, where "funerary workers were prohibited from entering the town except on official business and were forbidden to live closer to town than a tower where the local Grove of Libitina was located (*AE* 1971, 88II. 3 – 4)." Family members who suffered from similar pollution during the period of mourning (*funesta*) lost this status by performing cleansing rituals once the *funesta* had ended. Those who regularly came into contact with the dead by virtue of their profession however, appear to have been unable to achieve spiritual cleanliness.

The words of Martial (*Epigrams* II. 61.3 – 4) indicate that those involved in the funerary trade were afforded little respect: "Now that your sorry head has earned the scorn of undertakers and the disgust of a wretched executioner." This was probably largely due to their close physical association with the dead but may also be connected to the fact that they were paid to carry out a job that was the traditional responsibility of the family itself. Bodel (*ibid*.: 141) observes that "there was nothing inherently ignoble in the activity of burying the dead – on the contrary, laying the dead to rest was a *negotium humanitatis* (*Dig.* 11.7.14.7 [Ulpian]). Ignominy lay in performing for pay what was regarded as a natural obligation of humanity." Not only were funerary professionals paid for their services (paid employment was itself considered vulgar, unless it involved large scale commerce – see Chapter 3) in a context which rendered them spiritually unclean, but they performed duties that should have been conducted by all pious individuals. Perhaps a concealed sense of guilt on the part of those who employed such professionals lent further weight to the stigmatisation of funerary workers. Nevertheless, if any guilt *was* harboured by the elevated classes of society it evidently had little effect on their decision to continue to employ people to perform the appropriate funerary rituals and preparations for them. Herein lies a further explanation for the increased use of funerary specialists: display of wealth and status. Employing outsiders to cleanse and prepare the body, to play music, to lament loudly the passing of the deceased, to organise the cortège and prepare the place and means of disposal, allowed these families to ostentatiously demonstrate that they were providing the dead with the proper attention, at

---

[31] It is notable that only the latter occupation has been recorded epigraphically, thus intimating that there was indeed a higher degree of prestige (and/or wealth) associated with such a position.
[32] See Bodel (2004) for a detailed examination of this text and the funerary professionals of the Roman world.
[33] See Graham (forthcoming a and b) for a new interpretation of the rituals involved in these cleansing activities.

[34] See also Lindsay (2000).

the same time as displaying their economic status and ability to employ people to do these things for them.

The extent to which professional funerary workers were employed by the lower classes remains obscure. It is unlikely that the very poor were able to afford the expenses involved, despite the fact that when Festus (*Paul. Exc. Fest.* 368 –9) mentions *vespillones* he appears to refer directly to the poor. He noted that *vespillones* bore the corpses of those who could not afford a proper funeral and that their name derived from the fact that these activities occurred during the evening (*vespertino tempore*) (see Bodel, 2000: 138). However, questions can be raised regarding the identification of *vespillones* as professional corpse bearers employed specifically by the poor. On a purely practical level, if those carried to the grave were too poor to afford a "proper funeral" it seems unlikely that they could afford to hire specialist corpse-bearers when family members or friends could easily perform such duties. Bearing a bier, after all, requires relatively little specialist expertise. Perhaps the poor also wished to make a public statement by hiring funeral professionals for one of the most visible aspects of the funerary ritual? If Festus is to be believed, however, these funerals occurred at night when there were few people to witness such a display. Two suggestions can be made which go some way to explaining this. Firstly, it is possible that by "those without the means to afford a proper funeral" Festus refers not to the poorest members of society but those unable to afford the extremely extravagant displays of the elite; in comparison the funerals conducted by these people were considered to be "poor". Alternatively, the term may have been used to refer not to a specialist group of funerary workers but to *any* individual responsible for bearing a bier.

The belief that the funerals of the poor took place at night by the light of torches is based on three short passages by Servius, possibly derived originally from the works of Varro (Rose, 1923: 191). Despite Rose's early twentieth century examination of this assumption, scholars have continued to assert that the tradition of conducting funerals at night in early Rome was eventually abandoned for all but the funerals of children and the poor (see Paoli, 1963: 129; Toynbee, 1971: 46; Walker, 1985: 9).[35] Funerals probably *were* held originally at night, perhaps, as Bodel (2000: 142) suggests, in order to avoid crossing the path of magistrates and high priests, who would suffer damaging spiritual pollution as a result. Nevertheless, an adult member of the lower classes was no more spiritually contaminating than an aristocrat, and so there would appear to have been no specific religious reason for continuing to bury only the poor at night. Rose (*ibid.*: 194) points out that "one possible explanation of their nocturnal burials is simply that the mourners would then be likelier to have time to attend." This may certainly have been the case amongst those who were required to work long hours in order to survive. However, it seems

unlikely that all the burials of the lower classes took place at night. It is evident from written descriptions of Republican and Imperial funerals that these events commonly took place during the day, which was when the proceedings were at their most visible. The eulogy delivered in the forum was intended to reach the ears of as many members of the community as possible, including those going about their everyday business in the busy centre of the city. Equally, the procession through the city streets was designed to communicate on a grand scale. As we have seen in the previous chapter, these parts of the funeral were integral to the commemorative process and there is little reason to suggest that the lower classes were any less eager to capitalise on the opportunities they offered for display, remembrance and recognition. Even if these events lacked vast numbers of mourners, *imagines*, and elaborate shows of wealth, a passing funerary procession will still have attracted attention and probably made people stop, watch it pass by and perhaps even contemplate their own mortality and remember their own deceased ancestors. The suggestion that lower class funerals were "hurried nocturnal affairs" (Paoli, 1963: 129) has further contributed to a distancing of the customs of the lower classes from those of the elite, but there is no reason to believe that the lower classes held fundamentally different beliefs with regards to the appropriate time for funerals. They may have been more restricted by the structure of their daily routine and the need to bury the deceased quickly (those living in apartments will have had no *atrium* for lengthy lying in state, for example) but this did not necessarily compel them to conduct funerals at night. Moreover, although Juvenal (*Sat.* III. 232 - 238) complains of being kept awake by the noise of carts and traffic in the city he makes no mention of the loud lamenting and music traditionally associated with Roman funerals.

The funeral procession therefore provided further opportunities for display. Whether the increased funerary extravagance of the late Republic was the cause of, or a response to, the change from night to day, remains unclear. However, holding funerals at night restricted their ability to make public statements concerning the status and identity of the deceased and their family. As McDonnell (1999: 549) notes, "within the world of Roman aristocrats, in purpose and effect the funeral procession was about competition," and, as noted in Chapter 1, the procession was itself a means by which to create and display a desired image of the deceased. Moving through the city streets, the procession exhibited to the wider community the illustrious past of the family, their wealth and position in society. The power of this communication was heightened by the nature of the spaces through which the procession passed; these were public spaces filled with ordinary citizens going about their daily business. The extravagant funerals of the upper classes consequently became a form of public entertainment. As Bodel (1999: 263) states, "funerals were popular spectacles, and like other public entertainments at Rome that drew a crowd, they provided a powerful vehicle not only for elite self-promotion but

[35] See also Rushforth (1915) for a discussion of the significance of torches in Roman sepulchral monuments, particularly in terms of their religious associations.

30

also for popular expressions of pleasure or displeasure, approbation or censure." Although originally purely functional in nature (based on a simple practical need to move the body to the burial site) the procession became increasingly integrated within wider social processes.

Our reconstruction of the funeral procession (*pompa*) is again reliant on literary references which primarily focus on particularly ostentatious examples, and one or two funerary reliefs. Toynbee (1971: 46 – 47) uses a marble relief from Amiternum to illustrate her discussion of the procession. This relief, dated to the late-Republican or Augustan period, depicts the deceased reclining on a bier piled with pillows and mattresses and borne by eight men. The scene also depicts other people involved in the procession including the *dissignator* (directing and organising the procession), pipers (*tibicines*), a trumpeter (*tubicines*), two horn-blowers (*cornicines*), two *praeficae* (hired mourners) and the chief mourners, consisting of family members, friends and servants (*ibid.*: 46 – 47). The absence of *imagines* indicates that the relief is not a depiction of the funeral of an office-holding aristocrat, but it provides an opportunity to see the variety and wealth that such occasions could involve.

Clearly not all members of society could afford lavish processions. The comment of Martial (*Epigrams* VII.75.9 – 10) that, "Four branded slaves were bearing a corpse of low degree like a thousand that the pauper's pyre receives," has been interpreted as a description of a typically simple lower-class funeral,[36] but it is not possible to completely dismiss the existence of funeral processions amongst the less wealthy. Family and friends probably followed the bier, however simple and unadorned, on its way to the burial site. Moreover, unlike events immediately surrounding death or burial, the funeral procession appears to have had no specific religious significance. It was thus able to act on a purely secular level to communicate the desired image of the deceased to the wider community and could be manipulated without fear of breaking with religious custom. The absence of any real religious significance has connotations especially for understanding the funerary activities of the lower classes. Traditional religious rites, such as the last kiss, were probably carried out amongst these classes; there is no reason to suggest otherwise – they were not activities than depended on wealth or class but religious belief and piety. However, the funeral procession, lacking such associations, was probably considered to be less vital than rites connected with religious or superstitious beliefs. No superstitious fears compelled individuals to hold an elaborate (or as

elaborate as financially possible) funeral procession. Equally, therefore, there is no reason to assume that the lower classes did not recognise the opportunities this occasion presented for self-display and commemoration. The audience for processions undoubtedly varied in accordance with the status and identity of the deceased. Lavish funerals were probably witnessed by the majority of the urban community, as was suggested in the previous chapter, but those of the less wealthy were probably more low-key. The extent of the audience was largely a factor of the procession itself, with more elaborate displays attracting greater attention. Although the lower classes may not have expected to draw a large crowd, the procession still provided an opportunity for public expression and communication with their peers and anyone who saw the procession as it passed.

However, like commemoration, the importance of the funeral procession gradually decreased during the Imperial period, as the focus shifted away from extravert displays to internalised expressions of grief (*ibid.*: 267). Nevertheless, Bodel (*ibid.*: 270) observes that although the focus moved away from the procession it did so "toward the spectacular finale of the cremation itself" which, despite taking place in "the more personal suburban environment of the burial site" was probably no less extravagant.

Inhumation or cremation?

Cicero (*de Leg.* II. 22.56) and Pliny (*Nat. Hist.* VII. 187), both state that the primitive rite of burial at Rome was inhumation but that cremation had more recently become the norm, and it was now unusual for families to inhume their deceased relatives. Pliny (*Nat. Hist.* VII. 187), in particular, notes that the *Gens Cornelia* continued to practice inhumation at a time when it was more customary to cremate. Cremation was probably the predominant burial rite practiced at Rome from about 400 BC onwards (Toynbee, 1971: 40). Archaeological evidence certainly demonstrates increased concentrations of cremation burials between the fourth century BC and the end of the first century AD, and Morris (1992: 45 – 46) concludes that during the first century AD "cremation was probably virtually the only rite used at Rome." Two textual references shed further light on this issue. Tacitus (*Ann.* XVI. 6), in his description of the burial of Poppaea in AD 65, characterises cremation as the 'Roman *mos*', and Petronius (also writing around AD 60) refers in turn to inhumation as a 'Greek custom' (*Sat.* III.2). There was evidently widespread agreement on what constituted the traditional "Roman" method of burial.

Although cremation was the predominant burial rite during this period and appears to have encompassed all levels of society, the conclusion of Morris requires further qualification. Despite cremation being "the norm", not all members of urban society were incinerated after their death. There was no legal prohibition on inhumation – cremation was simply a widely observed *custom*. It is therefore unsurprising to find that

---

[36] Martial's reference to slaves here is interesting for it has already been established that those involved in the funerary business were professionals. It is possible that slaves were used for certain tasks, although these are likely to have involved the more unpleasant and less visible activities. The text from Puteoli (*AE* 1971, 88) noted above states that, "the contracting undertaker (*manceps*) is to keep a staff of thirty-two workers, who are to be of sound body and free of marks (*neve stigmat(ibus) inscrip(tus)*)" (Kyle, 1998: 163). These workers may have been slaves. It is also possible that Martial was referring not to employed bier bearers but individuals carrying the body of a fellow slave.

inhumation continued to be practiced during the Republic and early Imperial period, albeit to a lesser extent. The *puticuli* themselves (if indeed they represent a normal method of disposal – see Chapter 4) seem to demonstrate the persistence of inhumation and the continued use of the rite by the *Cornelii* suggests that they felt little compunction to alter family tradition. Cicero (*de Leg.* II. 22. 56) informs us that Sulla was the first of the *Cornelii* to be cremated, but as Kyle (1998: 169) points out, "cremation was also appealing because it meant that the body could not be disturbed (by animals or foes);" something that no doubt affected this decision given the circumstances surrounding his death. Since inhumation is generally considered a cheaper means of disposal (Nock, 1972: 282), requiring no combustible fuel or specialist knowledge, it may consequently be expected to have remained popular amongst the less wealthy members of the urban community.

Cremation remained dominant at Rome during the early Imperial period, as evidenced by the many *columbaria* and other tombs built specifically to accommodate cremation urns or chests, but the situation changed once more during the second century AD, as inhumation began to make a resurgence. Between *c.* AD 150 – 300 tombs were constructed specifically to accommodate inhumation burials, either in free-standing sarcophagi, *arcosolia* (arches built into the lower parts of the walls) or *formae* dug beneath the floor. Other existing tombs were modified, for example at Isola Sacra where the house tombs underwent significant alterations to their interior.

However, the change from a rite widely considered to be the "Roman *mos*" to that of "Greek custom" did not occur instantaneously and for a period of time the two rites probably existed simultaneously. The precise details of how and why the change came about have long been the subject of scholarly debate. Inhumation was generally less expensive than cremation and therefore we should be cautious in aligning fully with Morris (1992: 54) who states that "the richer classes at Rome, from the emperors down to wealthy non-magistrates, probably all took up the rite within the space of a generation or so, between about 140 and 180; the lower orders apparently took to it rather more slowly, as did those outside Rome." Not only had many members of the very poor probably continued to use the less expensive rite of inhumation regardless of so-called "custom", but Morris also fails to define precisely who he is referring to as "the lower orders." This group could conceivably include both the destitute and successful freedmen, shopkeepers, craftsmen and merchants. The latter have been shown to be particularly concerned with the opportunities for social advancement offered by the funeral and may thus have clung to cremation, and the high visibility of the luxuriously adorned pyre, for longer than wealthier members of the community. Morris (*ibid.*: 61) also observes that inhumation led to a reduction in the number of burials that could take place within the average sized tomb: "a tomb built after 175 would inevitably emphasise a narrower kin or professional group than previously." This mirrors the change from exterior to internal tomb

elaboration by many members of society, discussed in Chapter 1. Statements about identity and social status could continue to be made through these tombs but for freedmen, and those whose status had recently undergone significant improvement, the more traditional practices may have held greater appeal. As we have seen, aligning themselves with traditional Roman practices was an essential part of expressing their identity and negotiating a place within citizen society, and therefore the more successful members of the lower classes who could afford to cremate their dead may have clung to the tradition for longer. For the majority of less economically successful individuals, however, inhumation will have probably been the more commonly employed rite.

The proposal that the change in custom reflected a shift in religious beliefs has been largely discounted, with Nock (1972: 286) observing that, "the modes of honouring the dead man are commonly the same under both customs; we find libation tubes for ash-urns and for burials." Furthermore, he points out that the reasons given by contemporary Romans for inhumation, including clinging affection, were not associated with religion (*ibid.*: 286). Christianity may have strengthened the desire to inhume during later centuries but probably had little influence when the change initially occurred during the second century AD. Nock (*ibid.*: 306) also rejects the suggestion that it was brought about by an increase in the cost of fuel on the basis that it appears to have begun amongst the richer elements of society. The reasons for increased fuel costs are also obscure and, as Meiggs (1982: 257) points out, there was no shortage of wood for fuel available in the city. There also appears to be no legal reason for the change because legal texts continued to treat the two rites equally (*ibid.*: 306). Morris (1992: 67) concludes that the shift from cremation to inhumation was related to a change of form or fashion, with Nock (1972: 306) suggesting that the evolution of elaborate sarcophagi provided an opportunity for an ostentatious display of wealth by the rich which "might well appear a more solid and adequate way of paying the last honours to the dead." Morris (1992: 67) concurs, stating decisively that diffusion to the less wealthy classes of society was "a matter of competitive emulation," although, the majority of sarcophagi were probably placed inside tombs and were therefore invisible to members of the public. The conclusions of Nock and Morris imply that the lower classes played little active part in the transformation and were passive recipients of the change. However, inhumation had never completely disappeared amongst these groups and the image of the rite "filtering down" to the less wealthy therefore suggests an apathy that was not necessarily a reality.

Inhumation

Inhumation took several forms and these are discussed in more detail within their archaeological context in Chapter 5. For the purposes of this discussion it is necessary only to note that the body could be placed directly into the earth, either wrapped in a shroud or in a coffin made of wood, stone, lead or a combination of materials.

Alternatively the body or coffin was placed within a tomb, perhaps in *formae* below the floor or *arcosoli* in the lower parts of the walls. Sarcophagi, placed outside in a tomb enclosure, against the interior wall of the tomb, squeezed into *arcosoli* or freestanding, were also employed. Methods of inhumation evidently spanned the scale from cheap and simple to ostentatious and expensive, and could be customised to be as economical or costly, as basic or complex as resources and circumstances allowed. Presumably permission had to be obtained to use a piece of land for burial, and the price of plots undoubtedly varied considerably depending on their size and location. Large plots of land were probably bought, divided up and subsequently sold as individual plots for profit. Alternatively, permission may have been granted for slaves and freedmen to be buried in the family plot of their master, suggested by the clustering of burials around the house tombs of Isola Sacra. The *Digest* (11.7.2.2; 11.7.8.2 (Ulpian)) contains prohibitions against burial in land belonging to another person, thus indicating that this was a relatively frequent occurrence that required regulation.

Cremation

Cremation was a complex process and required a degree of specialist knowledge in order for it to be completely successful. The simplest form, the *bustum* type, involved the cremation of the corpse at the site of burial. Below the pyre was dug a shallow pit or trench, into which fell the ash, dust and bones of the deceased, the fabric of the pyre and the burnt remains of any goods or equipment that accompanied the body. These were then buried *in situ*. More complex and yet, according to Noy (2000b: 186), more common, was the use of a separate site (*ustrinum*) for cremation. Polfer (2000: 31) observes that *ustrina* built of durable materials and capable of being reused "are in most cases though not exclusively to be found on urban cemeteries, where the large number of cremations per year made permanent structures if not necessary then at least useful, as they allowed a more efficient and faster cremation." However, *ustrina* were not all permanent constructions, nor were they always used more than once. The use of an *ustrinum* required that the burnt remains be collected and placed in a container (an urn, ash chest or bag) in order to be buried. Noy (2000b: 186) suggests that "the force of the fire, the raking and collapse of the pyre during burning, and eventual quenching with cold liquid would together normally be sufficient to reduce the bones to small fragments which would fit easily into the container." However, McKinley (2000: 40) observes that this process rarely resulted in the collection of the entire remains of a cremated individual, with generally only 40-60% of the bone weight recovered. Nevertheless, this seems to have satisfied the requirements for proper burial.

The construction of the pyre and requirements of fuel, temperature and the appropriate attention differed very little. McKinley (*ibid.*: 39) summarises the situation: "there may have been slight variations in form but all pyres would require fuel and needed to perform the same function; to provide a stable, body-sized support for the corpse and any pyre goods, to allow circulation of oxygen to facilitate combustion, and to accommodate enough fuel to give sufficient time and temperature for cremation to complete." There is a scattering of literary descriptions of pyre structures, including the observation that pyres were built with layers of logs laid at right angles (Vitruvius, 2.9.15). This seems to be confirmed by two depictions of pyres found on sarcophagi which show logs of wood arranged on top of one another in regular layers (see Noy 2000c: 36).[37] Noy (2000b: 187) attributes the rarity of literary (and figurative) descriptions to the fact knowledge of how to construct a pyre was widely known and it was therefore felt unnecessary to comment upon it.

The temperature of the pyre was essential to ensuring that adequate incineration occurred. The archaeological recovery of cremation burials demonstrates that complete disintegration of the body was rarely achieved and was therefore probably not required, but high temperatures were nevertheless needed even for this and, as Kyle (1998: 170) points out, "the sordid but certain truth is that flesh, being mostly water, is not very flammable by itself. Funeral pyres were stuffed with papyrus to achieve the necessary large, hot fire." Noy (2000b: 157) proposes that an initial temperature of 500 °C was required but later in the process much greater temperatures must be reached. Modern crematoria operate at an average of 900 °C, a temperature which Wells (1960: 35) indicates could also have been achieved by an ancient pyre. He also observes (*ibid.*: 35) that "it is evident that for complete cremation of the body a pyre of very considerable magnitude would be needed – possibly augmented with stoking as the ritual progressed." Maintaining the high temperature of ancient pyres required taking account of other factors such as the weather, wind direction and the amount of fuel available. A degree of specialised knowledge was evidently required in order to sustain high temperatures at a consistent level for a considerable amount of time. In addition, the pyre needed periodical stoking and raking in order to prevent a build-up of ash. The term *ustor,* mentioned by ancient writers, is believed to refer to a professional pyre-burner, presumably responsible for overseeing the maintenance of the burning pyre (Noy, 2000b: 187).

The length of time that a full cremation took is also significant, and Noy (*ibid.*: 187) points out that ancient descriptions give a "misleading impression of speed," and "according to Varro, quoted in Servius (*In Aen.* 6.216), it was the normal practice for the crowd to remain around the pyre 'until the body was consumed and the ashes were collected, when the very last word *ilicet* was said, which signified that it was permitted to go (*ire licet*).' Yet McKinley estimates that a cremation by standard Roman methods would take 7 to 8 hours." It was clearly a time consuming process that would have occupied the best part of an entire day, especially if the cremation was

---

[37] According to Noy (2000c) one sarcophagus can be found in the Capitoline Museum (inv. no. 618) and is actually the lid of a sarcophagus dated to the second century AD. The other is in the Palazzo Sciarra. Both sarcophagi depict scenes from the myth of Meleager.

preceded by a procession and eulogy and followed by a funerary feast and other ceremonial activities. In addition, once the process was complete the burnt remains needed to be collected and, depending on the way in which this occurred, it may have been necessary to wait for the pyre to cool considerably (McKinley, 1989: 73).

The length of time and specialist skills required for cremation to be successful has significant implications for the burial practices of the lower classes. In the context of cremations which took, under proper supervision, up to 8 hours it is difficult to understand descriptions of pauper funerals as "hurried nocturnal affairs" unless these refer *only* to inhumation burials. These events may have lasted even longer if specialist *ustores* were not employed to ensure that the pyre was constructed correctly, suitably supplied with fuel and oxygen and the temperature strictly controlled. Even amongst the wealthiest classes cremations could go wrong; Pliny (*Nat. Hist.* VII. 186) cites the example of Marcus Lepidus whose corpse "had been dislodged from the pyre by the violence of the flame, and as it was impossible to put it back again because of the heat, it was burnt naked with a fresh supply of faggots at the side of the pyre." This raises questions about whether cremation could be carried out without professional assistance. The existence of *ustores* implies that a degree of knowledge was required for an efficient cremation, but rudimentary knowledge of how to construct a pyre was probably quite common. Noy (2000c: 31) notes that "in an emergency, friends or relatives would have to do it themselves, with any materials they could get their hands on," and highlights several examples from ancient literature which describe individuals building their own pyres. The basic knowledge of how to construct and burn a pyre was obviously widespread enough to allow individuals to conduct cremations without specialist assistance, although these did not always go to plan. Evidence from Isola Sacra (see Chapter 5) indicates that the poor *were* sometimes cremated and it must therefore be concluded that either the cost of fuel, the required knowledge, and the time needed were not beyond the reach of all members of the poorer classes, or that these difficulties were overcome in some way. Noy (2000b: 186), for example, observes that "the pyre should be built specifically for the deceased; having to use someone else's pyre was a sign of poverty, or an emergency procedure." Perhaps pyres were shared by the lower classes, thus helping to reduce the financial burden they placed on a single family unit.

Toynbee (1971: 50) describes the cremation ceremony itself:

> "The eyes of the corpse were opened when it was placed on the pyre, along with various gifts and some of the deceased's personal possessions. Sometimes even pet animals were killed round the pyre to accompany the soul into the afterlife. The relatives and friends then called upon the dead by name for the last time: the pyre was kindled with torches; and after the corpse had

been consumed the ashes were drenched with wine."

Paoli (1963: 131 – 132) also suggests that the pyre was "surrounded by cypress trees and decorated with pictures, hangings and statues. Friends and relatives also threw clothes, ornaments, arms and even food on to the pyre, objects which had belonged to the dead or been held dear by him." Both descriptions are again based largely on an amalgam of ancient accounts of luxurious cremations but archaeology attests the placing of items on the pyre, probably intended to accompany the dead into the afterlife. Similar goods are also found in inhumation graves. Toynbee (1971: 52), examining the goods found in such contexts, lists the common items as: "jewellery and other personal adornments, arms and pieces of armour and other items of military equipment, toilet boxes and toilet articles, some in precious metals, eating and drinking vessels and implements, dice and gaming-counters, children's toys, small funerary portraits, and small images of other-world deities." These items seem to be largely functional or personal in character rather than prestige objects designed to impress the living. As Toynbee (*ibid.*: 53) observes, "the purpose of these grave-goods was partly to honour the dead, but mainly to serve them and help them to feel at home in the afterlife." Commonly, a coin was placed in the mouth in order to pay the fee of Charon to take the dead across the River Styx, an action dictated specifically by traditional religious belief.

Although the goods and equipment burnt with the body do not appear to have played a significant role in competitive display, the pyre could also provide a backdrop for highly visible displays of conspicuous consumption. Friedländer (1909: 212) notes the extravagance witnessed by those attending the cremations of the aristocracy: "the pyre, too, no doubt was a work of luxury. Certainly we only know of those of the emperors, which in the third century consisted of several pyramidal tiers, covered everywhere with gold-braided carpets, pictures and reliefs, all abandoned to the flames. But as Pliny speaks of painted pyres, it is probable that private individuals imitated this extravagance according to their means."[38] Furthermore, "Lucian makes a widower say that he has proved his love of his wife by burning all her clothes and ornaments at her funeral. Regulus the orator made an ostentatious exhibition of his grief at the death of a son about 14 or 15 years old, and had all the boy's many ponies, dogs, nightingales, parrots, and blackbirds slaughtered at the pyre" (*ibid.*: 212) These actions have been attributed to the tremendous grief of the survivors (although were doubtless viewed as rather eccentric in their zealousness), but they also acted as a means by which to display the wealth and status of the family through the conspicuous destruction of high quality items. The pyre therefore served both a practical and social function that could be manipulated in accordance with the desires and resources of those responsible for the funerary rites. As with so many other aspects of the

---

[38] For Pliny's description see *Nat. Hist.* 35.49.

funerary process, it is likely that the lower classes were as much aware of this as the other members of the urban community and may have wished to capitalise on it if they could.

Religious beliefs

Life after death?

Opportunities for public display and the practical need to dispose of the corpse were undoubtedly significant forces affecting the burial rites of Roman city-dwellers but there were also other major factors which influenced these activities, including religious belief. The lack of consensus amongst modern scholars with regards to ancient beliefs about the afterlife parallels that of the Romans themselves. The dead had no central role within organised religious belief (Walker, 1985: 13) and there was no official doctrine categorically affirming or denying the existence of the afterlife. As a result, beliefs were largely a matter of personal conviction, although there did exist certain commonly held ideas. The teachings of the schools of Epicureanism and Stoicism are frequently cited in discussions of ancient concepts of the afterlife. According to Cumont's (1929: 7) comprehensive study of afterlife beliefs, Epicurus "taught that the soul, which was composed of atoms, was disintegrated at the moment of death, when it was no longer held together by its fleshly wrapping, and that its transitory unity was then destroyed forever." This rather dramatic fate, however, was not one to be feared since it could be no more painful than the time before one existed. Alternatively, Stoicism held that "souls, when they leave the corpse, subsist in the atmosphere and especially in its highest part which touches the circle of the moon. But after a longer or less interval of time they, like the flesh and the bones, are decomposed and dissolve into the elements which formed them" (*ibid.*: 15). Despite several differences, both philosophies ultimately shared the belief that the soul eventually ceased to exist.

Although these ideas were principally embraced by the more "cultivated circles" of society they also found adherents amongst the lowest classes, who expressed such ideas within their epitaphs (*ibid.*: 9 and 15). For example, variations of the phrase "I was not; I was; I am not; I do not care" are repeatedly found on grave monuments (*ibid.*: 9 – 10). The far-reaching influence of these philosophical doctrines can, however, be questioned. Toynbee (1971: 34) suggests that "there persisted and prevailed the conviction that some kind of conscious existence is in store for the soul after death and that the dead and living can affect one another mutually. Human life is not just an interlude of being between nothingness and nothingness." These rather more optimistic, and as a result perhaps more comforting, beliefs were manifested in the idea that the dead resided in or near the place of burial and were capable of moving amongst the living. Toynbee (*ibid.*: 34) proposes that this was "an ancient and deep-seated belief" but

acknowledges that the majority of evidence for afterlife beliefs does not predate the first century BC. However, Plautus (*c.* 250 – 184 BC) provides some details about common beliefs before this date: "His *Mostellaria* implies, of course, belief that the spirits of the dead can haunt the dwellings of the living; and two of its lines convey the notion that the lower world is barred to the souls of those who have died before their time" (Toynbee, 1971: 34 – 35). Equally, Ovid's *Fasti* sheds light on the traditional festivals of the dead during the early- and mid-Republic. During this period it was widely believed that the *Manes*, the spirits of the dead, existed as an undifferentiated mass that should be respected and honoured (Scullard, 1981: 37). By the late Republic the members of this nebulous mass had assumed greater individuality, and ancient sources (such as Cicero, *in Pis.* 16) begin to refer to the *Manes* as separate entities. This might reflect an increasing desire amongst the living to have their individual identity recognised, acknowledged and commemorated during their lifetime and also after their death. Use of the phrase '*Dis Manibus*' on tombstones implies, at least initially, a belief in some form of existence after death, although perhaps it is more accurate to suggest that these monuments express *hope* for life after death rather than firm belief in it.

The absence of an official authorised state doctrine on the issue of the afterlife left the matter open to discussion. The teachings of Epicureanism and Stoicism evidently did not become popular enough to be officially adopted and promoted by the state, something which suggests they were perhaps not as widely held as Cumont believed. Indeed, "Epicurus denied the afterlife, but in his will he provided for offerings in perpetuity to his father, mother, and brother, for celebrations of his birthday and the anniversaries of others of his intimates" (Nock, 1972: 286). If the founder of a philosophy which denied the existence of immortality was, ultimately, doubtful of its truth it is unlikely that many other members of society were more easily convinced. The persistence of early Republican traditions during the Empire implies that established customs exerted particularly strong influence over the population. These customs implied that individuality was retained after death – a far more optimistic view than that of the Epicureans or Stoics. Beliefs regarding the nature of the afterlife remained hazy, undefined and varied, but were always strong enough to influence aspects of burial practice.

Religious burial

That the shade of the deceased might continue to exist after death, either at the place of burial or amongst the living, was considered particularly fearful if the deceased was denied proper burial. This is a situation alluded to by Horace (*Odes*, I. 28 (2)):

"Me, too, Notus, whirling mate of setting Orion, overwhelmed in the Illyrian waves. But do thou, O mariner, begrudge me not the shifting sand, nor refuse to bestow a little of it on my unburied head and bones! Then, whatever threats Eurus shall vent against the Hesperian waves, when the Venusian woods are beaten by the gale, mayst thou be safe, and may rich reward redound to thee from the sources whence it can, – from kindly Jove and Neptune, sacred Tarentum's guardian god!

Thou thinkest it a light matter to do a wrong that after this will harm thine unoffending children? Perchance the need of sepulture and a retribution of like disdain may await thyself sometime. I shall not be left with my petition unavenged, and for thee no offerings shall make atonement. Though thou art eager to be going, 'tis a brief delay I ask. Only three handfuls of earth! Then thou mayst speed upon thy course."

Horace's words imply that the lack of a proper burial had serious repercussions for both the living and the dead. As Cumont (1922: 64) explains, "from the most ancient times the beliefs reigned from all the peoples of antiquity that the souls of those who are deprived of burial find no rest in the other life. If they have no "eternal house" they are like homeless vagabonds. But the fact that the dead had been buried did not suffice; the burial must also have been performed according to the traditional rites." Cicero (de Leg. II. 22. 57) also informs us that:

"...until turf is cast upon the bones, the place where a body is cremated does not have a sacred character; but after the turf is cast, [the burial is considered accomplished, and the spot is called a grave]; then, but not before, it has the protection of many laws of sanctity."

It was evidently considered essential that the remains of the deceased be covered with earth, a condition that applied to both inhumation and cremation. However, Horace suggests that a symbolic scattering of "three handfuls of earth" could satisfy the demands of the dead and was sufficient to protect the living.[39] Without minimal burial the shade of the deceased remained trapped between the world of the living and that of the dead, restless and vengeful (Hope, 2000a: 120). The very serious nature of this situation is illustrated by the fact that denial of burial was occasionally used as a form of punishment. Kyle (1998: 131) observes that "denial of even minimal burial was regarded as an abuse of decent humans, as a form of damnation beyond death, but it was acceptable when criminals' acts put them beyond the protection of any law." He cites the example of increased incidents of suicide during the reign of Tiberius "because, unless there was a suicide, conviction for treason brought confiscation of property (the denial of any will)

and denial of burial" (ibid.: 132 – 133). Denial of burial entailed eternal punishment for the individual and permitted the authorities to extend their power beyond death. In order for these punishments to act as a successful deterrent there must have existed a widely held belief that lack of burial resulted in a particularly fearful state of existence.

Further evidence for the strength and extent of these beliefs can be found in the ghost stories that are recounted by ancient writers, such as Pliny the Younger (Ep. 7. 27). He describes how one night Athenodorus the philosopher, the owner of a house in Athens that was haunted by a ghost, followed the spectral figure of an old man wrapped in chains. Having seen the ghost disappear in the middle of the courtyard he ordered the area searched the following morning and discovered the bones of an improperly buried individual, entangled with iron chains. He re-buried the remains according to the proper rites and the ghost was never seen again. In a similar manner, the ghost of Caligula, who was hastily cremated and buried after his assassination, was believed to haunt the area of the Lamian Gardens at Rome until his remains received proper burial rites (Suet. Calig. 59; Hope, 2000a: 106). That these stories were perpetuated over both time and space (the haunted house story was probably quite old before Pliny committed it to writing) implies a widespread belief in the restless spirits of the unburied. It was therefore important for both the safety of the living and the peace of the dead that deceased individuals received at least minimal burial. There is no reason to suggest that the beliefs of the upper and lower classes differed on this matter, and it is thus possible to propose that for the majority of the population of Rome the appropriate rites were always strictly observed.

Funerary festivals and feasting

The belief that the dead could haunt the living also influenced the practice of funerary banqueting and religious festivals. A meal (silicernium) was consumed at the grave as part of the funeral ritual on the day of interment and on the ninth and final day of mourning (cena novemdialis). These meals were an essential part of the funeral rite, and they provided sustenance for the departed as they passed to the world of the dead. Cumont (1922: 50) states that "the dead are hungry; above all they are thirsty. Those whose humours have dried, whose mouths are withered, are tortured by the need to refresh their parched lips. It therefore is not enough to place in the tombs the drinks and dishes, the remains of which have often been found beside skeletons; by periodic sacrifices the manes must be supplied with fresh food also. If they are left without nourishment they languish, weak as a fasting man, almost unconscious, and in the end they would actually die of starvation."[40] There was

---

[39] The rather obscure rite of *os resectum* (also known as *os exceptum*) has often been viewed as further evidence that a token gesture was deemed acceptable. This rite appears to have involved the removal of a piece of the corpse (usually a finger bone) for separate burial in instances of cremation. However, recent re-assessment of the archaeological and literary evidence for this rite suggests that the custom was more closely associated with the ritual purification of the living and the shade of the dead, than the provision of proper burial. See Graham (forthcoming a and b).

---

[40] Although this description is particularly evocative, Cumont does not make it entirely clear what he has based it on and we must remember that these are his words, not those of the ancient Romans themselves. The ordinary Roman city-dweller probably would not have described his beliefs so eloquently.

evidently considerable concern for the welfare of the dead wherever they lay, either beyond or within the grave, and this, like proper burial, was associated with a desire to make their existence more comfortable and to placate the spirits of the dead lest they become troublesome.

Beliefs that the dead required food and drink are also reflected by annual festivals such as the *Parentalia*. This took place in February (13th – 21st) and was a week long festival of the family dead, culminating on the last day (the *Feralia*) with public ceremonies. Ovid (*Fasti*, II. 533 – 542) describes the activities:

> "Honour is paid, also, to the grave. Appease the souls of your fathers and bring small gifts to the tombs erected to them. Ghosts ask but little: they value piety more than a costly gift: no greedy gods are they who in the world below do haunt the banks of Styx. A tile wreathed with votive garlands, a sprinkling of corn, a few grains of salt, bread soaked in wine, and some loose violets, these are offerings enough: set these on a potsherd and leave it in the middle of the road. Not that I forbid larger offerings, but even these suffice to appease the shades: add prayers and the appropriate words at the hearths set up for the purpose."

Offerings, predominantly of food, were made to the dead during this festival, and the family reprised the meal that had taken place originally during the funeral. According to Cumont (1922: 54), "it was believed that at funeral feasts the Manes of ancestors came to sit among the guests and enjoyed with them the abundance of the food and wines." Families could thus satiate the hunger of the dead through the sharing of food whilst at the same time honouring and commemorating their memory. These festivals thus acted as a means to both placate the dead and to continue the commemorative process. As a result they can be included amongst the 'incorporating practices' of commemoration defined by Connerton and discussed in the previous chapter. Such events should therefore be considered as a very important aspect of the funerary process for all social groups. Rich and poor alike could be involved in activities such as these, at minimal expense.

The fact that the *Parentalia* was an officially recognised festival[41] again implies that it was closely observed by the majority of the urban population who believed it to be of great importance for their own welfare as well as that of the dead. Indeed, Ovid (*Fasti*, II. 547 – 556) tells a cautionary tale about neglecting these sacred festivals:

> "But once upon a time, waging long wars with martial arms, they did neglect the All Soul's Days. The negligence was not unpunished; for tis

said that from that ominous day Rome grew hot with the funeral fires that burned without the city. They say, though I can hardly think it, that the ancestral souls did issue from the tombs and make their moan in the hours of stilly night; and hideous ghosts, a shadowy throng, they say, did howl about the city streets and the wide fields. Afterwards the honours which had been omitted were again paid to the tombs, and so a limit was put to prodigies and funerals."

The *Parentalia* was a family festival and a period in which to personally commemorate and appease one's kinfolk. It therefore had significance to all members of society, regardless of wealth or rank and during this time the tomb became a focus for social interaction (Heinzelmann, 2001: 186; Graham, 2005a and 2005b). Hopkins (1983: 233) pictures the scene: "we have to imagine Roman families picnicking *al fresco* at the family tomb, where, according to Christian critics, they often got boisterously drunk, with their dead relatives around them." One of Trimalchio's dinner guests arrives after attending a funeral and is described as "already drunk, and had put his hands on his wife's shoulders; he had several wreaths on, and ointment was running down his forehead into his eyes" (Petronius, *Sat.* 79).

During these festivities the area of the cemetery would have been particularly busy, although this was not the only time of the year that the dead required attention. The family also returned to the grave to mark the anniversaries of the birth and death of their relatives by pouring libations directly into the burial via tubes or holes, and consuming ritual meals. Toynbee (1971: 63) also observes that "provision could be made for the lighting of lamps at the grave on the Kalends, Ides, and Nones of every month." Wills occasionally arranged for items to be offered at the tomb and it can be assumed that some, or a combination, of these were given as libations when the family returned to the grave. Toynbee (*ibid.*: 62) lists the following: "food (*cibus, esca, edulia*), bread (*panis*), wine and grapes (*vinum, escae vindemiales*), cakes (*liba*), sausages (*tuceta*), ceremonial meals (*epulae*) thought of as shared by the living with the dead, incense (*tus*), fruits (*poma*), flowers of all kinds, particularly violets (*violae*) and roses (*roscae, escae Rosales*)." Ovid referred also to the giving of "loose violets" as part of the *Parentalia* offerings. There was also a festival specifically associated with roses: the *Rosalia*. This festival took place in May and June and, although "by no means exclusively connected with the dead, the Rosalia (*dies Rosalium, Rosariorum, Rosationis*) undoubtedly afforded specific occasions for scattering roses on the grave and decking the funerary portrait with them" (*ibid.*: 63). Images of roses were also occasionally painted on the walls and vaults of tombs, such as those at Isola Sacra and were apparently "regarded as pledges of eternal spring in the life beyond the grave" (*ibid.*: 63) (**Fig. 12**). Activities such as these that required the living to return to the grave and perform certain ceremonial rites may have originated as pious religious responsibilities but

---

[41] During this time the law-courts and temples were closed and no public business was conducted (Hopkins, 1983: 233).

Figure 12. Niches painted with flowers in Tomb 77, Isola Sacra (photo: author).

symbolic or status oriented role by virtue of their location *outside* the tomb. Unlike other cemeteries, such as the *Via Laurentina* at Ostia, where dining provisions are located within the structure of the tomb or enclosure, there appears to have been an overriding desire to place the Isola Sacra dining provisions *outside* the tombs in a highly conspicuous and public location. The owners of the tombs could therefore have used the physical accoutrements of religious festivals and dining activities to advertise their identity and social status (see Graham, 2005b). This was particularly significant given that the cemetery community was composed largely of members of the freedman class and more humble levels of society whose ambiguous social or legal status led to an increased desire to publicly exhibit, and thus confirm, their legitimacy as free members of society. Visibly dining outside the tombs allowed families to advertise their ability to afford the expense of a substantial banquet. Furthermore, in light of the predominance of non-Roman freedmen in the Isola Sacra necropolis, these dining structures allowed them to conspicuously align themselves with Roman traditions and religious beliefs; the use of a *biclinium* further underlined their familiarity with high status Roman dining habits. For individuals attempting to strengthen or legitimise their position within the community and emphasise a newfound social or legal status, this provided an excellent opportunity for a public display of wealth and embracing of Roman custom. Ritual dining activities and the religious festivals with which they were associated were therefore capable of acting as more than a means by which to appease and commemorate the dead and their impact extended into the world of the living. The dead always remained the focus of these occasions, the family simply capitalised on the opportunities they offered for competitive display.

they acted equally as 'incorporating' forms of commemoration that allowed the living to recall the dead and celebrate their memory. This was a process in which all members of the community, regardless of their economic status, could participate.

The need to regularly return to the grave implies that the cemetery was an environment that was heavily frequented by the living; a situation which facilitated other social processes, such as those involved in status display and competition (Graham, 2005b). Funerary dining structures at the necropolis of Isola Sacra, for example, highlight the ways in which aspects of the funerary ritual acted on multiple levels. Wells and ovens attest to regular ritual dining activities at Isola Sacra, but the most common provision associated with dining in the cemetery takes the form of two-sided masonry dining couches, or *biclinia* (**Fig. 13**). These sloping benches flank the entrances of many of the house tombs and are found occasionally in association with the smaller chest-tombs (*cassone*). The only practical function performed by these structures was to facilitate formal ritual dining within the environment of the cemetery, allowing mourners to recline in the proper Roman manner. However, these structures may also have adopted a

Another festival of the dead, the *Lemuria*, took place on the 9th, 11th and 13th of May. This was a time in which "the apparently kinless and hungry ghosts, the *Lemures*, and the mischievous and dangerous *Larvae*, were supposed to prowl around the house" (Toynbee, 1971: 64). In contrast to the celebrations of the *Parentalia*, the *Lemuria* was an occasion centred on a fear of restless spirits, presumably those who had not been suitably placated by the *Parentalia* a few months earlier or who had not received proper burial. The events of the *Lemuria* were of domestic character, and although Toynbee (*ibid*: 64) observes that the festival is entered on some calendars and Ovid (*Fasti*, V. 485 – 490) informs us that temples were closed and "she who married then, will not live long," any public ceremony that occurred as part of it remains unknown. However, Ovid (*Fasti*, V. 429 – 454) describes the activities that took place in the home:

"When midnight has come and lends silence to sleep, and dogs and all ye varied fowls are hushed, the worshipper who bears the olden rite in mind and fears the god arises; no knots constrict his feet; and he makes a sign with his thumb in the middle of his closed fingers, lest in his silence an unsubstantial shade should meet

Figure 13. Masonry *biclinium* outside Tomb 15, Isola Sacra (photo: author).

him. And after washing his hands clean in spring water, he turns, and first he receives black beans and throws them away with face averted; but while he throws them, he says: "These I cast; with these beans I redeem me and mine." This he says nine times, without looking back. The shade is thought to gather the beans, and to follow unseen behind. Again he touches water, and clashes Temesan bronze, and asks the shade to go out of his house. When he has said nine times, "Ghosts of my fathers, go forth!" he looks back, and thinks that he has duly performed the sacred rites."

The ritual activities of the *Lemuria* were undoubtedly connected with the removal of restless spirits, lending further weight to the proposal that there was a deep-seated fear of the unhappy dead. Alcock (1980: 64) makes the following observation:

"Sir James Frazer once commented that 'Customs often live on for ages after the circumstances and modes of thought which gave rise to them have disappeared and in their new environment new motives are invented to explain them' (Frazer 1931, 490). But people would remain attached to practices which possibly seemed dangerous to omit for this omission might bring retribution from the powerful, and perhaps vindictive, spirits of the dead."

In light of such an observation, the persistence of the festivals of the dead, funerary banquets and the offering

of libations discussed here may not necessarily reflect a direct continuation of the original beliefs that gave rise to them. It is likely that these activities underwent a degree of transformation in order to align with the needs of contemporary society, as demonstrated by the multi-faceted activity of funerary dining at Isola Sacra. Nevertheless, beliefs concerning the fate of the soul and the afterlife, the need for proper burial and the placating of the dead with food and celebrations in their honour, continued to exert considerable influence over the burial practices of the urban community. The physical manifestation of these may have varied in accordance with economic resources, status and ambitions, but it is evident that certain beliefs were widely shared regardless of social position.

The Law

A further factor which exerted a particularly strong influence over urban burial practice was the law, which again transcended the boundaries of social class and wealth and, with the occasional exception of the Imperial family, was applicable to all those living and dying in Rome.

Reconstructing and understanding Roman burial laws

The XII Tables, dating to 451 – 450 BC, represent the earliest collection of Roman laws and provide a starting point for both ancient and modern discussions of Roman law. The law of the XII Tables was "largely a statement of long-observed principles sanctioned by immemorial custom," (Wolff, 1951: 59) and was predominantly based on traditional principles transformed into official laws. Much of the XII Tables has been reconstructed from references in other, often much later, sources and although many of these appear to be direct quotations from the original tablets (for example, Cicero, *de Legibus*) the possibility of corruption remains high. Wolff (1951: 58) observes that "ancient writers had no strict views about scrupulous accuracy of quotations and saw no harm in adapting the texts of their authorities to the needs of their own time," and it is probable that what exists today are "the clauses of the Twelve Tables, as they were known in the Middle and Late Republic" (Crawford, 1996: 556).

The precise wording of the XII Tables may be questioned, but there was a strong sense of traditionalism within Roman law and the recognised importance of the *mores maiorum* (customs of the forefathers) allows a fairly confident reconstruction of their basic content. This probably changed relatively little between their initial formulation and the late Empire; a supposition strengthened by the high esteem in which Roman writers held the code. The first century AD jurist Labeo and his second century colleague Gaius, for example, wrote commentaries on the Tables, Livy (III. 34) described them as "the source of all public and private law" and Cicero (*de Leg.* II.23.59) states that as a schoolboy he was required to learn the laws by heart. The fact that later legal writings, such as those produced under Justinian, incorporate elements of the Tables into their own system, and the distinct absence of any further codifications of the law in the intervening period, also imply that they were considered relevant. Indeed, Robinson, (1975: 185) writing of the later Empire, states that "we are clearly in the same world as the Republic; it is just that in the declaration of sacral law the emperors have replaced the pontiffs and in secular law they are in the process of superseding the jurists." This, however, highlights one of the difficulties encountered when examining burial regulations: the main sources date to the chronological extremes of the Roman period and we again run the risk of creating anachronistic amalgamations of the evidence. Furthermore, a lack of evidence for change may not necessarily reflect a static situation. However, the importance of tradition, the lack of direct evidence for radical change and the persistent references to the XII Tables during the late Empire, indicate that the basic content of these regulations remained both relevant and active for many centuries after their initial codification.

Table X of the XII Tables concerns funerary activities. Crawford (1996: 583) provides the following translation:

> X,1 He is not to bury or burn a dead man in the city.
> X,2 He is not to do more than this: he is not to smooth the pyre with a trowel.
> X,3 ... < three veils > ... a little purple tunic ... ten < flautists > ...
> X,4 Women are not to mutilate their cheeks or hold a wake for the purposes of holding a funeral.

> X,5 He is not to collect the bones of a dead man, in order to hold a funeral afterwards, < but ... >.
> X,6 < He is not to place perfumed liquid on a dead man. > (Prohibition of *circumpotatio*) < He is to scatter a pyre with not more than ??? wine. >
> X,7 Whoever win a crown for himself or his < *familia* >, or it be given to him for bravery, < and it is placed on him or his parent when dead, it is to be without liability.> ... < incense altars > ...
> X,8 ... nor is he to add gold, < but > for whomsoever the teeth are joined with gold, and if he shall bury or burn it with him, it is to be without liability.
> X,9 <<< He is not to place a *bustum* within sixty feet of another's house >>>.
> X,10 <<< A fore-court or *bustum* is to be *religiosus*. >>>[42]

The first regulation of Table X is the most widely known Roman burial law. The clearest evidence that the rule prohibiting burial within the city continued to be enforced throughout later periods can be found in the concentration of tombs beyond the walls of Roman towns and cities. However, as Robinson (1975: 176) points out, "this does not seem to spring from any absolute taboo, for Vestal Virgins and a few others continued to be buried, or to have the right to be buried, within the City," further supported by the observation of Lindsay (2000: 170) that the law "was never applied to children under four days old, who would be buried *sub grundo*, that is under the porch facing into the courtyard (Ful. *serm. ant.* 560.13)." Despite these allowances, the law was reinforced several times after its initial formulation in the XII Tables. For example, Lindsay (*ibid.*: 170) notes a decree of the senate dating to the consulate of Duillius in 260 BC, a further senatorial decree of 38 BC in which the distance beyond which burning was allowed was set at two miles, and that Hadrian, "prescribed a pecuniary penalty for those who contravened the restriction on burial within two miles of the city, as well as for the magistrates who turned a blind eye." The regulation contained within the XII Tables evidently remained relevant for many centuries, albeit with certain refinements. However, the original regulation (with Crawford's translation) asserts that burial or burning should not take place "*in the city*". Crook (1967: 135) interprets this as "no-one's remains must rest within the *pomerium* of the city of Rome." This sacred boundary did not always align with the physical boundary of the city (i.e. the encircling walls) and it is therefore unclear which was intended by the original law. Given the close association of burial regulations with sacral rather than civil law, it may be suggested that the *pomerium* originally marked the limit of burial or burning, although as the city expanded and

---

[42] The text contained within <<< ... >>> represents "where we believe that a text can be reconstructed with reasonable plausibility, but no source claims to report it" (Crawford, 1996: 557), thus further highlighting the problems we must face when assessing the reliability of the sources.

the *pomerium* was consequently extended, this may have altered. The rule prohibiting the placing of a *bustum* within 60 feet of another person's house (X,9), appears closely connected with this first regulation and was presumably influenced by the risk of fire inherent in placing pyres adjacent to buildings.

The final prohibition, stating that a *bustum* became a *locus religiosus*, was equal to the first in terms of continued relevance. Berger (1953: 679) defines *res religiosae* as: "things 'dedicated to the gods of the lower regions' (*diis Manibus* Gaius *Inst.* 2.4) such as tombs or burial grounds," in contrast to *res sacrae* which were consecrated to the gods in heaven. Other sources, most notably Cicero and jurists of the later Empire, provide further insight into this regulation. Cicero (*de Leg.* II.22.55; 57) states that the approval of the pontiffs was required in order to officially make a burial place religious, but as Robinson (1975: 177) suggests, this approval was probably implicit in most cases. Cicero (*de Leg.* II.22.58) goes on to explain that the pontiffs had declared it unlawful for a grave to be placed in a public place (a *locus publicus* could not be a *locus religiosus*), and any remains buried in such a place must be removed. He cites as an example the circumstances surrounding an area outside the Colline Gate, on which was to be built a temple: "But as there were many graves in that place, they were dug up; for the college decided that a place which was public property could not receive a sacred character through rites performed by private citizens" (*de Leg.* II. 23. 58).

The law was usually interpreted to mean that the actual *place of burial* became *religiosus* and thus a cenotaph could not receive such status (Robinson, 1975: 178). This is supported by the observation that "a place where a coffin was left temporarily, as in the carriage of Augustus' body from Nola to Rome, did not become religious" (*ibid.*: 183). The law concerning the religious status of graves also appears to have remained active during later centuries, with evidence found in the *Institutes* of Gaius (II.3.6 and 9) and summarised by Crook (1967: 133): "the place containing human remains put where they have a right to be is *locus religiosus*, subject to divine law and therefore not susceptible of human ownership or possession or alienation of any kind (by sale or gift or legacy or anything else). It is *res nullius*." Crook (*ibid.*: 134) also notes that, "one text in the Digest says: 'Not the whole *locus* intended for burial is *religiosus*, only the place where remains actually lie'"(*Digest* 11.7.2.5) thus reasserting the earlier rule that cenotaphs were not religious, nor could they bestow this status on the place in which they were raised. Berger's (1953: 491) observation that *illatio mortuo* made the place "a *locus religiosus* even when the dead was a slave" (*Digest* 11.8), reminds us of how the law applied to all levels of society equally.

In light of these regulations, it can be assumed that the interment of bodies in a mass grave also rendered the location *religiosus*, but Bodel (1994: 39) suggests that this was not the case. He examines a passage of Varro

(*L.L.* 5.25) in which the writer "states that the pauper's graveyard at Rome was officially designated a *locus publicus*, that is, a parcel of land owned by the *populus Romanus* and intended for the public use of all" (Bodel, 1994: 39). As a result Bodel proposes that the *puticuli* of Rome "were not regarded in law as *loca religiosa*" (*ibid.*: 39). He (*ibid.*: 39) suggests that because the essential element of Roman burial was inhumation, requiring a symbolic covering of earth, and because the *puticuli* on the Esquiline do not demonstrate evidence that they were covered in any way, they may not have been regarded as proper graves. However, he concludes (*ibid.*: 39):

"Whatever the official religious status of the Roman *puticuli*, popular belief seems to have held that any location where a body was consigned to its final resting place was bound by a *privata religio*, regardless of the state's claim to jurisdiction over public land. Similarly, in the case of Roman burials in the provinces, most authorities, according to Gaius, maintained that the land could not be made *religiosus*, because it was owned by the emperor or the state; but, he adds, it was nonetheless treated as if it were."

The implications of these observations are examined more thoroughly in Chapter 4, but they highlight some significant issues for this current discussion. Firstly, ordinary members of Roman society were apparently not always aware of the specific legal regulations in place and did not always adhere to them. The written law codes can thus not be used as an unquestionable foundation on which to base a reconstruction of burial practice, although they remain useful for the insights they provide into the impact of religious issues on the legal regulations concerning burial. The example of the *puticuli* also highlights the potential unreliability of the sources that have been used to reconstruct these laws, Varro for example, possibly misunderstood the legal status of the mass graves at Rome, which he terms as "*locus publicus*." It is conceivable that the area *was* intended for public use, as a cemetery, but that Varro misunderstood either the legal status of the area or the meaning of the legal term.

Local funerary regulations

Funerary regulations were also recorded epigraphically. The following is an extract from the *lex Coloniae Genetivae Iuliae seu Ursonensis* (translation by Crawford, 1996: 424), described by Robinson (1975: 182) as "a model of municipal organisation":

LXXIII No-one is to bring a dead person within the boundaries of a town or of a colony, where (a line) shall have been drawn around by a plough, nor is he to bury him there or burn him or build the tomb of a dead person. If anyone shall have acted contrary to these rules, he is to be condemned to pay the colonists of the colonia Genetiva Iulia 5,000 sesterces, and there is to be a suit and claim for that sum by whoever shall wish < ? according to this statute ? >. And whatever shall have been built, a IIvir or aedile is to see to its being demolished. If a dead person shall have been brought in or deposited contrary to these rules, they are to make expiation as shall be appropriate.

LXXIV No-one is to prepare a new *ustrina*, where a dead person shall not (previously) have been burnt, nearer the town than 500 paces. Whoever shall have acted contrary to these rules, is to be condemned to pay 5,000 sesterces to the colonists of the colonia Genetiva Iulia, and there is to be a suit and claim for that sum by whoever shall wish according to this statute.

Although inscribed in this form during the Flavian period, the original charter was probably of Caesarian date (Crawford, 1996: 395) and is very similar to sections X,1 and X,9 of the XII Tables. In this context the original regulations have been expanded and defined more precisely to suit the needs of the colony, with fines established for individuals who broke the rules. The *lex coloniae Genetivae* therefore further emphasises that the content of the XII Tables remained relevant and that areas outside Rome adapted them to local circumstances. As Bodel (2004: 147) warns, we cannot assume that the burial laws of any two Roman towns were exactly the same: "at Puteoli the contractor was forbidden to employ tattooed workmen (*stigmat(ibus) inscript(i)*) (P. II, 7) and the removal of the dead from the town was not envisioned after dark (P. II, 23), [but] Martial mentions tattooed corpse-bearers at work at night in Rome (8.75.9 – 10).' However, it is clear that local regulations, such as these, drew heavily on the traditional laws of Rome and their fundamental regulations concerning the location of burial remained consistent. It was only in the details that they differed.

During the 1870s two travertine cippi inscribed with a late Republican praetor's edict (Edict of Sentius) that prohibited certain activities (cremation, dumping and corpse abandoning) were discovered *in situ* near the Esquiline Gate at Rome (Bodel, 1994: 42) (**Fig. 14**). A third stone inscribed with the same text was recovered in 1942.[43] Bodel (*ibid*.: 44) suggests these were:

"intended to mark off not only the section of the *campus Esquilinus* destined for pauper burial and the disposal of unclaimed corpses, but also the surrounding areas; especially to the north, where more prominent and wealthy Romans, including even some members of the nobility, continued to be buried in individual tombs down to the final years of the Republic."

Figure 14. One of the *cippi* bearing the Edict of Sentius found on the Esquiline, now in the Capitoline Museum, Rome (photo: author).

This interpretation supports the suggestion that this was public land and that action was taken in order to ensure that the area did not receive the status of *locus religiosus*. The protection of a specific area on the Esquiline from burial activities and dumping was later reasserted by the *senatusconsultum de pago Montano*.[44] This text was inscribed on a large travertine block raised outside the Esquiline Gate and assigned to the first century BC (*ibid*.: 47). Bodel (*ibid*.: 48) argues that this *senatusconsultum*, protecting the area against illegal dumping, was issued *after* the Edict of Sentius, given the fact that it does not specifically mention the dumping of corpses. He suggests that because the area was no longer used for this purpose no such prohibition was required. However, it is equally possible that the *senatusconsultum* was issued first, but that the public continued to dump beyond it and began to introduce corpses to the region. This, in turn, may have led to the need to be more precise, leading ultimately to the Edict of Sentius.[45]

---

[43] Bode (1994: 44) provides the text from the second stone to be recovered (CIL I² 839) as: *L. Sentius C. f. pr(aetor) | de sen(atus) sent(entia) loca | terminanda coer(avit). | b(onum) f(actum). neiquis intra | terminos propius | urbem ustrinam | fecisse velit neive | stercus, cadaver | iniecisse velit*. The other stones bear the same text.

[44] Bodel (1994: 48) provides the fragmentary text with the tentative restoration of Mommsen: *... eisque curarent tu[erenturque | ar] bitratu aed[i]lium pleibeium | [quei] comque essent; neive ustrinae in | eis locis recionibusve nive foci ustri | nae{ve} caussa fier⌐e⌐nt; nive stercus terra[m] | ve intra ⌐ea⌐ loca fecisse coniecisseve veli[t] | quei haec loca ab paaco Montano || [redempta habebit; quod si stercus in eis loceis fecerit terramve | in ea] loca iecerit, in ... [uti HS ... | ma]nus iniectio pignorisq(ue) ca[pio siet.]*

[45] The relevance of these inscriptions to burial activity on the Esquiline during the Republic and their relationship to the *puticuli* are examined in Chapter 4.

A final inscription, the *lex Lucerina*, provides some parallels with those examined above and, "records a local ordinance prohibiting three activities – dumping dung (or refuse), abandoning corpses, and performing sacrifices in honour of the dead – and prescribes a statutory fine to be exacted from transgressors, either by a private party on behalf of the *populus* or at a magistrates discretion" (Bodel, 1994: 3).[46] The *lex Lucerina* also appears to have been intended to mark off a public area, probably within an existing graveyard, which was no longer to be used for burial or dumping activities (*ibid.*: 4).

Regardless of the circumstances surrounding these regulations, they highlight the use of specific rules for the control of burial activities in certain locations that were more precise than the overarching laws of the XII Tables on which their fundamentals were ultimately based. The examples presented here indicate how local authorities limited the extent and location of burial around the outskirts of towns and cities but that these restrictions continued to be influenced by the original rules of the XII Tables. Robinson (1975: 181) writes: "the law at the end of the Republic seems essentially the same as that of the early Republic," although it is clear that it has become more precise in its limitations.

Tomb regulations

Even more specifically directed were the prohibitions and formal notices that were occasionally included within the wording of the epitaphs which adorned tombs or monuments. Such inscriptions frequently record the dimensions of the burial plot in terms of its frontage (*in fronte*) and depth (*in agro, retro*) (Toynbee, 1971: 75) (**Fig. 15**), in order to assert legal ownership of the land (for example, Thylander, 1952, A83, A149, and A263). In addition, inscriptions often included the phrase *H(oc) M(onumentum) H(eredem, -eredes) N(on) S(equitur, -equeter)* or *H(oc) M(onumentum) H(eredem) E(externum) N(on) H(abebit)*, which was "designed to prevent the property from passing to the owner's heir or heirs or to the heir or heirs of someone else" (*ibid.*: 75). Close control was evidently exercised over access to family tombs or burial plots.

The passage cited above by Petronius (*Sat.* 71) in which Trimalchio states that "It will certainly be my concern in my will to provide against any injury being done to me when I'm dead. I am making one of my freedmen guardian of the tomb to prevent folk running up and shitting on it," demonstrates the widespread fear of disturbance after death. Trimalchio relied on the living to safeguard his tomb but, on occasion, the supernatural was also called upon to punish those who defiled or damaged a place of burial. For example, an epitaph from Rome ends with the lines:

"...Stranger, so may the earth rest lightly upon you after death as you do no damage here; or if anyone does damage, may the gods above not approve of him and the gods below not receive him, and may the earth rest heavily upon him."

(CIL VI 7579)[47]

Another reads:

"To the spirits of the departed. Gaius Tullius Hesper built [this] tomb for himself, where his bones are to be placed. If anyone do violence to them or removes them hence, I wish for him that he may lie a long time in bodily pain, and that when he dies the gods below may not receive him."

(CIL VI 36467)[48]

The great fear that one's interred remains might be disturbed can be understood in the context of beliefs about proper burial and restless spirits discussed above, but the presence of these warnings on tombs and monuments is also particularly revealing given the fact that it was already a criminal offence to disturb buried remains. Toynbee (1971: 76) remarks, "*Violatio sepulcri* was, indeed, a criminal offence and the subject of repeated imperial enactments, as the legal compilations testify," and Hope (2000a: 123) states that "those accused of deliberately violating graves suffered *infamia*. Anyone who despoiled a corpse could endure the death penalty or the mines (*Digest* 14.12.3.7)." The fact that a great many individuals considered it necessary to reassert such regulations on their tombs and to call on the supernatural to lend further weight to the threats, may indicate that the law was not successfully enforced and that they consequently felt the need to take the matter into their own hands. It also emphasises once more the close relationship between religion and the law – it was obviously not seen as strange to support the words of one with the other. Although not all legally recognised, these phrases were regarded as official declarations of ownership and indicate a desire for control over one's last resting place. However, as Hope (2000a: 124) points out, "we can only speculate how long such measures were honoured and thus effective." It is probable that most were disregarded within a few generations. Subdivision of tombs at Isola Sacra into smaller units by people unmindful of the original inscriptions forbidding use of the tomb by non-family members illustrates particularly well the short-lived effect of these provisions.

The law and burial practice

The reasoning and motives behind these laws and regulations is as important as their existence for

---

[46] Bodel (1994: 2) provides the following text: *in hoce loucarid stircus | ne [qu]is fundatid neve cadaver | proiecitad neve parentatid. | sei quis arvorsu hac faxit, [in] ium | quis volet pro ioudicatod n(umum) ⌐L¬ | monum iniect<i>o estod, seive | mac[i]steratus volet moltare, | [li]cetod.*

[47] Cited in Lewis and Reinhold (1966b: 286).
[48] Cited in Lewis and Reinhold (1966b: 283).

Figure 15. Two burial plot markers recording the size of the plot with the formula
in fr(onte) and *in agr(o)*, Rome (photo: author).

understanding burial practice. Practical issues or concern for public safety may have played an important role in their formulation, especially in the establishment of regulations concerning the location of graves or pyres. Fire was a major concern for the inhabitants of urban areas; the devastation that could be caused was vividly illustrated by the Great Fire of Rome in AD 64. Cicero believed that this was the logic behind the rules on cremation (*de Leg*. II.24.61), although Bodel (1994: 33) asserts that it was more likely to reflect the reality of his own day than that of the XII Tables. Concern for public health and safety was probably partly responsible for the regulations limiting the dumping of corpses and rubbish on the Esquiline which, according to Bodel (*ibid*.: 34), "was treated on a par with public rowdiness and other forms of littering as a general problem of public order rather than a matter of religious taboo." As Rome expanded the availability of land on which to build became increasingly important and Cicero's description of the activity outside the Colline Gate reflects these concerns.

This discussion has highlighted two other possible significant motives behind Roman burial legislation: hygiene and religion. The existence of the *puticuli*, regardless of the capacity in which they were used, and the need to regulate dumping activities implies that hygiene was generally considered to be unimportant by most city-dwellers, and although its significance may have increased over time, Robinson (1975: 176) believes it unlikely that at the time of the XII Tables hygiene was a motive for prohibiting burials within the city. The religious character

of the XII Tables is, however, unquestionable and it seems most probable that many of the burial regulations were influenced by religious beliefs. The pontiffs were vital to the process of making a grave religious for example, something which demonstrates the influence that such attitudes had on early funerary regulations. Fear of ritual pollution may also have been responsible for keeping burial at a distance (Lindsay, 2000: 152). Nevertheless, the original religious reasoning behind these regulations was gradually replaced by concerns for civil law and more practical considerations. The Edict of Sentius and the *senatusconsultum de pago Montano* provide little indication that superstition played any role in their creation and they appear to be concerned primarily with issues of public safety and land availability. Various motives probably co-existed of course, especially during later periods when the reasoning behind the original restrictions of the XII Tables had been forgotten or were no longer considered relevant, even if the laws themselves remained in use.

Continued observation of long-standing traditions was of the utmost importance to burial legislation. Long-observed customs shaped the original XII Tables which subsequently became the traditional source of all law and formed the basis, albeit with alterations and refinements, of Roman funerary law for many centuries. The fundamental rules that governed the disposal of the dead at Rome were evidently applicable to all members of society and would thus have influenced the practices of both rich and poor, particularly in terms of how and where corpses were buried. That the place of burial received the status of *locus religiosus* is particularly significant, for it conferred both a legal and religious status on even the simplest burial, thus legally protecting it from damage and legitimising its existence as the spiritual home of the deceased.

Burial clubs

The desire for some form of commemoration (of either the inscribing or incorporating variety), proper burial in accordance with the correct religious rites and the subsequent continuance of ritual activities, were evidently of great importance to all levels of society. However, not all members of the urban community had access to the resources required to adequately satisfy these demands, and it has been suggested that these pressures were largely responsible for the creation of funerary clubs or *collegia*. Paoli (1963: 129), for example, claimed that "men dislike death almost as much as they dislike the idea of not having a decent funeral after death. In every age men have toiled laboriously all their lives merely to save enough to pay their funeral expenses. This human sentiment gave birth to the *collegia funeraticia* in Rome."

A *collegium* consisted of a group of individuals who shared a common profession, trade, religious belief or who were the dependants or slaves of a single household. They engaged in various social activities and met regularly for banquets, meetings and festivals. Many of these associations owned burial plots or monuments (often *columbaria* which allowed for the burial of large numbers of individuals in one place) with space in which to hold funeral feasts and celebrate religious festivals, in addition to a separate place in which they met to dine on other occasions (see Patterson, 1992b: 20 – 21). Associations of any sort were regarded with suspicion by authorities fearing political rebellion, and the legal situation surrounding such organisations consequently fluctuated. According to Kaser (1965: 79) "the formation of an association for any lawful purpose was allowed by the XII Tables," but during the first century BC the situation appears to have varied considerably. Crook (1967: 265) summarises the legal situation:

"... a *senatusconsultum* of 64 BC suppressing *collegia* and a law put through the assembly by Clodius in 58 restoring them; a *senatusconsultum* in 56 suppressing *sodalities decuriatique* (which sounds like the pressure-groups of the aristocracy) and a *lex Licinia de sodaliciis* of 55, apparently again directed against mass bribery; and finally a *lex Iulia* which seems to have settled the law fairly effectively for the future."

The final *lex Iulia* mentioned here permitted the existence of certain societies provided they were licensed by the Emperor (*ibid.*: 265). These laws were concerned with regulating *all* forms of association, in particular those with a political agenda, but a shift in policy during the first century AD related specifically to burial clubs. Crook (*ibid.*: 266) continues: "the innumerable small groups of

the humble folk who paid small sums for an occasional beano and a proper burial were permitted to enlist unlicensed, by a *senatusconsultum*." Increased numbers of associations during the first century AD may be attributed to this change in the law which allowed for the easy creation of informal societies. An examination of the surviving charters of these *collegia*, however, highlights the extent to which they were frequently highly structured organisations rather than *ad hoc* groups of friends or colleagues.[49]

The extant constitution of a burial club at Lanuvium dedicated to Diana and Antinous and dating from AD 136 (CIL XIV 2112) provides an excellent insight into a *collegium*. In addition to regulations concerning the dates and conduct of feasts (including a list of those responsible for their organisation and the provision of the appropriate food), specific religious festivals and the celebration of the birthdays of Diana and Antinous, the charter makes specific reference to the process of entry to the *collegium* and its response to the death of a member:

"It was voted unanimously that whoever desired to enter this society shall pay an entry fee of 100 HS and an amphora of good wine and shall pay monthly dues of 5 asses (1 ¼ HS) ... If anyone has not paid his dues for six consecutive months and the common lot of man befalls him, his claim to burial shall not be upheld ... It was voted further that upon the death of a paid-up member of our club, there will be due to him from the treasury 300 HS ... from which will be deducted a funeral fee of 50 HS to be distributed at the pyre ...."

(CIL XIV 2112)[50]

Following these regulations are instructions on the appropriate action to be taken should a member die whilst away from town, if a slave's owner refused to hand over his body for burial, or if a member committed suicide.

Several significant details emerge from this document, including an insight into the types of people who were members of *collegia*. Freeborn, freedmen and slaves were all permitted to join, and in the case of the *collegium* of Lanuvium, "if any slave who is a member of this club should be freed, he shall be bound to pay an *amphora* of good wine." Patterson (2000a: 278) attributes this to a desire to collectively celebrate the good fortune of the former slave. Clearly legal status was not considered to be a major issue for the club members. However, although the majority of *collegia* members belonged to the lowest classes of society, Patterson (1992b: 21) demonstrates that they were unlikely to have included the poorest members of the community, stating that "the

---

[49] More informal *collegia* no doubt existed and the surviving charters simply reflect the organisation of clubs structured enough to produce one. However, the existence of these reminds us of quite how seriously members of the ancient urban community took funerary activities and responsibilities.
[50] Cited in Hopkins (1983: 215).

evidence available for the cost of funerals in Roman Italy suggests that the 250 HS received by members of the association of Diana and Antinous at Lanuvium was on a par with the cheapest recorded funerals from elsewhere in Italy. again, this suggests a comparatively exalted position for members of the clubs, as anonymous funerals will have been much cheaper." As Hasegawa (2005: 85) reminds us, these *collegia* never functioned as charitable groups. There were entrance fees to pay, ranging from 125 sesterces for the college of Aesculapius and Hygia on the Via Appia, to 100 sesterces for the *familia Silvani* at Trebula Mutuesca, or 100 sesterces and an amphora of wine at Lanuvium (Duncan-Jones, 1982: 131), plus monthly dues and the provision of banquets. Furthermore, some *collegia* owned large tombs and meeting places in which they held regular events. Members must have had access to a certain amount of financial resources in order to construct and maintain these facilities, although some may have been financed by wealthy patrons. This evidence is vital to understanding the *collegia* for it highlights that although their members derived from the lowest groups of society, the destitute and poorest members of the community, who would have benefited most from the services of the *collegia*, could not afford to join. This throws into question the common view that the poor joined burial clubs and those that couldn't found their way into the *puticuli*. In this case, a vast majority of the poor would have faced the horror of the mass grave. Whether or not this was logistically feasible is discussed in Chapter 4.

Although Patterson (2000a: 279) states, "in some cases it seems that wives and children of club members were themselves buried in a club's monument," there is a widespread absence of female *collegium* members. The constitution from Lanuvium, for example, does not refer to women or children and the names listed are male. Women and children were generally excluded from these organisations (Price, 2000: 301) and although they may in some cases have received burial if their husbands or fathers belonged to a *collegium*, this is unlikely to have occurred regularly. The Lanuvium charter asserts strictly that only fully paid-up members are entitled to financial assistance for burial. That few families are recorded within the monuments of *collegia* may be due to the fact that men with families experienced a reduced fear of being left kinless and alone upon their death and therefore did not require a socially created family to assist them.

A large proportion of the population (women, children, and possibly married men) were therefore unable to obtain, or did not seek, burial assistance from *collegia*, and although these organisations have been interpreted as a means by which the lower classes ensured good company in life and a decent burial in death, it is clear that their effect in this regard was limited. Nevertheless, although the observation of Hopkins (1983: 214) that *collegia* "saved men from the anonymity of mass graves and guaranteed each man's individuality in death" may not have been a comfort to all those facing the prospect of an ignominious burial without proper rites, it certainly eased the minds of those who did join an association.

Moreover, as the Lanuvium constitution reveals, *collegia* operated as more than a burial club, providing opportunities for social interaction and friendship. *Collegia* have been described as "characteristically urban institutions" (Bassett *et al.*, 1992: 6) and their development within urban environments has supported the interpretation of these clubs as a reaction to the loss of individuality experienced by members of large communities (Hopkins, 1983: 214). Patterson (1992b: 23) suggests they were "a means of 'humanizing the city,'" and "a remedy against the anonymity of life in a city of a million people." Brought together by a common profession, religious belief or other shared interests, the members of these clubs met regularly for meetings and dining activities, allowing them to create an artificial extended family on which they could rely after death. Consequently, the *collegia* cannot be viewed primarily as "burial clubs" but rather as social institutions which allowed members of the lower classes, with access to the necessary resources, to interact and socialise whilst ensuring that their remains received proper rites after death.

The funeraticium

Towards the end of the first century AD, Nerva instituted a funeral grant (*funeraticium*). Evidence for the grant is limited to a reference from AD 354, stating that he gave "*funeraticium plebi urbanae instituit* of 62 ½ denari," plus a small number of inscriptions and a reference in the *Digest*.[51] The precise meaning of the term and the process that it entailed consequently remain rather obscure. Degrassi (1962: 698) rejects the interpretation of Mommsen that Nerva provided 250 HS (62 ½ denarii) in his will for each member of the *plebs urbana* who attended his funeral, and also that of Sutherland who associated the grant with the funeral of Domitian. Although conceding that money was distributed to those attending the funerals of the rich,[52] Degrassi (*ibid.*: 698) observes that specific terms describing this (*sportula* and *exequiarium*) already existed. After an examination of inscriptions which refer to the *funeraticium* and those stating the amount granted by city councils for burial of prominent individuals,[53] he states that it is impossible to deduce the precise cost of a funeral, suggesting that it was probably modest compared to attested figures (which probably included the cost of the monument and donations to those in attendance) (*ibid.*: 701). Degrassi (*ibid.*: 701) therefore proposes that 250 HS was sufficient for a "modest" funeral at Rome and that the *funeraticium* was thus granted at times of need to members of the *plebs urbana* in order to cover burial expenses.

---

[51] Chron. 354, Mommsen *Chronica Minora* 1, p.146; CIL III p.924; VI 9626, 10234; XII 736, 4159; XIV 2112; *Digest* 11, 7, 30.
[52] He points also to the charter of the *collegium* from Lanuvium which stated that out of the 300 HS provided for the funeral, 50 HS was to be distributed at the pyre (*ad rogus*) (Degrassi, 1962: 698).
[53] At Pompeii 2,000 HS appears to have been the standard amount granted to important members of the community, for example CIL X 1019, 1024.

Eligibility for the grant is equally unclear. On the basis of the reference to the *plebs urbana*, Degrassi (*ibid.*: 701) suggests that only Roman citizens resident at Rome and eligible for the grain dole were included within the scope of the *funeraticium*. Numbers receiving the grain dole were strictly controlled (see Chapter 3) and eligibility for this was not determined by need, hence many of the poor found themselves excluded. This is a particularly significant observation for it suggests that many of the urban poor were probably also ineligible for the funerary grant and thus those who would have benefited most from assistance with burial costs were denied it. The *funeraticium* cannot, therefore, be interpreted as a funeral grant distributed to 'the poor', since many members of the *plebs urbana* as defined by Degrassi, lived well above the poverty line. Equally, the *funeraticium* appears not to have continued after Nerva's death. Degrassi (*ibid.*: 702), observing the impact that such a scheme would have on the state (an annual cost of approximately 1,000,000 HS), suggests that it was essentially a popularity seeking measure that was quickly revoked by Trajan. The *funeraticium* therefore existed for less than two years, a fact which explains the scarcity of textual and epigraphic references to the scheme. The temporary nature of the grant is further hinted at by the fact that, whilst the grain dole became an established symbol of poverty, a topos within Latin literature, the *funeraticium* did not. The absence of direct association of the scheme with the very poor emphasises this further. A grant that was theoretically available to *all* members of the urban plebs was unlikely to become a symbol of destitution.

Whether the *funeraticium* represented awareness on the part of the state of the problems facing those unable to afford decent burial or was simply an attempt to curry favour with the masses can be debated. Had Nerva ruled for longer the burden placed on the state may have forced a change in policy, the results providing evidence for the motives behind it. However, that it was quickly revoked by Trajan,[54] suggests that its success as a vote winner was outweighed by the financial pressure it exerted on the state. What is more, the scheme appears not to have been revived during subsequent centuries. The *funeraticium* was evidently not active for long enough to become an established means by which the poor financed burial.

Conclusions

Proper burial and commemoration were evidently fundamentally important on a social, religious and legal level to all groups of Roman society, and there is little reason to assume that opinions differed widely on these matters. The law applied to rich and poor alike, and wealth or class did not significantly influence religious beliefs about disposal. The physical responses to these factors doubtless varied in accordance with status and wealth, but essentially all members of urban society were influenced by the same pressures, needs and fears surrounding the death of a relative or friend. They were not, however, all affected by the same economic constraints. In order to assess the impact of economic resources on the responses of the lower classes to the demands posed by death, it is necessary to examine in detail the economic position of this sector of the urban community and to define more precisely who this group of people were.

---

[54] Something which occurred apparently without significant complaint on the part of the recipients – perhaps implying further that they did not consider it an inalienable right.

CHAPTER THREE

THE URBAN POOR

"It is no easy matter, anywhere, for a man to rise when poverty stands in the way of his merits: but nowhere is the effort harder than in Rome, where you must pay a big rent for a wretched lodging, a big sum to fill the bellies of your slaves, and buy a frugal dinner for yourself."

(Martial, *Epigrams* III. 164 – 167)

The importance of commemoration and proper religious burial during the late Republic and the early centuries of the Imperial period has been vividly illustrated in the previous two chapters. It has been shown that these concerns transcended the boundaries of wealth and social or legal status and affected the lives, deaths, attitudes and actions of a variety of individuals within the urban community of Rome. Although much of the evidence used in the reconstruction of these beliefs and reactions must necessarily focus largely on the upper echelons of the urban community, it has been shown that this evidence can also be used to make inferences regarding the practices and beliefs of the more humble members of society. However, if we are to gain a comprehensive understanding of the circumstances, emotional responses and activities surrounding death for these poorer social groups it is necessary to define in more precise terms who the 'poor' members of that community were. In the early chapters of this volume the phrases "the lower classes", "the less wealthy" and "the poor" have been used indiscriminately to refer to what was, in reality, a heterogeneous conglomeration of people, with varied social, legal and economic status. It is however highly inaccurate, and particularly unhelpful for a study of this nature, to continue to describe the vast majority of the population of Rome using such vague and indiscriminate terminology. It is therefore essential at this point to identify to whom the term "poor" can be applied and the economic implications this status entailed.

Roman attitudes to poverty

Attempts to classify 'the poor' can be approached in several ways, utilising various terms of definition, including social and legal status, economic wealth, and living conditions. Before these can be assessed in detail though, it is also essential to place the discussion in context and to examine contemporary definitions and attitudes in order to understand the ways in which both the upper and lower classes conceived of 'poverty.'[55]

Unfortunately (although unsurprisingly) there is no extant account of ancient poverty composed by those who directly experienced such a condition and we are therefore compelled to rely on the writings of elite members of society in order to gain an impression of contemporary attitudes to, and definitions of, poverty. However, as usual, these sources reflect the attitudes and biases of the wealthy elite who held particular views and opinions of the lower classes and were unlikely to have fully understood the realities of urban poverty, let alone to have experienced it first hand. Nevertheless, although these attitudes may be divorced from reality, they remain essential to understanding poverty in the Roman urban world. Such attitudes cannot be used as a basis on which to construct a definition of 'the poor' but they do illuminate contemporary opinions and definitions that contribute toward a thorough examination of this social group and the factors that shaped their identity.

The lower classes were generally considered too insignificant to play a major role in ancient literary or historical texts, unless involved in political activities in their incarnation as "the mob", but certain texts do refer to poverty. A cursory glance at these writings (especially those of Cicero, Seneca, Horace, Juvenal and Martial) leads to two conclusions. Firstly, the writers of these texts (and, by implication, their intended audience) did not fully understand the hardships of true poverty, often idealising and romanticising its apparently simple and frugal lifestyle; and, secondly, they despised those stricken by it in its most desperate form – beggary.

The first of these is illustrated particularly well in a passage by Seneca (*Ep.* 18.7, cited in Whittaker, 1993: 20) in which he says that bored members of the aristocracy would often "play at living like the poor in their small cells, eating simple meals and sleeping on mattresses." As Whittaker (*ibid.*: 20) has observed, Seneca boldly claimed that this gave no real insight into the hardships of poverty, but even his own attempt at simple living included a carriage of slaves and food that

---

[55] See Graham (2006) for further discussion of how ancient and modern attitudes towards the "lower classes" of ancient Rome have influenced our understanding of this sector of the urban community, particularly in terms of their attitudes towards the disposal of the corpse.

took only one hour to prepare (*Ep.* 87). Furthermore, Juvenal, who puts considerable effort into complaining about his own wretched poverty-stricken state and miserable living conditions, was not actually "sorry for the very poor or working-class; he is sorry for the middle-class men like himself who cannot get advancement" (Hands, 1968: 64). Juvenal provides further confirmation of this when he writes:

"And what of this, that the poor man gives food and occasion for jest if his cloak be torn and dirty; if his toga be a little soiled; if one of his shoes gapes where the leather is split, or if some fresh stitches of coarse thread reveal where not one, but many a rent has been patched? Of all the woes of luckless poverty none is harder to endure than this, that it exposes men to ridicule."

(*Sat.* III. 147 – 153)

To suggest that to be mocked for a shabby appearance was the most unbearable aspect of poverty clearly indicates a lack of understanding or experience of poverty on the part of Juvenal. Fear of ridicule more accurately reflects the anxieties of elevated members of the community concerned about their social position, than the hungry individual worried about the source of his next meal. Juvenal's words highlight the way in which wealthier members of urban society defined poverty using their own frame of reference. Whittaker (1993: 7) has also observed that Juvenal, "thought a person poor if he had less than 20,000 *sesterces* a year (9. 140 – 41)," which, in reality, represented a fortune to the majority. Furthermore, Veyne (1987: 141) spotlights the example of Horace who "said he was prepared to see his ambitions come to nought, for his poverty would serve as his life raft. This "life raft" consisted of two estates, one at Tivoli and the other in Sabine, where the master's house covered some 6,000 square feet." For the wealthy (and indeed also the moderately well-to-do) member of urban society, the concept of "poverty" clearly entailed being unable to live in the splendour and luxury that one desired whilst remaining comfortable, well fed and with at least a single roof over their head. Occasionally this "poverty" was equated with honour and "would be praised as the teacher of good and honest living, and equated with virtues such as *parsimonia*" (Hands, 1968: 63). Members of the city community who were constantly concerned with their social position and the future of their name and fortune were envious of the apparently simple and uncomplicated lifestyle of the 'poor'. They did not, however, envy the beggar, of whom they were very aware but spoke of only rarely. Essentially, in the eyes of the elevated sections of society, or at least those who have left textual evidence of their opinions, "the poor were the rich who were not very rich" (Veyne, 1987: 141). The rich were not necessarily blind to the plight of the many poorer members of the urban community but they were simply uninterested in understanding or discussing the existence of people who made little or no direct impact on their lives.

This vague acknowledgement of true destitution did, however, evoke strong *opinions* amongst ancient authors and a clear distinction was drawn between 'the poor' and 'beggars'. Unlike those perceived to be 'poor', who were essentially slightly unfortunate versions of themselves, the truly destitute were considered contemptuous, vile and unworthy of assistance, illustrated by Martial's comment (*Ep.* XII. 57. 13) that begging was something which Jewish children were taught by their mothers to do. There was a commonly held belief that the destitute chose to be unemployed and to live idle lives, leading consequently to the related conviction that the poor were quite content with their lot (Whittaker, 1993: 2). Paradoxically, however, those that did find employment were considered equally dishonest, sordid and untrustworthy. Brunt (1987: 714) points out that to the elite "a man was not truly free if he depended on wages," and Cicero (*de Off.* 1. 150) states unequivocally that, "wage labour is sordid and unworthy of a free man, for wages are the price of labour and not of some art," suggesting that "all retail dealing too may be put in the same category, for the dealer will gain nothing except by profuse lying, and nothing is more disgraceful than untruthful huckstering." It was not so much the work that was despised, but the "ties of dependence which it creates between the artisan and the person who uses the product which he manufactures" (Mossé, 1969: 27).[56] Hands (1968: 85 – 86) suggests the rich were "accustomed to seeing the poor free man and the slave at work together, so it would be easy for them to think of their dealings with both in much the same way," but their attitudes were seemingly shaped by more than just visual association. The close working relationship between slaves and lowly freemen may have confirmed their opinion of the latter as sordid and worthless but it was the fact that these individuals had opted to work for somebody else, and were thus degrading and enslaving themselves, which led to the contempt and scorn evident in the textual sources.

More sordid and vile than those who were compelled to find paid employment were those who, in the minds of the rich, actively chose not to. Balsdon (1969: 268) remarks that "one of the most striking features of our extensive literary evidence about life in ancient Rome is that it hardly ever mentions a beggar." This was evidently due in part to the fact that beggars were of no interest, politically or socially, to the upper classes, and although their presence on the streets of Rome was presumably unavoidable, those who believed themselves to be superior could easily ignore their outstretched hands. What is more, there was no desire or compulsion to help the indigent through the provision of food or money. The grain dole (discussed below) was designed more as a means to keep the peace than appease the social conscience of the ruling class and was, at any rate, not available to everyone. Plutarch (*Moralia* 235A) voices the feelings of the upper classes on the subject of charity when he writes of a Spartan's response to a beggar: "But

---

[56] See also Joshel's (1992) investigation of the working members of the Roman urban community and attitudes towards these occupations held by both rich and poor.

if I gave to you, you would proceed to beg all the more; it was the man who gave to you in the first place who made you idle and so is responsible for your disgraceful state." This is an attitude echoed by a Pompeian graffiti which reads: "I hate poor people. If anyone wants something for nothing, he's a fool. Let him pay up and he'll get it" (CIL IV 9839b). These passages and the attitudes they engender are frequently quoted in modern discussions of the ancient poor due to the relative small number of references to the destitute in literary sources – a symptom of the lack of interest in their welfare. Similarly, the following passage by Martial has received much attention from modern scholars and provides perhaps the most extensive ancient description of a beggar:

> 'Whoever he be, despiser of stole or purple, that has assailed with impious verses those whom he ought to respect, let him wander through the city, exiled from bridge and slope, and, last amongst hoarse beggars, crave morsels of shameless bread, fit only for dogs. May a long December and a wet winter and a closed archway drag out for him miserable cold. May he call them happy, acclaim them fortunate who are borne in an Orcivian litter. But when the threads of his final hour have come and his tardy day of death, let him hear the wrangling of dogs and flap his rags to drive off noxious birds. And let not his punishments end with a simple death, but let him weary all the fables of the poets, now lashed by the thongs of stern Aeacus, now crushed by the mountain of restless Sisyphus, now dry amidst the waters of the old chatterbox. And when the Fury commands him to confess the truth, let conscience betray him and let him cry out: "I wrote it."

(Martial, *Ep*. X. 5)

Martial was evidently aware of the suffering endured by the destitute, but demonstrates little concern for them; in fact, he wishes such misery upon the subject of the *Epigram*. This passage supports the claim that "since a poor man or a slave might be thought to have deserved his lot because of bad character, we should not expect Romans to see poverty and slavery as social problems which required cure" (Treggiari, 1996: 886). Martial's attitude was that the "despiser of stole or purple" deserved misery, hunger and a distressing death as a result of their bad character which was, in turn, their own fault. It was because of perceptions such as this that the destitute rarely received financial or nutritional support, since in order to benefit from donations of money or food the recipient was first required to demonstrate that he was worthy of receiving it (Whittaker, 1993: 2). However, the qualities required by the upper class were, as Hands (1968: 74) observes, "those qualities of mind or character which could either serve or be appreciated by that class, qualities which could scarcely be possessed unless the approved recipient had at some time enjoyed comfortable circumstances and the education which made these possible." Former slaves, who had acquired certain skills

and observed the practices and manners of their upper class masters, were therefore probably more capable of securing this sort of support than homeless freeborn beggars. Furthermore, these freedmen generally had patrons to whom they could turn in times of need.

The perception of the poor as contemptuous parasites was further reinforced by the concept of *"panem et circenses"* (bread and circuses). Juvenal's statement (10. 78 – 81) that the Roman people looked forward only to bread and games was reasserted in the second century AD by Fronto (*Princ. Hist.* 17), who suggested that "Trajan knew that the Roman people was held fast by two things, the free corn distribution (*annona*) and the shows (*spectacula*)" (cited in Balsdon, 1969: 267). The frequency with which this phrase was used in characterisations of the lower class population of the city indicates the existence of a commonly held belief that the majority of the population depended on the state for food and entertainment and were, consequently, of bad character. Horsfall (2003: 28 – 29) has recently pointed to the interesting history behind this statement and shown that its origins can be traced to ancient Greece and Egypt. It was evidently an established way of perceiving the lives of the poor. These conclusions resulted in a decreased desire to assist the very poor and reinforced the conviction that they had actively chosen this state of existence and were adequately fed and entertained by the state.

Certainly there were varying degrees of indifference to the plight of the destitute and whereas Sallust, writing during the late Republic, described the poor as "those who "envy the good and praise the bad"," (cited in Whittaker, 1993: 3), during the later Empire "a pagan did pity "the mendicant poor, covered with rags and sunk in the calamity of their wretchedness"" (MacMullen, 1974: 87; Firm. Matern., *Math.* 4.14.3). The latter example may reflect later Imperial attitudes, but it remains probable that individuals were aware of the plight of the very poor in earlier periods. There was, however, no commonly held sense of duty to help the poor and any assistance that occurred did so on an *individual* basis. The wealthier classes were certainly aware of the presence of impoverished people since Seneca (*Ad. Helv.* 12.1) observed "how great a majority are the poor," but they displayed little active concern for their welfare.

These attitudes were, of course, also greatly affected by the conventions of the genre in which many of them were written. The epigrams, comments and poems of authors such as Martial and Juvenal in particular, were designed to deliberately polarise behaviour and to create stereotypes that could be ridiculed. As Joshel (1992: 63) has pointed out, the attitudes expressed in these works "engender and in turn reinforce stereotypes that constitute a vital element in satire: lying, cheating, vulgar tradesmen are stock figures along with rich, obnoxious freedmen, greasy foreigners, decadent nobles, needy clients, insensitive patrons, and unchaste women." To this list should also be added the beggar – a character who could be safely mocked by the wealthier members of society. Given the genre in which these poets were writing we should not expect to find the true feelings of the authors hidden within their words. Martial and Juvenal probably had more experience of life in the streets of Rome than many of the other ancient authors and may well have been aware of the terrible living conditions experienced by the poor, but this was of no use for their satire. Where was the fun in showing concern for the destitute?[57] This must, as a result, be taken into account when studying these attitudes towards poverty but it must also be remembered that Juvenal and Martial were writing what their audience wanted to hear, and as much as the stereotypes were fictional, they reinforced the already existing opinions of the more elevated members of society that the poor were worthless and undeserving of their attention or charity.

Ancient literary sources can therefore not be relied upon in order to establish a realistic definition of 'poverty.' Those whom they described as 'poor' were very different from those they considered vulgar and idle. This renders their accounts relatively unhelpful for gaining an insight into the *conditions* in which the latter struggled to survive, but does illustrate the attitudes they had to confront. Faced with this distaste and contempt, the poor may have felt more strongly about making themselves appear respectable in the eyes of the urban community and it doubtless affected their sense of individual and collective identity, as well as their responses to the opportunities offered by the funeral process to assert their true selves.

Modern definitions of "the Roman poor"

Similarities can be detected between the attitudes observed in ancient literary sources and modern scholarly treatments of Roman society. Modern discussions of ancient society often pay scant attention to the lower classes, preferring to focus on wider political issues and social competition between the elite, amongst other subjects. In many of these accounts it seems to be considered unnecessary to provide a more precise definition of 'the lower classes' because they did not feature highly in social or political negotiations and serve simply to provide a contrast to the issues being discussed. This approach has created many rather vague descriptions of the poor, such as Patterson's (2000a: 268) observation that "the vast majority of the population must of course have occupied a position somewhere between the wealthy political class on the one hand and the destitute on the other." Whilst this may suffice for a general discussion of urban society, it has also led to the lower classes being repeatedly viewed as a single entity, or, to use the words of Garnsey (1998: 250), "one monolithic block."

On occasion, ancient descriptions of idle and lazy poor individuals concerned only with "bread and circuses" have been adopted almost unquestioningly by modern scholars. Such dismissive attitudes are most evident in the literature of the 1960s and 1970s, including that of

Salmon (1974: 64) who went so far as to suggest that the *plebs* "made little contribution to the civilisation in which they were living; they were scarcely a part of the living organism of the Empire." Both Cowell (1961) and Carcopino (1964)[58] assumed, like Juvenal, or at least his readers, two thousand years before them, that the grain dole was the most significant feature of the lives of the poor, and Paoli (1963: 122) takes the words of Martial (*Ep.* XII. 70) at face value when he suggests that "even the poorest took at least three slaves with them to the baths. Not to have one slave was a sign of the most degrading poverty." As noted above, the 'poor' that were referred to in these texts were either literary stereotypes or were actually the "less rich" – a distinction that Paoli does not make. The unquestioning perpetuation of these ancient attitudes has generated an image of the lower classes as a vague homogenous group of people living in wretched conditions, who were nevertheless well fed, entertained and content.

More recent archaeological and historical literature has challenged this perception by attempting to examine this group of people in more detail and to highlight the existence of various levels of status and wealth within it. Veyne (1987: 133 – 134), for example, distinguishes between three grades of economic status:

"(1) A plebeian owned nothing, simply earning his daily bread day after day ... (2) A poor shopkeeper (a cobbler, say, or a tavernkeeper) disposed of so little ready cash that every morning he had to buy the merchandise he would sell during the day. If a demanding client asked for a good bottle of wine, the tavernkeeper would have to go out and buy that wine from a wealthy wine merchant in his neighbourhood ... (3) A wealthy merchant was one who could afford to keep on hand several barrels of wine or sacks of flour or sides of beef. He was not a wholesaler but a merchant who sold to private individuals as well as to lesser merchants."[59]

This description highlights the existence of varying levels of economic success amongst the 'lower classes,' an observation with particular significance for a study of the access that people had to the resources required for burial and commemoration. Divisions such as these suggest that status competition may also have prevailed between these various levels, perhaps being manifested in funerary activities as seen amongst wealthier groups.

---

[57] Thanks to Valerie Hope for her comments on this issue.

[58] Cowell (1961: 143): "thousands seem to have survived on the charity of the rich, supplemented by free wheat and water supplied by the state." Carcopino (1964: 78): possibly one-half of the population of the city lived on public charity."

[59] It is unclear exactly what Veyne has based these divisions on – there is certainly no extant literary evidence that distinguishes between members of the lower class in this way. It is perhaps derived from a combination of textual evidence for life and work in the ancient city, epigraphy, archaeology, cross-cultural comparison and common sense. As a result, his divisions must be viewed with a degree of scepticism concerning their accuracy. Nevertheless, Veyne's divisions appear to represent a plausible and useful understanding of the situation. The same is true of the Garnsey quote which follows.

Even more revealing is the distinction made between the "permanent poor and the temporary poor" by Garnsey (1998: 226), who also subdivides the former into "the very poor and the ordinary poor":

> "The very poor were the truly destitute: they spent their lives in search of food, work and shelter. The ordinary poor lived at the edge of subsistence; they had some kind of lodgings, and provided unskilled, part-time or seasonal labour, when they could get it. By the temporary poor I mean small shopkeepers and artisans, who enjoyed a somewhat higher social and economic status, but were liable to slip into poverty in times of shortage or at difficult points in their life cycles."

(*ibid.*: 227)

These subdivisions hint further at the fluidity of life in the city of Rome. It was evidently possible to move from one level of poverty to another, depending upon economic circumstances, and these groups should certainly not be regarded as fixed or static. Indeed, Purcell (1994: 657) suggests that true destitution was a highly fatal state that was not long endured at Rome, and that survival depended upon bettering oneself. This need not imply that death quickly followed as a natural consequence of economic deterioration, since the comments of Martial and Juvenal demonstrate that beggars did survive, but it does indicate that there was a certain degree of movement within and between these levels. These groups were not real in the sense that poor people identified themselves as belonging to one and were anxious to progress to the next. They should be viewed simply as a means by which to understand poverty at Rome and to emphasize the existence of fluid gradations of wealth and status within the lower classes similar to the rest of society.

An economic definition of the Roman poor

Although ancient Roman concepts of poverty have been shown to be of limited value to this investigation they do highlight the existence of a large community that was living precariously on the edge of poverty. Similarly, modern definitions such as those of Veyne and Garnsey illustrate the various levels of poverty *within* the "lower classes" and allow us to begin to understand the fluidity of wealth and status within this sector of society. However, in order to understand the impact of burial demands and costs on the attitudes and behaviour of the poor it is necessary to examine the economic resources that were available to the poor inhabitant of Rome that may in turn have influenced their decisions regarding burial and commemoration.

Wage rates

Evidence for the economic resources that were available directly to poorer members of Roman society is limited to Cicero's statement (*Q. Rosc.* 28) that during the late Republic an unskilled labourer earned 12 *asses* (3 HS) per day.[60] Wage levels doubtlessly varied in relation to the type of work carried out and the season, and presumably did not remain static throughout the period in question, but this information can be used to provide an insight into the basic resources of ordinary workers. For individuals lacking particular skills or a craft, employment could probably be found on one of the public building projects at Rome, and "the narrow entrances and multiple levels of Roman warehouses demonstrate that goods were transported by manpower alone without the use of carts or draft animals. Such a system would have required an enormous number of labourers employed solely as porters" (Mattingly and Aldrete, 2000: 148). This latter demand was doubtless very high at busy ports such as Ostia where, increasingly during the summer months, "one could readily suppose that it was supplied partly by the casual labour of persons normally resident in Rome" (Brunt, 1980: 93). DeLaine (2000: 132) suggests that some 12,000 – 20,000 men were employed in the construction industry at Rome. The people employed in these sorts of jobs were probably the unskilled labourers of which Cicero speaks and probably could not hope to earn very much more than this "minimal wage" of 3 HS. Of course, 3 HS cannot be confirmed as the daily wage of *all* unskilled labourers at *all* periods of Roman history, but in light of the absence of any other information pertaining to such matters and because Millett (1999: 1615) suggests that "wage rates were fixed more by custom than by demand and supply and were slow to change," the following discussion is based on the assumption that it represents a plausible average income.

Assuming the unskilled labourer in question found employment for 365 days each year, his annual income would have totalled 1095 HS. However, there are several other variables that require consideration when calculating annual income. It is highly unlikely that employment was secured for every day of the year, not least because of the unreliable and temporary nature of unskilled employment, which was probably seasonal or dependent upon the availability of public building projects. As Brunt (1980: 93) observes, public building was by no means a continuous process: "under Tiberius, for instance, there was very little. Indeed building was always in some degree a seasonal business: Frontinus says that it was best done between April and November, subject to intermission in a time of great heat, which had as bad an effect as frost (*de aquis* 123)." Furthermore, it is important that we take into account public holidays, with business suspended on *dies nefasti*. Although Balsdon (1969: 74) argues that "it is absurd to exaggerate the impact of festival days on the working life of Romans

---

[60] Comparison has been made between this amount and that of wealthier members of society by Whittaker (1993: 6) who observes that "Seneca tells us that one of Caesar's contemporaries, the younger Cato, who sang the praises of simple living, had property valued at four million sesterces, which would have yielded him an income of 550 – 650 sesterces a day." The difference is considerable, with Cato potentially earning more in a single day than a labourer could hope to make in a year (see **Table 1**).

Period	Number of working days	Annual income (HS)
Pre-Sulla	306	918
Post-Sulla	272	816
Caesar	215	645
Claudius	206	618
Marcus Aurelius	230	690

Table 1. The effect of public holidays on the annual income of an unskilled worker.

and to imagine that on all these days shops were shut and work ceased ... workers had simply to down tools and stand about if a sacred procession was passing, since holy days were polluted if priests caught sight of men at work," it is likely that certain public holidays *were* observed in such a way, in addition to days on which games were held. Examination of the theoretical impact of public holidays on the wage earning capabilities of the unskilled allows greater understanding of the effects of the *unreliability* of employment and how *not* working 365 days a year may have influenced annual income. Before the time of Sulla there were apparently 59 public holidays each year but this rose to 159 under Claudius, before being reduced to 135 by Marcus Aurelius (*ibid.*: 75). Taking into account the various numbers of festival days during different periods, the annual income of an unskilled labourer can be calculated (**Table 1**). It is unlikely that a major city such as Rome could have continued to function with any degree of efficiency with only 206 working days each year and these figures should therefore not be viewed as an accurate reflection of the reality of wage earning. However, they do provide an adequate illustration of the impact that temporary and casual employment may have had on the wages of unskilled workers and are therefore used in the following discussion as a means of quantifying *unreliable* employment.

Acquiring grain

The average unskilled worker would have required most of their income to purchase food. It has been well established that wheat or grain generally formed the basis of the ordinary Roman's diet,[61] and Shelton (1988: 81) explains how this was "either crushed and boiled with water to make porridge or *puls*, or ground into flour and baked as bread ... Boiling was probably more common than baking because few poor people would have their own oven." At various periods grain was distributed free of charge (the *frumentario*) and this has consequently led to the conclusion that those at the lower end of the economic scale had access to a regular source of nutrition. However, the circumstances surrounding grain distribution require closer examination.

In 123 BC Gaius Gracchus fixed the price of grain at 6⅓ *asses* (about 1½ HS) per *modius*, for a maximum of 5

modii per month for each individual.[62] This system continued until 82 BC when Sulla abolished all subsidised grain distributions. However, the 70s BC witnessed a re-establishment of subsidised distributions and although the *lex Aemilia* of 78 BC, supported by the consul Lepidus, was perhaps annulled relatively quickly, the *lex Terentia Cassia* of 73 BC ensured the continued provision of 5 *modii* per month at the original Gracchan price. These prices were evidently still in effect in 62 BC when Cato's *lex Porcia* maintained the price but reduced the number of individuals eligible to receive (or, more accurately, to purchase) subsidised grain to approximately 200,000, the previous figure having presumably increased to an unmanageable level. A mere four years later, in 58 BC, P. Clodius Pulcher, as part of an attempt to gain political support for Julius Caesar, took the unprecedented step of making grain distributions free, although the number of recipients was again reduced by Caesar to 150,000 (Cowell, 1961: 137 – 138). From this period onwards grain distributions remained free, although the number of recipients fluctuated (Augustus reduced the number from 320,000 to 200,000 in 5 BC) and with a short-lived hiatus after the Great Fire of AD 64, when Nero was compelled to discontinue free distributions but imposed a low maximum price of 3 HS per *modius* on grain available to the entire urban population (Dio 62.18; Robinson, 1992: 155). During the late second century AD Septimius Severus added free olive oil to the dole that was by now received by 170,000 individuals, and Aurelian later introduced free pork and cheap wine, in addition to replacing the grain with bread.

Several significant issues emerge from this brief history of the grain dole. Firstly, it provides useful information regarding the prices at which grain was sold that can be used in the context of this study to assess its impact on the economic resources of the ordinary city-dweller. In addition, it highlights the fact that limitations were imposed on the number of recipients of grain; those not receiving subsidised or free grain were evidently forced to purchase it elsewhere. The grain-market beyond the dole appears to have been largely unregulated (Garnsey, 1983: 63) and the action that was taken after the catastrophic fire of AD 64 illustrates how the availability and price of grain was also dependent on external factors. Disasters such as that could severely disrupt the dole.

---

[61] See Cowell, 1961: 76 – 77; Robinson, 1992: 144; Garnsey, 1998: 229.

[62] For the reasons behind this action and its political implications, see Garnsey and Rathbone (1985).

This presumably occurred at other undocumented times, perhaps as a result of poor harvests, military activity or epidemic disease that affected the production, transportation or distribution of the grain. The dole should thus not be considered as a reliable source of nutrition for all members of the population since only a limited number benefited from it.

The circumstances surrounding eligibility for the grain dole unfortunately remain relatively obscure, although it is known that citizenship was essential and that women were excluded from it at all times. It is also known that freedmen were eligible, because, as Cowell (1961: 138) notes, "a number of slave-owners freed their slaves, so that they no longer would need to feed them."[63] Residency at Rome was also essential. Caesar and Augustus compiled lists based on their sub-division of the city into *regiones* and *vici*, "with vacancies filled by a lottery procedure, *subsortitio*" (Purcell, 1994: 648). Augustus also seems to have reduced the age of eligibility from an unknown level to ten years of age (Cowell, 1961: 138 – 139). It is evident, therefore, that the dole was restricted to a relatively small section of the population, on the basis of adult male citizenship and residency at Rome. What is more, there was no means test, which rendered it even more unlikely that those most in need of free or cheap food would receive any assistance. It was apparently considered to be an honour to be eligible for the dole, and this fact was occasionally alluded to on funerary monuments as a mark of status (*ibid.*: 139; ILS 2049, 6062 – 6070; see also Veyne, 1990: 243 – 44). The system also operated within the context of ideas about the 'good' and the 'bad' poor, with those of "bad character" deemed unworthy of support. As a result, the poor and needy were not necessarily the recipients of the dole; indeed, senators and equestrians seem to have been included at least until the time of Augustus (Robinson, 1992: 153).

Market prices also inevitably fluctuated in reaction to political, economic, military and social circumstances, as the actions of Nero attest. The price could rise to extortionate levels in times of shortage, with Eusebius noting that in AD 6 prices rose as high as 5½ *denarii* (HS 22) per *modius*. Such prices presumably were not sustainable for long periods, but they do highlight the instability of prices at Rome – a city whose food supply was largely at the mercy of external events. It is, however, generally accepted (Duncan-Jones, 1982; Garnsey, 1998) that, under normal circumstances, a *modius* of grain cost 6-8 HS at Rome during the early Imperial period.

A further significant point that emerges from this discussion concerns the amount of grain that was distributed. Whether sold at a reduced price or given away free there appears to have been a standardised amount allocated to each individual – 5 *modii*. Garnsey

(1988: 229 – 230) has examined the nutritional value of the corn distributions and he concludes that:

> "Wheat scores well as a source of food energy. Operating with the figure of 1,625 – 2,012 kcals per person per day as a minimum requirement (Clark and Haswell (1970) 58) and taking 3,330 kcals as the food energy of 1kg of soft wheat, we can estimate that basic needs, if met completely by wheat, would be satisfied by consumption of 490 – 600gm of wheat, or, at a high extraction rate, 650 – 800gm of wholemeal bread (or 2 – 2.4 Roman lbs). A side-glance at the *frumentario* shows the recipient of 5 *modii* (about 3,700 kcals per day) was getting more than 1 kg of wheat per day or more than double his basic requirement."

He also observes that, despite the fact that grain distributions provided a maximum of 60 *modii* per annum, if we assume that an individual obtained 25% of their calorific needs from other foods, their *minimum grain requirement* was approximately 22.5 *modii* per annum, with the *average grain consumption* likely to be approximately 30 *modii* (Garnsey, 1998: 191 – 192). These figures indicate that the grain dole was sufficient to provide a married couple with the calorific intake they required, although it evidently could not provide sufficient nutrition to support children without the parents considerably reducing their own consumption. On the basis of these observations the following prices can be calculated for the period during which the Gracchan prices (6⅓ *asses* per *modius*) were in effect (123 – 58 BC):

Consumption rate	Grain price per annum (HS)
Minimum (22.5 modii pa)	35.6
Average (30 modii pa)	47.5
Family (60 modii pa)[64]	95

Table 2. The price of purchasing grain in the Gracchan period (123 – 58 BC).

Assuming, therefore, that an unskilled labourer, employed for 365 days a year, earned 1095 HS, these expenses would leave that individual with between 1047.5 HS and 1,000 HS for other essentials (other food, clothing, fuel, rent etc). However, as we have already noted, employment was unreliable and if this factor is considered in conjunction with these rates of consumption, the remaining income would be significantly reduced, as can be seen in **Table 3**.[65]

---

[63] Although this of course may not indicate that they received the dole, simply that acquiring food was now their own problem and not his.

[64] This figure is based on a married couple sharing.

[65] The unreliability of employment is represented in the table by the data we possess regarding public holidays given the problems we face trying to quantify this factor in any other way. The figures are designed to give an impression of how differing levels of unemployment might affect an individual's income.

Number of working days	Annual income (HS)	Consumption rate	Remaining income (HS)
306	918	Minimum Average Family	882.4 870.5 823
272	816	Minimum Average Family	780.4 768.5 721
215	645	Minimum Average Family	609.4 597.5 550
206	618	Minimum Average Family	582.4 570.5 523

Table 3. The effects of grain expenditure at Gracchan price levels (6 ⅓*asses*) on the annual income of an unskilled worker experiencing unreliable employment.

Consumption rate	Grain price		
	6 HS	7 HS	8 HS
Minimum (22.5 modii pa)	135	157.5	180
Average (30 modii pa)	180	210	240
Family (60 modii pa)	300	420	480

Table 4. The cost of market priced grain at various consumption rates

These figures are obviously hypothetical, but it is clear from the data presented here that even the benefits offered by subsidized grain could seriously impact upon the economic resources of the very poor, perhaps leaving a family with as little as 523 HS per annum after the purchase of essential grain. The introduction of free grain was an undeniable benefit to those who were fortunate enough to receive it, but it must again be emphasized that this was restricted to between 150,000 and 200,000 members of the population and did not necessarily include those most in need.

Garnsey (1998: 236) suggests that grain received from the state was not necessarily suitable for human consumption in its entirety. He writes (*ibid.*: 236):

"The grain had travelled far; if of Egyptian origin, it was at best the grain of the year before. More likely it was older than this by the time it reached the consumer, having been stored in warehouses for some time. Not all of it would have been fit for human consumption. It would have deteriorated further after distribution, while stored in some dark corner, waiting to be processed and eaten. Wheat easily deteriorates if not stored in optimum conditions (such as were not available in the crowded tenements of Rome), and it is prone to attack by sundry pests and diseases."

This may not have prevented the desperately hungry from consuming unsuitable grain, but it does imply that a certain, possibly considerable, amount of the 60 *modii* per annum was inedible and perhaps required supplementing with grain that was purchased on the open market. This was also probably necessary for families with several mouths to feed, amongst which 60 *modii* would not go far. Equally, those who did not receive the dole presumably also had to purchase it in the market. **Table 4** shows the expenses that a price range of 6 – 8 HS would have entailed for the various rates of consumption that have already been established above.

If we now factor in to this equation the unreliable nature of unskilled employment then these grain expenses can be seen to have had an even more significant impact on the casual labourer's annual income. **Table 5** demonstrates that an unskilled labourer, who was potentially earning only HS 3 per day, may have been left with very minimal financial reserves with which to

Working days	Income (HS)	Consumption rate	Money left after grain			Remaining income (%)
			6 HS	7 HS	8 HS	
365	1095	Minimum	960	937.5	915	88 – 84
		Average	915	885	855	84 – 78
		Family	795	675	615	73 – 56
306	918	Minimum	783	760.5	738	85 – 80
		Average	738	708	678	80 – 74
		Family	558	498	438	61 – 48
272	816	Minimum	681	658.5	636	83 – 78
		Average	636	606	576	78 – 71
		Family	516	396	336	63 – 41
215	645	Minimum	510	487.5	465	79 – 72
		Average	465	435	405	72 – 63
		Family	345	225	165	53 – 25
206	618	Minimum	483	460.5	438	78 – 71
		Average	438	408	378	71 – 61
		Family	318	198	138	52 – 22

Table 5. The impact of unreliable employment (holidays), various grain prices and consumption rate on the income of unskilled labourers.

purchase commodities other than grain. Indeed, if such an individual was required to feed a family, or a wife, in the time of Caesar (or at least only able to secure employment for approximately 215 days per year) he could expect to spend only 25 – 53% of his earnings on non-grain items if he was unfortunate enough not to receive a free dole.[66]

Buying the grain was not the end of the story, or of the expense. Once it had been purchased the raw grain required often complex processing and storage, which again resulted in more expense for the consumer. Unfortunately there are no extant references to the costs of processing, or storing grain that had either been purchased or received from the state. Cowell (1961: 139) suggests that people "must have been compelled to entrust it to some baker-miller to turn into food," and it is highly likely that the latter accrued considerable profit in the process, perhaps retaining a portion of the grain for themselves. The original owner of the grain would have been forced to place a considerable degree of faith in the miller and hope that he would receive what he was rightfully his once the grain had been processed. Although it is impossible to discuss in detail the costs of grain processing it is possible to state that this would have entailed further expense for those with already limited financial resources. Coupled with the original cost

of the grain, the whole process consumed a substantial portion of an unskilled labourer's potential income.[67]

Purchasing other foodstuffs

Garnsey (1998: 239 – 240) has suggested that grain represented only 75% of the food energy requirement of an individual's diet, and that for a reasonably balanced diet the remaining 25% took the form of other foods such as vegetables. He (*ibid.*: 241) continues: "wine, oil and dry legumes are commonly regarded as staples throughout the Mediterranean region, and special reasons have to be found for denying their presence to some degree in the diet of the ordinary people of Rome." There is again little extant evidence for the price of these foodstuffs. It was not until the reigns of Septimius Severus and Aurelian that oil and wine respectively were provided free to residents of Rome; before this such items had to be purchased at market prices. Garnsey (*ibid.*: 242) has noted that an average of 20 litres of oil were probably consumed per person each year but that mass production of oil in the Mediterranean region presumably resulted in varying degrees of quality and price levels – undoubtedly low quality produce was available for low prices.

---

[66] Clearly individuals required to feed only themselves, were at an advantage but the extent to which people remained "dependent free" in order to save money remains doubtful. As has been discussed above, it is human nature to form relationships and families and these provided a vital source of economic support for members of the lower classes.

[67] It is also important to note here, as Garnsey (1999: 21) has, that the quality of the processing that took place affected the phytate content of the flour: "the higher the phytate content, the more deprived of vital minerals the body was likely to be. Galen's survey of breads encompasses four classes, which range from 'extra dirty' branbread to 'clean', fine-ground bread (VI. 480-6). The passage should be read with an eye to the class differences that were a feature of Graeco-Roman society." The health of the poor would therefore have been seriously affected by their ability to pay for adequate processing.

Similarly, wine was probably available at a wide range of prices, with Warde Fowler (1908: 39) suggesting that "rough wine ... was at times remarkably cheap," and Stambaugh (1988: 154) proposing that prices varied from an *as* to a *sestertius* (although this may also have reflected the quantity as much as the quality). Garnsey (1998: 241) reasons that wine could be purchased at Rome for 1-2 HS per litre – half the daily wage of an unskilled labourer. Although it is tempting to view wine as a luxury item, especially in light of the plentiful supply of water provided by the aqueducts of the city, it would have made an essential contribution to the maintenance of a balanced diet. Moreover, although free water perhaps did form a large part of the liquid consumption of the poorer members of society, the complaints of the *populus* on one occasion that the price of wine was too high and was in short supply (Warde Fowler, 1908: 40; Suet. *Aug.* 42) perhaps implies that wine was generally preferred and widely consumed.[68]

Significantly, Garnsey (1998: 242) also remarks that:

> "lentils, chickpeas and broad beans, were the main source of protein as of calories in the Mediterranean basin as a whole ... Beans are associated by Martial with artisans (*faba faborum*, 10.48.16), chickpeas are the food of the humble section of the theatre audience, according to Horace (*Ars. P.* 249), and a would-be politician is depicted by the same poet as having impoverished himself by showering the Circus crowd with chickpeas, beans and lentils (*Sat.* 2.3.184)."

The price of these foodstuffs remains unknown but their close association with the poorer elements of society perhaps suggests that they were inexpensive and readily available. Purchase of these items would, however, still have had an impact on the "shopping budget" of the ordinary Roman. Similarly, fruit and vegetables are vital to maintaining a balanced diet and "[c]heap vegetables such as cabbage, leeks, beet, garlic and onions, are associated in imaginative literature with the poor (cf. Juv. 1.134; 3.293; 5.87; Pers. 3.114; Mart. 13.13.1; Plaut. *Poen.* 13.4; etc)" according to Garnsey (1998: 242). Vegetables may have been relatively cheap and could possibly have been obtained cheaper still as they neared the end (or exceeded) their "best before date." Opportunities to grow fruit and vegetables were doubtless denied many city-dwellers given the dense occupation of small upper storey apartments in the city. Nevertheless, Rome was probably supplied with adequate fruit and vegetables by the small market gardens and farms in its immediate hinterland and so supply was probably rarely a problem.

In order to maintain a balanced diet the poorer city-dweller (whether a recipient of the corn dole or not) was evidently compelled to purchase commodities in the market in order to supplement the grain that formed the basis of their diet. These products may have been relatively inexpensive (depending of course on their quality) but in light of the very low income of these individuals and families, they still consumed a substantial amount of the resources they had at their disposal. The extent to which these people were concerned with ensuring their diet was nutritionally balanced is unclear, and we should be wary of transferring modern scientific concepts of diet to the situation in ancient Rome. However, a lack of biological knowledge does not negate the need for a balanced diet and malnourishment was probably widespread. It is evident from this discussion that Brunt (1966: 18) was correct when he observed that: "it is an illusion that in the late Republic the urban plebs was usually well and cheaply fed by the state."

Other household expenses

In addition to expenditure on food, the ordinary Roman also had to clothe himself and his family. Prices for everyday clothing are not forthcoming from ancient textual sources, with the exception of the Price Edict of Diocletian (AD 301). The prices outlined within the latter are unfortunately not applicable to this discussion because they reflect the economic situation of the later Empire, but the Edict does demonstrate the way in which clothing prices, as expected, varied in relation to the quality and style of the garment. The women of the Roman household were traditionally responsible for spinning and the production of clothing and, although this may have become no more than an upper-class ideal by the time of the early Empire, it does suggest that many garments were probably produced in the home. Unprocessed wool and other material was probably less expensive than "ready made" clothing, but would still have to be purchased. Clothing may have been worn for long periods of time, being constantly repaired and patched, as Juvenal's (*Sat.* III. 147 – 153) description cited above demonstrates, and therefore perhaps does not represent a regular expenditure. Nevertheless, it is still necessary to consider it within this discussion.

Fuel, in the form of oil (for lighting) and wood (for heat and cooking) was also required. The price of fuel is unknown (although, as noted above, oil could apparently be obtained inexpensively), but could probably be readily obtained in small quantities from a variety of sources at fairly minimal expense.[69]

A place to live

An individual may have equipped himself (and his family) with suitable clothing and fuel, and prevented starvation through the purchase of adequate food supplies on a basic and unreliable wage, but as Yavetz (1958: 517) points out "the heaviest monetary burden from which the

---

[68] The expenses involved in the purchase of wine could presumably have been balanced by watering it down considerably prior to consumption, thus making it last longer.

[69] See Meiggs (1982) for a discussion of the timber supply of Rome and its uses, including fuel.

Working days	Income (HS)	Annual rent (HS)	Remaining income HS
365	1095	365	730
306	918	365	553
272	816	365	451
215	645	365	280
206	618	365	253

Table 6. The effect of rent prices on variable income.

urban plebs suffered was the necessity to pay their rents." Many of the truly destitute inhabitants of Rome, those that Garnsey defines as the "permanent" or "very poor", were homeless, sheltering in doorways or narrow alleyways between buildings. Scobie (1986: 402 – 403) observes that:

"Several ancient sources refer to huts erected against or on top of public buildings, or between the columns of porticoes in front of shops. Such structures were likely to be demolished from time to time by city officials. The destitute also found refuge in tombs which also served on occasion as improvised brothels and lavatories. Others slept in spaces under the stairs of insulae (*subscalaria*), in underground cellars (*crypta*), vaults (*fornices*), or in the open air."

However, it is evident from the earlier discussion of the gradations of poverty within Roman society, that other poor people could, and did, afford more permanent accommodation. Not all of those stricken by poverty were homeless, and large numbers seemingly resided in small apartment rooms in high-rise *insulae*. As with so much of the evidence for the everyday lives of the urban poor, information concerning the cost of renting a room or apartment at Rome during the late Republic and early Empire is scarce. The majority of references to house prices concern the large houses of the wealthy or the more expensive ground floor apartments of individual buildings.[70] The only direct reference applicable to this discussion concerns the actions of Julius Caesar in 48 BC (Suet. *Caes.* 38.2; Dio 42.51.1). Returning to Rome triumphant after the Civil Wars, Caesar "remitted all Roman rents up to HS 2,000 a year, all Italian rents to HS 500 a year" (Frier, 1977: 34); a fact that has led to several scholars suggesting that "the humblest tenant had to pay a rent of 2,000 sesterces" (Carcopino, 1964: 56). A glance at the earnings of an unskilled labourer (even one who successfully secured regular employment *and* received free grain) reveals that this amount was beyond the capabilities of the ordinary person. It thus seems unlikely that 2,000 HS truly

represents the lowest level of rent in Rome, especially as Caesar remitted rents *up to* 2,000 HS, thereby implying that accommodation could be secured for less. Frier (1977: 34) proposes that minimum rent was perhaps closer to the figure of 500 HS, although "Tenney Frank suggested HS 360 a year, or about 1 HS a day." Even this latter figure was a significant financial investment for those with an unreliable income. **Table 6** illustrates the effect that rent payments of 1 HS per day (365 HS per annum) could potentially have on the income of a casual labourer experiencing varying levels of employment. It is possible that temporary accommodation could be secured for as little as 1 *as* per night, but as Frier (*ibid.*: 34) points out, "for those who demanded conditions of even minimum decency, the price swiftly rose."

A brief examination of the urban rental system leads to a greater understanding of how the very poor may have dealt with the situation. Frier (1977: 28) explains how "it was legally permissible for the owner of an entire housing unit (or lessee from the owner, acting as an entrepreneur) to rent out portions of that unit to various tenants ... the tenant of the *cenaculum* might have in turn the right to sublease parts of the flat to various subtenants; this practice, which he could use for his profit, was called *cenaculariam exercere*." It is therefore conceivable that poorer tenants shared apartments or rooms, either as a sub-letting tenant or the sub-tenants; a system that would have reduced the rent owed by a single individual or family. It was therefore probably not surprising to find several individuals or families sharing small rooms. According to Frier (*ibid.*: 29), "the rental contracts envisaged in the legal texts concerning *locatio conductio rei* (leasehold) of urban dwellers normally run for a year or multiples of years, and the shortest payment period envisaged is for a full half-year payable *at the conclusion of the period*." As he points out, this shows an immense amount of trust on the part of the landlord. But payment in a single lump sum may have posed problems for those with an unstable source of income. As a result, landlords were probably unwilling to rent property on a long-term lease to poorer members of society, thus further rendering their lifestyle unstable. Short term leases were presumably more common than the literary sources attest,[71] perhaps with payment being made in some cases on a daily basis, such as suggested above. What is more, sharing an apartment or room allowed the poor not only to reduce the amount of rent they owed but also to gain an extra degree of stability. Scobie (1986: 428) writes: "An unskilled worker who paid rent on a daily basis, might not be able to find employment for every day of the year, a circumstance which could cause eviction through default if he rented a room by himself. However, this consequence of temporary unemployment would not be so likely to occur when a room was shared, and a degree of privacy afforded through subdivision by means of wooden partitions." Presumably sub-tenants supported

---

[70] The *aedile* and praetor Caelius reportedly paid 30,000 HS per annum for a ground floor apartment during the mid first century BC (Carcopino, 1964: 37).

[71] As we might expect – such matters were probably irrelevant to the authors and audience of these texts and therefore unworthy of mention.

Consumption rate (modii)	Working days	Annual income (HS)	Annual rent (HS)	Annual grain (HS)			Income after deduction of rent and grain (HS)
				6	7	8	
Minimum (22.5 pa)	306	918	365	135	157.5	180	418 – 373
	272	816	365	135	157.5	180	316 – 271
	215	645	365	135	157.5	180	145 – 100
	206	618	365	135	157.5	180	118 – 73
						Total expenditure: 500 – 545 HS	
Average (30 pa)	306	918	365	180	210	240	373 – 313
	272	816	365	180	210	240	271 – 211
	215	645	365	180	210	240	100 – 40
	206	618	365	180	210	240	73 – 13
						Total expenditure: 545 – 605 HS	
Family (60 pa)	306	918	365	360	420	480	193 – 73
	272	816	365	360	420	480	91 – -29
	215	645	365	360	420	480	-80 – -200
	206	618	365	360	420	480	-107 – -227
						Total expenditure: 725 – 845 HS	

Table 7. The effect of both rent (HS 365 pa) and grain purchases on unstable income during period of Gracchan prices (123 – 58 BC).

Consumption rate	Working days	Annual income (HS)	Annual rent (HS)	Annual grain (HS)	Income after deduction of rent and grain (HS)
Minimum (22.5 modii pa)	306	918	365	35.6	517.4
	272	816	365	35.6	415.4
	215	645	365	35.6	244.4
	206	618	365	35.6	217.4
Average (30 modii pa)	306	918	365	47.5	505.5
	272	816	365	47.5	403.5
	215	645	365	47.5	232.5
	206	618	365	47.5	205.5
Family (60 modii pa)	306	918	365	95	458
	272	816	365	95	356
	215	645	365	95	185
	206	618	365	95	158

Table 8. The effect of both rent (HS 365 pa) and grain purchases on unstable income during the Imperial period.

one another in times of financial crisis.[72] The conditions may have been unhygienic and cramped but sharing at least provided them with a roof over their heads and those living in such conditions may have developed close relationships.

The economic resources of the poor

The data gathered and discussed above concerning financial resources and sources of expenditure can be drawn together into a single table for each period (the Gracchan period when subsidised grain was available and the early Imperial period when prices were fixed. See **Tables 7** and **8**). Although these figures do not take into account other foodstuffs, clothes and fuel it is evident that many members of society dependant on unreliable or temporary employment for a low wage lived their lives balanced precariously on the edge of subsistence. A sudden increase in prices, major disaster or lack of employment was likely to lead to complete destitution. As Garnsey (1998: 239) observes, "employment was crucial. Tacitus says that the flood of AD 69 deprived the common people of food and the jobs with which they might have earned the money to buy it (*Hist.* 73)."

There are many factors that have not been considered here, including higher (or lower) wage rates for different jobs or at different times of the year.[73] The size of the families, which required food, shelter and clothing, has also largely been ignored.[74] Other expenses have also not been considered, including the purchase of household utensils, equipment and furniture, luxuries for special occasions and religious festivals or the repayment of debts. The discussion has also focused predominantly on the male "breadwinner" of a family mainly due to the scarcity of references to female employment and wage rates. But as Garnsey (*ibid.*: 238) points out, other members of society were at more of a disadvantage, including widows who "must have been in a particularly precarious position," being ineligible for state grain and unlikely to find regular employment, if any.

However, despite these problems and the fact that the calculations made above cannot be viewed as totally definitive, this discussion has demonstrated that large numbers of people in the city of Rome lived dangerously close to the boundary between destitution and basic subsistence. Life was inherently unstable and fortunes could rise and fall on a daily basis. There was consequently little room for lavish expenditure or

personal savings that might eventually be spent on burial.

The cost of burial

The figures calculated above highlight the financial constraints imposed by daily survival on the poorer members of Roman society and do not take account of unexpected expenses such as those that arose as the result of a death in the family. The expenses involved in conducting a proper funeral and erecting a commemorative monument are commonly cited to support the suggestion that these members of society were unable to bury or commemorate their dead. But what did these expenses actually entail? A comprehensive study of costs during the Roman period has been conducted by Duncan-Jones (1965 and 1982), during which he examined the range of epigraphically recorded burial costs from Italy and North Africa. Although his investigation largely ignores evidence from Rome itself, it remains a useful insight into the varying amounts spent on tombs and monuments. This data is presented in **Table 9**.

HS	Italy	Africa
500,000 – 100,000	10 (11%)	–
99,000 – 50,000	7 (7.7%)	2 (3.9%)
49,000 – 20,000	13 (14.3%)	5 (9.8%)
19,000 – 10,000	17 (18.7%)	2 (3.9%)
9,000 – 5,000	13 (14.3%)	4 (7.9%)
4,000 and below	31 (34%)	38 (74.5%)
TOTAL:	91 (100%)	51 (100%)

Table 9. Burial costs in Roman Italy and Africa (after Duncan-Jones, 1982: 128)

Within these figures he observed (*ibid.*: 128) a degree of standardisation at both 20,000 HS and 2,000 HS, with 11 and 10 recorded instances respectively. Further support for standardised prices exists in the funerary grants awarded to distinguished citizens of Pompeii which he observes were also 2,000 HS (*ibid.*: 128). However, he points out that "one of the Pompeian magistrates who received the grant was buried in a fortress-like tomb whose cost must have been much more than HS 2,000" (*ibid.*: 129). Using the example of several known military salaries and tombstones stating both the rank of the deceased and the price of the stone, Duncan-Jones proposes that an insight can be gained into the relationship between income and the amounts spent on funeral costs (*ibid.*: 129). He suggests that the greatest outlay involved not less than 1¼ year's pay for a *primipilii* and the lowest, about one-fifth that of a *tribuni militum* and *optio praetorianorum* (*ibid.*: 129). There would therefore seem to be little standardisation in this respect and the amount that was spent

---

[72] Although of course it should not be taken for granted that all neighbours were friendly enough with each other to do this the close living conditions and the unstable lifestyle they led may have created close bonds of dependence.

[73] 3 HS has been used consistently because it is the only attested figure available but should not be viewed as necessarily fixed.

[74] A large family will have placed added pressure on economic resources, at least until any sons became eligible for the dole or old enough to find employment, at which time the fortunes of the family may have improved.

presumably depended upon individual circumstances, and, in the case of military personnel, the length of service.[75]

There are also noticeable differences between the Italian and African samples, with an absence of very expensive monuments (between 500,000 HS and 100,000 HS) in the latter but a higher concentration of "inexpensive" burials (4,000 HS and below). Duncan-Jones (*ibid*.: 128) proposes that these differences "are partly accounted for by social variants." Furthermore, it is to be anticipated that prices were higher in Italy than the provinces, with those in Rome probably being even greater than those of surrounding towns. Certainly there is evidence for particularly expensive burial at Rome: "The cost of burying Vespasian was anticipated as HS 10 million, according to a jocular anecdote in Suetonius. The tomb of Sulpicius Similis at Rome cost HS 400,000. And the burial of Nero, now a fugitive, cost HS 200,000" (*ibid*.: 128). These examples may be rare (and exaggerated) but prices were generally higher in the capital and the evidence from Italy and Africa supplied by Duncan-Jones should therefore be used only as a guideline for discussions of burial and commemoration at Rome.

Other factors must also be taken into account when assessing this data. Firstly, as Duncan-Jones himself remarks (1965: 199), the practice of recording epigraphically the expenses involved in the burial and commemorative process were "always very much a minority practice" and there are strict chronological limits within which it occurred. The largest concentration of recorded costs is found during the first century AD, with the practice "beginning to die out completely in Italy by the beginning of the second century AD" (*ibid*.: 199). Furthermore, it is often unclear whether the sum represents only the monument or whether it includes other related burial expenses. Saller and Shaw (1984: 128, n.21), for example, observe that in one inscription (CIL VIII, 3079) the funeral is mentioned as an additional item of cost, although the price is not given. As Hopkins (1987: 114) has noted, "inscribed tombstones cost money, though not necessarily a lot of money; but in all the ceremonies and expenses surrounding death, inscribed tombstones were only one element in all the costs to be borne by the bereaved." The cost of funerals probably varied considerably and, in addition to the cost of a commemorative monument or tomb, money was required for funerary professionals (possibly 50-60 HS), disposal costs (fuel for cremation, for example), banquets and the purchase of a burial plot. The sums recorded epigraphically therefore probably do not reflect the *entire* cost of the burial process. What is more, there also remains the possibility of number rounding.[76]

Most importantly, when using the costs recorded on gravestones or tombs to reconstruct the expenses involved in the commemorative process, it is essential to consider the context in which they were erected and the motives behind the recording of this information. The practice of recording costs was not extensive, indicating that it was not widely considered to be an essential part of the commemorative process. However, stating the cost of a tomb may have played an additional active role in establishing or displaying the social status and wealth of those responsible for the memorial. Advertising one's economic success by stressing the amount spent on commemoration may have been particularly important amongst freedmen who, as has been demonstrated, often wished to display their success in life on their funerary monuments. Duncan-Jones (1965: 201) notes that higher tomb costs often belong to freedmen and cites the example of L. Numisius L. lib. Agathemerus, "a *sevir Augustalis* of Ostia who described himself as a merchant from Hispania Citerior, [who] spent the large sum of HS 100,000 on his tomb." It was, however, only beneficial to the display and promotion of the status and identity of the deceased and their family if the sum recorded could be considered indicative of success. In the case of Agathemerus, HS 100,000 represents a considerable sum for a former slave and merchant and consequently advertised his success through a display of economic resources. The natural corollary of this is that it is unlikely that the amounts recorded in this context represent an accurate cross-section of the costs of funerary monuments. Although sums as low as 120 HS (in Italy) and 96 HS (in Africa) are recorded, these are very uncommon compared to those in the 10,000 – 49,000 HS bracket. There was nothing to be gained by recording the cost of very cheap memorials. Finally, if a statement of expense can be viewed as a status symbol or indicative of economic success there remains the possibility that some figures may have been exaggerated.

Conclusions

Despite the limitations of the evidence provided by Duncan-Jones, it can be concluded that various amounts were spent on funerary monuments and burial of the dead. It is possible to suggest that whilst 100 HS may have been the lowest amount worth recording, lower prices were probably available. The cost of such activity is, however, likely to have been far greater at Rome than elsewhere in light of the fact that prices were generally higher in the capital (*ibid*.: 251). Saller and Shaw's (1984: 128) broad definition of the lower classes allowed them to assert that "the cost of modest memorials was not so high as to be prohibitive for working Romans ... memorial stones were within the

---

[75] Those who had progressed further in their career presumably had more opportunity to save their salary for such an occasion than newer recruits.
[76] Moreover, although Duncan-Jones provides details of the identification, date, location and reference for examples of stones recording expenses, he discusses no other aspects of the stones. Thus

the statement that the lowest recorded price was 120 hs, found at Cremona (dating to the period after ad 161), is limited by the fact that the dimensions and decoration of the stone remain unclear. Exactly what could be purchased for 120 hs is obscure.

means of modest men," but in light of the economic data above, even a simple funerary monument costing less than 100 HS may have been beyond the reach of poor members of the urban community.

An inability to afford a permanent stone monument need not imply a disinterest or lack of concern for the processes of commemoration and proper burial. This is, however, the prevailing view; a view that has been strengthened and supported by descriptions of mass graves, *puticuli*, on the Esquiline at Rome. But, given the evident concern for commemoration and proper religious burial demonstrated by the activities of all members of the urban community, how do these unusual burial features relate into the disposal practices of the poor? These people evidently had access to very limited economic resources that prohibited them from erecting substantial memorials to the dead, but did these economic restrictions override all of the fears and demands posed by death and force them to dispose of their loved ones in anonymous graves?

CHAPTER FOUR

THE *PUTICULI*

"Outside the towns there are puticuli 'little pits', named from putei 'pits',
because there the people used to be buried ...."

(Varro, *De Lingua Latina*, V.25)

Some form of burial or disposal is eventually necessary for the mortal remains of all members of any society, regardless of the economic resources at their disposal. As we have seen, there were varying degrees of wealth, status and poverty amongst the urban poor of Rome and, although for many the prospect of a funerary monument, even of the simplest type, undoubtedly lay out of reach, disposal of their deceased remains was essential. In order to understand the responses of both the poor themselves and the city authorities to these demands, it is first necessary to examine the scale of mortality at Rome before considering the evidence for these responses in light of the discussion of commemoration and religious burial seen in Chapters 1 and 2. The practical issues surrounding disposal must also be considered.

Mortality at Rome

The population of Rome during the late Republic and early Imperial period has formed the focus of much scholarly discussion, with figures being posited usually between 750,000 and 1,000,000 inhabitants based on examinations of epigraphic data and attempts to repopulate the domestic buildings of the city.[77] These figures remain, however, estimates that are based on rather unreliable and incomplete sources of evidence and there are many variables that must be taken into account when attempting to assess the size of the urban population of Rome at any period. Not only is it difficult to know exactly how many individuals made up each domestic unit but the number of slaves attached to the households of the city is almost impossible to predict. Many members of the community, particularly amongst the lower classes, will have left no trace of their existence. Calculating precise figures is complicated further by the instability of a population that fluctuated in response to the seasons, levels of employment, disease and a variety of external factors, including war and the success or failure of the harvest. Purcell (1994: 649) has also suggested that, "the urban population was probably not a huddle, however huge, of lifelong urbanites, inhabitants of a Rome around which a tight boundary

could be drawn." People would have been drawn to the city at different times of the year for various reasons, including potential employment possibilities and, during great spectacles such as a triumph or spectacular games, the temporary urban population would have swelled dramatically. Conversely, not all of those employed within the city on a daily basis would have lived permanently within its limits.

Bodel (1994 and 2000) favours a slightly conservative approach, suggesting that approximately 750,000 people resided within the city around the time of Augustus. Within this 750,000, he further proposes (1994: 41; 2000: 129) that 1 in 20 (5 per cent) fell into the category of those who "lacked the means to ensure for himself and his dependents even a modest burial;" people who can be equated with the "truly destitute" as identified in Chapter 3. Bodel admits that the figure of 5 per cent is "pure guesswork" but is certainly unlikely to overestimate the situation (1994: 41). Since no definitive figures on the matter are forthcoming from either ancient sources or modern studies of the subject, the numbers suggested by Bodel represent plausible estimates. It is in the context of these estimates that he suggests "if we further postulate an annual mortality rate comparable to that of other preindustrial European urban populations of roughly 40 per thousand ... we must figure that some 30,000 residents died in the city each year, or (on average) more than eighty a day" (2000: 128 – 129). If 5 per cent of this population were "truly destitute", it can be proposed that approximately 1,500 of these deaths were those of individuals without the means to afford proper burial and commemoration; a figure that aligns with parallels from early-modern and modern cities (*ibid*.: 129 – 130). In reality, however, the figure was probably much higher since the "truly destitute" will have been far more susceptible to outbreaks of disease, malnutrition and violent death. It is also important to note that a large proportion of infants aged 0–1 years (30 percent of total mortality) and young children aged 1–5 years (15 percent of total mortality) would also be included within this figure (A. Chamberlain, *pers. comm.*).

These estimates reflect urban mortality under what might be termed 'normal' circumstances, but during the regular epidemics that ravaged the urban population they would

---

[77] See for example Oates, 1934; Hermansen, 1978; Brunt, 1987*a*; Lo Cascio, 1994; Storey, 1997.

have risen considerably.[78] As Morley (2005) points out, the Roman capital was particularly vulnerable to such events given high levels of immigration and poor urban living conditions which provided "a hospitable environment for the reproduction of parasitic micro-organisms." The most comprehensive surviving record of major epidemics that afflicted Rome during the Republic is provided by Livy who often acknowledged the occurrence of plague in the city and elsewhere. According to Duncan-Jones (1996: 111) these references "occur in Livy's earlier narrative roughly once every eight years (a mean of 8.25 between 490 and 292 BC). In Livy's later narrative, presumably because it is much fuller, mentions are twice as frequent (a mean of once every 4.8 years between 212 and 165 BC)." Severe epidemics were evidently a familiar occurrence at Rome, to the extent that "all surviving adults and most adolescents would typically have experienced serious epidemic at least once, and the old several times" (ibid.: 109). Livy (41.21.5 – 8) provides an account of a plague at Rome in 174 BC, which vividly illustrates the affect that pestilence might have on the community:

> "The slaves especially died, and along all the roads there were piles of their unburied bodies. Libitina did not suffice even for the funerals of free men. The corpses untouched by dogs and vultures, were consumed by decay; it was generally observed that neither in this nor in the previous year, in spite of the great mortality of cattle and men, was a vulture seen anywhere …"

Some ancient texts claim to report the number of deaths that occurred during specific epidemics, although the accuracy of this information must be questioned. The claim that almost 10,000 people died every day over a period of several weeks during AD 77 (Chron. 2096I, p.188 Helm, cited in Bodel, 2000: 129) is doubtful, not least because it would have quickly decimated the population; but Cassius Dio's claim (72.14.3–4) that the plague of AD 189 was "the worst he ever knew" and sometimes killed 2,000 people per day is perhaps more plausible (Duncan-Jones, 1996: 115). Regardless of their accuracy, these figures demonstrate vividly that disease regularly claimed large numbers of lives and it is possible to surmise that the majority of deaths, although certainly not all, were those of the lower classes. Not only could the wealthy flee the city for their comparatively healthy country estates during times of pestilence – a luxury denied those whose daily survival was itself precarious – but they also had access to superior nutrition and, to a limited extent, hygiene.

Purcell (1987: 32 – 33) has shown how a population of approximately 750,000 – 1,000,000, within Rome and its surrounding area, put considerable pressure on space for burial, even under 'normal' circumstances. He estimates, on the basis of the higher figure, an annual "average burial-space demand" of almost 8 tombs in every square kilometre of the suburb (ibid.: 32 – 33) and, as the description provided by Livy shows, this pressure rose dramatically during times of disease.[79]

Not every member of the population could afford to be buried in their own individual tomb. In addition to the approximately 1,500 destitute individuals who died in the city every year (150,000 each century) there were thousands of "ordinary poor" who also required burial but did not have the economic stability to allow them to invest in a family mausoleum or even an individual burial plot. If their remains did not end up in one of the 8 tombs per square mile posited by Purcell where were they laid to rest?

The *puticuli*: the evidence and their traditional interpretation

Modern scholars have suggested that communal graves were the primary response to the disposal problems posed by the large numbers of "unclaimed" corpses and those of individuals unable to afford proper burial created by the immense population of Rome and its related high levels of mortality. The evidence on which this proposal is based was provided by excavations at Rome conducted by Rodolfo Lanciani during the late nineteenth century, during which he uncovered "many hundred" large pits which were subsequently identified as *puticuli*: ancient mass graves.[80]

The *puticuli* were discovered during the construction of the Via Napoleone III between the churches of St. Antonio and St. Eusebio on the Esquiline in the 1870s (Lanciani, 1874: 48; 1875: 43; no. 1, **Fig. 16**). In his initial report on these discoveries, published in the *Bullettino della Commissione Archeologica Comunale de Roma* in 1874, Lanciani was reticent to reveal too much information, stating that it was unnecessary to make public the section drawings and photographs of his finds because excavations continued to bring new discoveries, and he promised to publish the full details at a later date. Unfortunately, apart from his popular (and frequently reprinted) 1888 publication, *Ancient Rome in the Light of Recent Discoveries*,[81] this more detailed publication never appeared. Writing again in the *Bullettino* in 1875, Lanciani focused largely on the pottery finds of the area in order to present a guide to the Esquiline material that was on display in the newly created "Sala di Terracotta"

---

[78] See Littman and Littman (1973), Jackson (1988) and Scheidel (2003) for specific discussion of the diseases in question.

[79] It must be stressed that all of the figures cited here correspond to estimates and cannot be viewed as exact. However, they represent the most plausible "guesses" that modern scholarship has been able to produce on the basis of the available evidence. Although they are treated in this discussion as definitive, it is important to remember that there are many problems with calculations of both ancient population size and levels of mortality. See, for example, Hopkins (1987) on calculating patterns of mortality from funerary epigraphy.

[80] Although it will be suggested here that the pits uncovered by Lanciani are not *puticuli* in the truest sense of the word, the term will continue to be used in this discussion to refer to these discoveries since it is that by which they are most commonly known.

[81] The 1891 edition is used here.

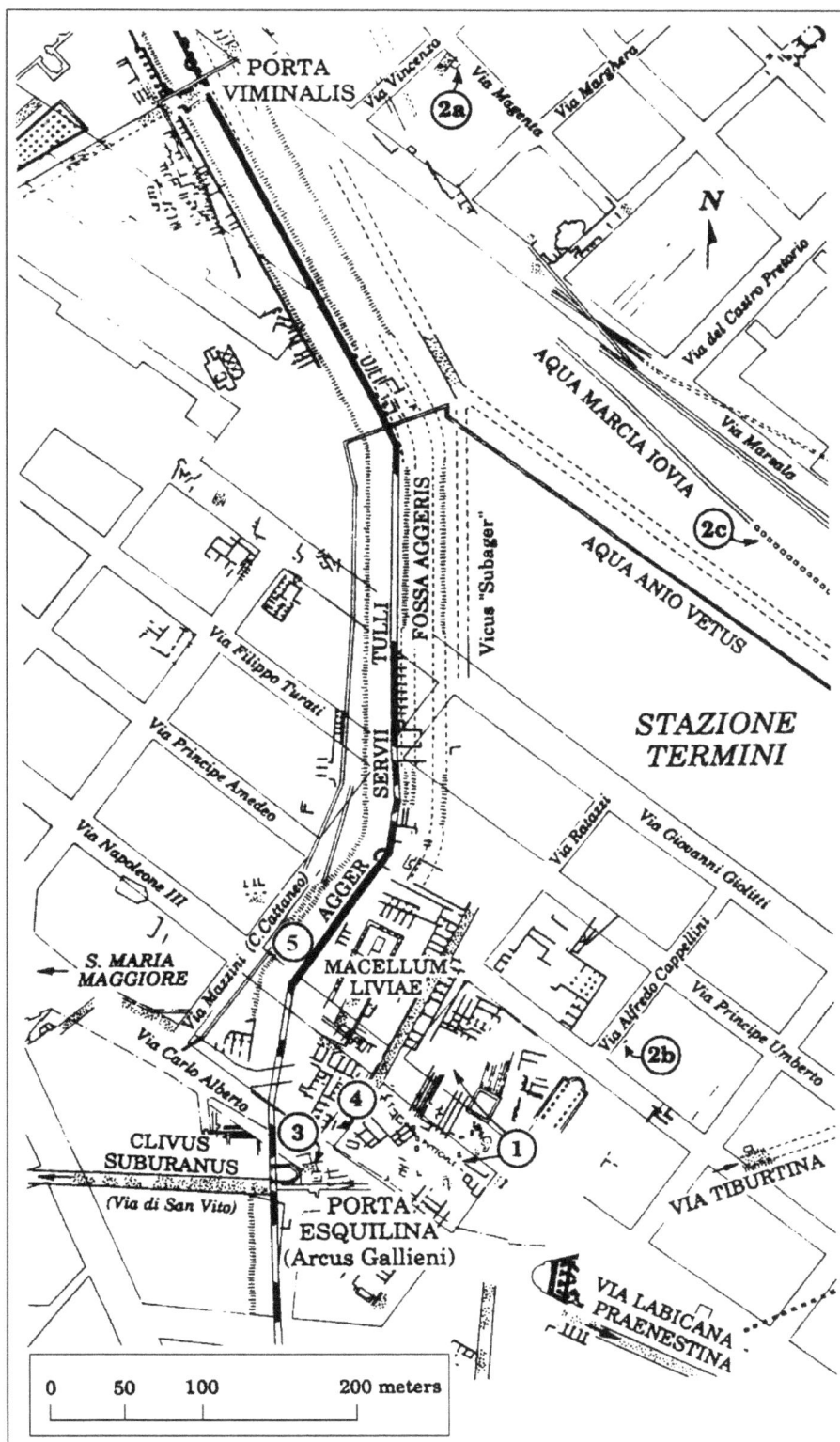

Figure 16. The *Campus Esquilinus* between the Viminal and Esquiline gates (after Bodel, 1994 fig. 1).

1. Lanciani's *puticuli*
2. The edict of L. Sentius
   2a = *CIL* I² 838
   2b = *CIL* I² 839
   2c = *CIL* I² 2981
3. The *sc de pago Montano* (*CIL* I² 591)
4. The inscription of the *collegium tibicinum* (*CIL* I² 989)
5. Section of *agger* filled with corpses

in the Palazzo dei Conservatori.[82] He provides a few more details about the structure of the *puticuli* and their orientation (more or less exactly aligned with the meridian line (Lanciani, 1875: 43)) and expresses a wish to provide an accompanying "topographical plate to demonstrate the limits and the arrangement of these mortuary pits, their structure and relationship with the new roads, but since the excavations of that ground have still not reached an end, we judge it superfluous to present a plate still full of gaps" (*ibid.*: 43).[83] Unfortunately, this plate was never produced, even once the excavations were complete, and the modern scholar is thus forced to rely on two sketchy preliminary reports and a few passages in a popular volume in order to recreate the circumstances surrounding the discovery of these mass graves.

Lanciani (1874: 48) describes the *puticuli* as a series of rectangular cells of various sizes forming an angle of approximately 52° with the axis of the Via Napoleone III, their walls lined with an irregular mass of *cappellaccio* stone. He notes that the area was surrounded by a "channel of travertine of which we have found one well preserved part that does not seem to be the remains of a wall" (*ibid.*: 51).[84] Further details concerning the dimensions of the pits and their contents can be found in one of his later publications, where he states that the vaults were "twelve feet square, thirty deep" and that he had "brought to light and examined about seventy-five" (1891: 64). There then follows his infamous, and much quoted, description of the fill of the pits:

"In many cases the contents of each vault were reduced to a uniform mass of black, viscid, pestilent, unctuous matter; in a few cases the bones could in a measure be singled out and identified. The reader will hardly believe me when I say that men, beasts, bodies and carcasses, and any kind of unmentionable refuse of the town were heaped up in those dens. Fancy what must have been the condition of this hellish district in times of pestilence, when the mouths of the crypts must have been kept wide open the whole day!"

(*ibid.*: 64 – 65)

In a letter to *The Athenaeum* (November 27th, 1880) Lanciani describes the discovery, also on the Esquiline, of a *cappellaccio* quarry near the church of St. Bibiana in which had been cut several galleries (Lanciani, 1988: 87).

Some square blocks had been cut and were awaiting transportation, others had either been cut on two or three sides or their dimensions marked out (*ibid.*: 87). Lanciani identified this as "the archaic stone quarry from which the materials for the *Puticuli* of Horatian fame, have been taken," and which was seemingly abandoned "in the first or second century of the Republican era" (*ibid.*: 87).

The use of the term *puticuli* by Lanciani to describe the Esquiline pits is based largely on a passage from Varro's *De Lingua Latina* (V.25), composed between 47 and 45 BC, in which he writes:

"From *putei* 'wells' comes the town-name, such as Puteoli, because around this place there are many hot and cold spring-waters; unless rather from *putor* 'stench', because the place is often *putidus* 'stinking' with smells of sulphur and alum. Outside the towns there are *puticuli* 'little pits', named from *putei* 'pits', because there the people used to be buried in *putei* 'pits'; unless rather, as Aelius writes, the *puticuli* are so called because the corpses which had been thrown out *putescebant* 'used to rot' there, in the public burial-place which is beyond the Esquiline. This place Afranius in a comedy of Roman life calls the *Putiluci* 'pit lights', for the reason that from it they look up through *putei* 'pits' to the *lumen* 'light'."

The designation of an area outside the Esquiline Gate as a public burial ground in which the corpses of lowly members of the community were left to rot is further supported by the words of Horace (*Sat.* 1.8.8 – 16), who describes the area around the Servian *agger* before its reclamation in the late first century BC:

"Hither in other days a slave would pay to have carried on a cheap bier the carcasses of his fellows, cast out from their narrow cells. Here was the common burial-place fixed for pauper folk, for Pantolabus the parasite, and spendthrift Nomentanus. Here a pillar assigned a thousand feet frontage and three hundred of depth, and provided that the graveyard should pass to no heirs. Today one may live on a wholesome Esquiline, and stroll on the sunny Rampart, where of late one sadly looked out on ground ghastly with bleaching bones."

It was on the basis of these two passages, which seem to indicate that the Esquiline was a place in which unclaimed corpses and the bodies of the humble members of society were dumped without ceremony into *putei* 'pits', that Lanciani interpreted his discoveries.

Lanciani makes little real attempt to establish a precise date for the pits, assigning them only to the late Republic. He does, however, refer to the closure of the area to further burial activity during the late first century BC, at which time (possibly around 35 BC) Maecenas was invited by Augustus to redevelop the space beyond the Esquiline Gate and transformed the burial ground

[82] These are not, it would appear, exclusively from the pits. Indeed, he speaks only of finds that appear to be contemporary with them, or from the same stratum, rather than the fill of the *puticuli* themselves.
[83] "Avremmo voluto corredare il nostro racconto con una tavola topografica dimostrante I confine e la disposizione dei pozzi mortuarii, la loro struttura e relazione con le nuove strade; ma poichè l'escavazione di quell suolo non è ancor giunta a termine, giudicammo superfluo di presentare una tavola ancor di lacune." All translations, unless stated otherwise, are my own.
[84] "... era circoscritta tutt'attorno da un canale di travertine, di cui abbiamo rinvenuto una parte ben conservata, ed al di là del quale non appaion vestigial dei muri."

66

into the famous *Horti Maecenati*. Lanciani recovered evidence for this redevelopment which appeared to suggest that the entire area was buried in order for the gardens to be constructed. He describes a deep layer of limestone blocks and bricks with carbon and pottery fragments which was overlying the *puticuli*; perhaps materials transported to the site from structures that had been destroyed by fire (Lanciani, 1874: 52) (**Fig. 17**). Virgin soil was deposited above the layer of demolition rubble, again presumably transported from elsewhere, within which he was unable to identify any organic remains or industrial products (*ibid.*: 52). He later described this embankment as "twenty-five feet high and a third of a square mile in area" (Lanciani, 1891: 67). Lanciani also records the recovery of three square travertine *cippi* each inscribed with the text of the Edict of Sentius (see Chapter 2) stating that the dumping or burning of corpses, carcasses and other rubbish was strictly forbidden in the region (*ibid.*: 66) (no.2 **Fig. 16**). He (*ibid.*: 67) describes the discovery of one *cippus* in characteristic style:

> "On the day of the discovery of the above-mentioned stone, June 25th, 1884, I was obliged to relieve my gang of workmen from time to time, because the smell from that polluted ground (turned up after a putrefaction of twenty centuries) was absolutely unbearable even for men so hardened to every kind of hardship as my excavators."

The discovery of mass burial on the Esquiline did not, however, cease with the *puticuli*. The Servian *agger*, a defensive embankment comprising an external ditch (100 feet wide, 30 feet deep) and a huge bank supported by a wall of large stone blocks with a smaller wall along its interior slope (Lanciani, 1988: 30 – 31), passes through the area of the Esquiline in which Lanciani uncovered the *puticuli*. During extensive development of the region in the years following his initial discoveries, workmen stumbled across another site of mass burial that was directly associated with this feature (no. 5, **Fig. 16**). Lanciani (1891: 65) describes the events of that day in 1876:

> "In building the foundations of a house at the corner of Via Carlo-Alberto and Via Mazzini, the architect, deceived by the presence of a solid bed of tufa on the northern half of the building-ground, began to lay his masonry and fill up the trenches to the uniform depth of twelve feet below the level of the street. All of a sudden the southern portion of the ground gave way, and one half of the area fell through into a chasm thirty feet deep."

Reporting this in a letter to *The Athenaeum* (November 10th, 1877) he identifies the chasm as part of the ditch (*fossa*) of the Servian *agger* which was "used in process of time as a burial-ground for slaves and domestic animals – a supposition confirmed by the discovery of a stratum of fossil bones nineteen feet six inches thick"

(Lanciani, 1988: 44). These remains reportedly crumbled when brought into contact with the air but he was able to calculate that there were "thousands upon thousands of corpses" deposited within an area measuring 160 feet in length, 100 feet wide and 30 feet deep (Lanciani, 1891: 65 – 66). Allowing, a more than adequate, average space of twenty cubic feet per corpse he postulated that, "there were not less than twenty-four thousand bodies in a comparatively small space" (*ibid.*: 66). Beyond the proposal that these depositions took place "on the occasion of a stupendous mortality," (*ibid.*: 65) Lanciani advances no specific theory to explain the presence of such a large quantity of corpses (and rubbish) in this area of the ditch, simply linking them to the wider use of the Esquiline for dumping of corpses and general refuse.

A critical examination of the *puticuli*

Since the publication of these discoveries, at the end of the nineteenth century, few scholars have seriously questioned the validity of Lanciani's conclusions. The vaults continue to be seen as the pits into which "paupers and abandoned slaves – in short, all those who had failed to provide a last resting-place for themselves, or who had no relations, friends, or burial clubs to secure them proper interment, were thrown by thousands and by tens of thousands, to rot in the company of dogs and cattle" (Thomas, 1899: 165). Attempts have been made to examine the use of the *puticuli*[85] but there persists an unquestioning perpetuation of Lanciani's statement that the pits are the *puticuli* described by Varro, and the place in which the corpses of all the poor and enslaved members of the urban community were left to rot amongst animal carcasses and rubbish. For example, despite suggesting that "Rodolfo Lanciani's gothic and repulsive account of what he took to be the communal *puticuli* of the Republican cemetery has perhaps led to misrepresentation of the cemetery," Purcell (1987: 34, n. 40) proposes that the area did indeed represent the primary response to the demands of mass mortality (*ibid.*: 37). Equally, despite a comprehensive examination of the mechanisms in place for the disposal of unclaimed corpses in Roman cities, Bodel continues to perpetuate the conclusions of Lanciani, stating that "it is in any case clear that, except in times of plague, when extraordinary and frequently inadequate measures were taken to dispose of diseased corpses in the Tiber and the public sewers (Dion. Hal. *Ant. Rom.* 10.53.2 – 3; 9.67.2 ...), the bodies of Rome's indigent, wherever found, wound up in the same place" (Bodel, 2000: 131).[86] However, in order to understand the ways in which the various poverty-stricken groups that were described in Chapter 3, disposed of their dead and responded to the need for

---

[85] See, for example, Bodel (1994 and 2000) who, despite an excellent in-depth examination of the *puticuli*, is primarily concerned with the mechanisms of disposal rather than the legitimacy of Lanciani's claims; and Kyle (1998) who examined the possibility of a link between the pits and arena spectacles.
[86] See also Le Gall (1980-81); Sartorio (1983); Pellegrino (1999: 11); Schoen (2000: 285); Heinzelmann (2001: 180 – 181) and Jongman (2003: 107) for other recent examples.

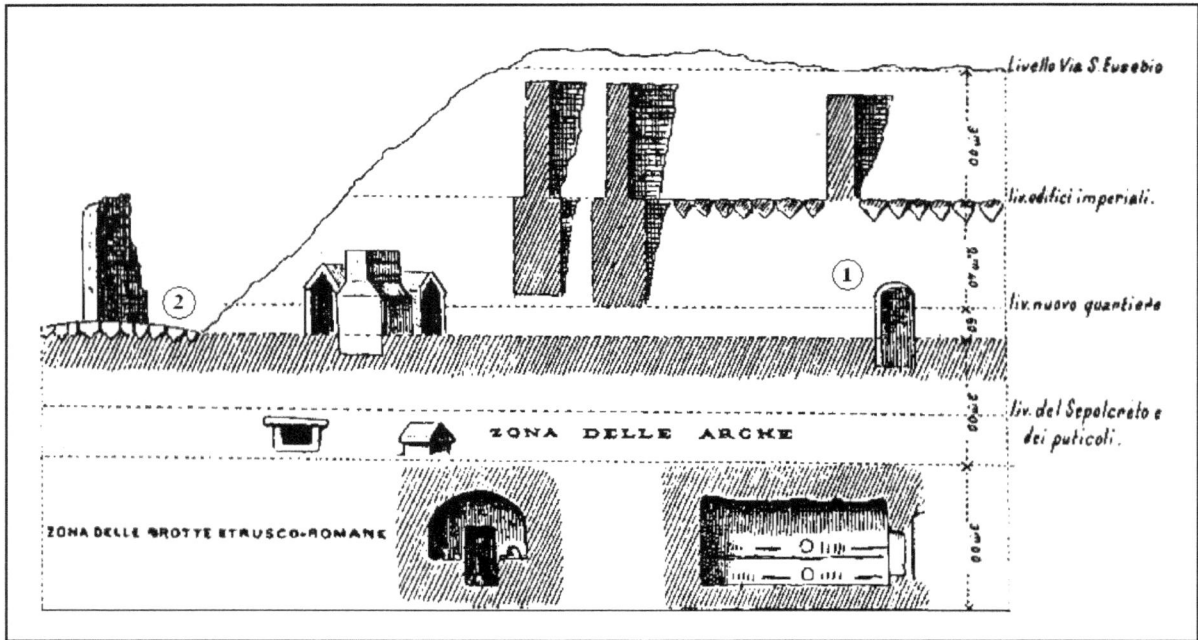

Figure 17. Schematic section drawn by Lanciani showing the archaeological strata of the Esquiline burial ground.

1. the *senatus consultum de pago Montano* (CIL I² 591).
2. the Republican "via consolare" leading from the Esquiline Gate. The level of the *puticuli* is also indicated (after Bodel, 1994, fig. 2).

commemoration and proper burial, it is essential to critically examine the archaeological and textual evidence for the *puticuli* as described by both Lanciani and Varro.

Chronology

Regular dumping of household waste on the Esquiline is attested by the epigraphically recorded efforts of the state to bring about the cessation of such activities. The Edict of Sentius and the *senatus consultum de pago Montano*, both prohibiting the abandoning and burning of refuse and corpses on the Esquiline, have been discussed in their legal context (Chapter 2) but these regulations are also useful for elucidating the chronological aspects of the use of the region for burial and/or dumping.

Two travertine *cippi* bearing the edict issued by the praetor L. Sentius during the early first century BC were discovered *in situ* and delineate an area, approximately 200 metres from the *agger*, in which the dumping of corpses and refuse was forbidden (Wiseman, 1998: 15). These can be linked with another stone discovered during construction of the Stazione Termini in 1942.[87] Although this last *cippus* was no longer *in situ*, Bodel (1994: 42) points out that its estimated weight of almost a ton makes it unlikely that it had been moved far. He interprets these boundary stones in the context of a more extensive attempt to regulate dumping activities within a much

wider region than the 60m² occupied by the *puticuli* (*ibid.*: 42).

This information facilitates the establishment of a chronology for the exploitation of the region for disposal purposes during the later Republic. Examining Lanciani's limited stratigraphic records, Bodel (*ibid.*: 45 – 47) concludes that the *puticuli* were sealed by the charred debris and rubble during the pre-Augustan period *before* reclamation of the region by Maecenas.[88] He suggests that the *cippi* bearing the Edict of Sentius (including one recovered only 120 metres from the *puticuli*) were contemporary with this levelling and reflect an earlier attempt to control the use of the area (*ibid.*: 45 – 47). He proposes that this pre-Augustan levelling and regulation was directly associated with the construction of a new "via consolare" which emerged from the Esquiline Gate and can be seen in the section drawn by Lanciani (*ibid.*: 45 – 47) (**Fig. 17**). It would appear, therefore, that the disposal ground of the Esquiline was closed *before* Maecenas took action to transform the area. This is supported further by the fact that the large travertine block, inscribed on both sides with the text of the *senatus consultum de pago Montano* forbidding the dumping of refuse but, significantly, not corpses, was embedded *in situ* in the pre-Augustan layer (see **Fig. 17**).[89] Bodel

---

[87] Edict of Sentius: CIL I² 838, 839, 2981.

[88] For useful discussions of the stratigraphy of the Esquiline necropolis see Ryberg (1940) and, especially, Taloni (1973).
[89] *Senatus consultum de pago Montano*: CIL I² 591.

(*ibid.*: 47 – 49) interprets this as evidence for successful regulation of burial but continued widespread use of the area for dumping and burning refuse. He connects the *senatus consultum* with the *libitinarii*, at whose headquarters he postulates the *cippus* may have been posted (*ibid.*: 49). However, the *senatus consultum* makes no reference to burial or corpses, which would be expected if it was directly linked with the activities of the *libitinarii* whose primary function was to dispose of the dead. Is it possible, therefore, that the activities of the *libitinarii* also extended to the disposal of rubbish?

Bodel's argument for the chronology of the Esquiline is generally convincing. Although the *puticuli* were probably closed prior to when Maecenas assumed control of the area, the region probably continued to be used for the disposal of refuse and thus required further regulation. The large dimensions of the area employed in this capacity are indicated by the fact that the measures taken to prevent dumping encompassed an area much wider than that containing the *puticuli*, which comprised only a small section of it. Perhaps the area is thus better interpreted as one in which a variety of dumping activities took place in different zones. Perhaps one or more areas were reserved for burial, others for rubbish. The *Horti Maecenati*, that famously turned an area of pestilence into one of beauty, have been definitively located to the south of the Esquiline Gate, between the *Via Labicana-Praenestina* and the eastern slope of the *Mons Oppius* (Wiseman, 1998: 13, citing Häuber), and not in the immediate vicinity of the *puticuli* uncovered by Lanciani (**Fig. 18**). This area was perhaps one in which general disposal had continued despite attempts to prevent it, and consequently required further regulation by Maecenas. Horace, after all, does not specifically mention burial pits and the *Horti Maecenati* do not necessarily have to have replaced the *puticuli*, just an area of burial that was considered particularly offensive.

Topography

The text of Horace's *Satire* 1.8 points strongly towards the existence of a cemetery that was recognised both in legal and religious terms, in the vicinity of the Esquiline Gate and the Servian *agger*. The first half of the *Satire* is concerned with the area around the *agger*, both before and after its transformation by Maecenas. Allowance must of course be made for extensive poetic license, it was, after all, Horace's intention to glorify the achievements of his friend, but this passage allows several observations to be made about the region. Firstly, Horace describes the area as "the common *burial-place* fixed for pauper folk" (my italics) and puts into verse of the epigraphic formula *Hoc monumentum heredes non sequetur*, found commonly on tomb inscriptions of the period, to state that the "monument" (in this case the entire cemetery) should pass to no heirs. This is a clear reference to the presence of tombs in the area that probably bore this very formula. The irony of Horace's statement is that the closure of the area by Maecenas ensured, once and for all, that the tombs would definitely not pass to any heirs. His use of the past tense suggests

that burial no longer occurred there, and importantly he does not refer to the area as a rubbish dump, but uses terminology and formulae derived directly from a funerary context. In addition to that already noted, he includes a reference to a pillar which "assigned a thousand feet frontage and three hundred of depth" – an unequivocal reference to the way in which the dimensions of burial plots were recorded epigraphically. The image he conjures of slaves carrying their fellows to the site for burial also points towards the existence of a recognised site of burial; something which is supported further by the statement that "a slave would *pay* to have carried on a cheap bier the carcasses of his dead fellows" (my italics). If the slaves concerned intended to unceremoniously dump the corpse in a pit, incurring the expense, however small, of *paying* for a bier is difficult to understand. His description of "ground ghastly with bleaching bones" also does not seem to align with Lanciani's description of large pits and more strongly implies that bones were strewn over a wide area, perhaps the result of disturbed shallow graves.[90] These features are easily understood in the context of a graveyard that was probably used predominantly by the poor who dug graves personally, rather than incur the expense of hiring a professional *fossor*. This is strengthened by the second half of the *Satire* in which the poet describes witches digging easily into the earth and disturbing the souls buried within it.

The absence of any direct (or even indirect) reference by Horace to *puticuli* or mass graves in the area during the years prior to Maecenas's transformation is also particularly striking given that he intended to praise the actions of his friend in turning a pestilential region into a wholesome park. That he should ignore evidence which could further promote dramatically the achievements of Maecenas is curious. Finally, Horace states that, "You might see serpents and hell-hounds roaming about, and the blushing Moon, that she might not witness such deeds, hiding behind the tall tombs" (*Sat.* 1.8.34 – 36). A remark that again points strongly towards the presence of an official cemetery in the vicinity; the "tall tombs" indicating that it was of significant size and that people of note (or at least wealth) had built substantial structures within it. Archaeological evidence reinforces these observations. The Esquiline was used for burial for much of its history, beginning with the simple trench or *fossa* graves of the very early Republic (Davies, 1977: 16). Chamber tombs dating to the fourth century BC have also been located in the region, in addition to a "transitional type of tomb" taking the form of an open vault constructed with blocks of tufa laid in courses (*ibid.*: 16). Furthermore, Cicero informs us that, like the *Campus Martius*, the *Campus Esquilinus* was a favoured location for the burial of notable members of the community who had been awarded an honorary monument or place of burial (Cicero, *Philippics* 9.17). Use of the Esquiline as a

---

[90] Of all the scholars to examine the Esquiline cemetery, the only one who appears to have interpreted this description of the cemetery in this way is Middleton (1892: 267).

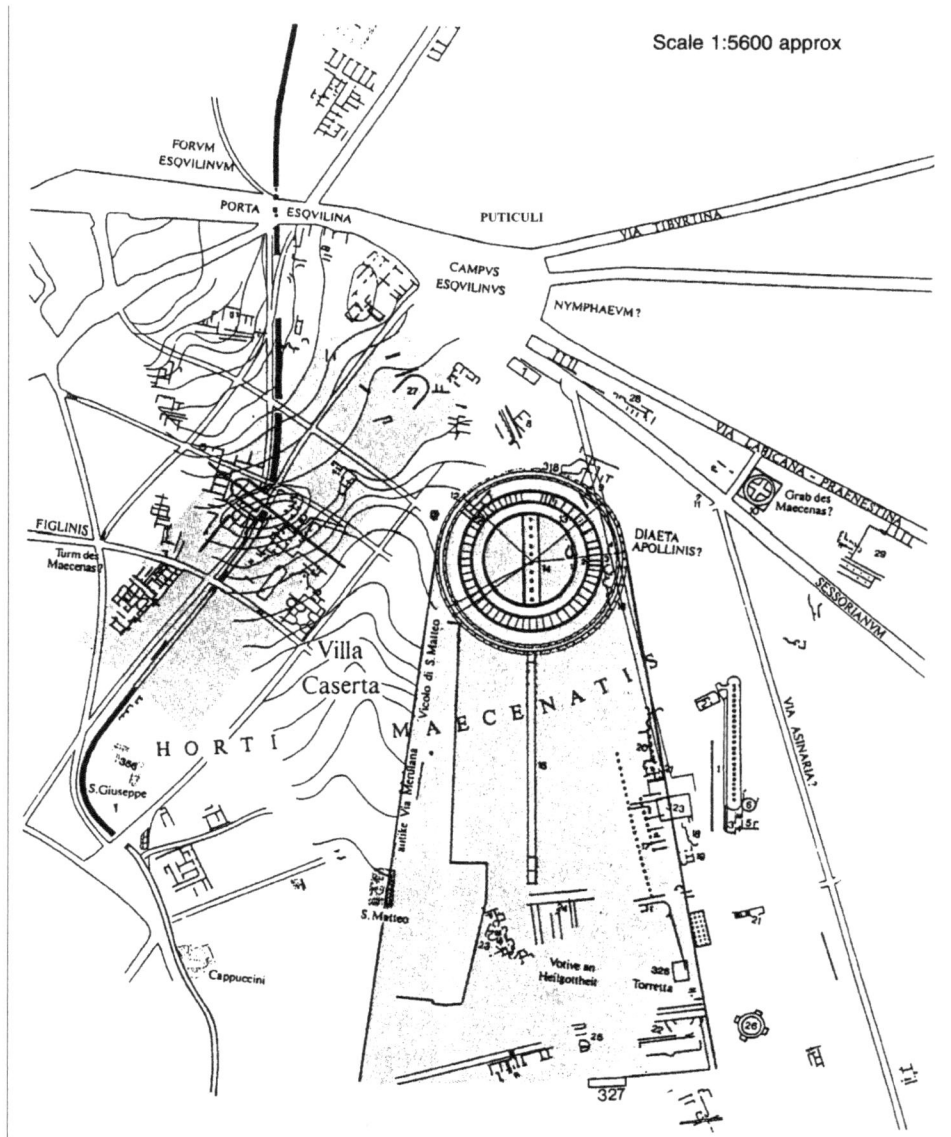

Figure 18. Map of the Esquiline showing the area believed to contain the Gardens of Maecenas and the *puticuli* (after Purcell, 1996 fig. 46).

cemetery also continued subsequent to the reclamation of a section of it by Maecenas despite Bodel's proposal (1994: 47 – 49) that such activities had ceased by this time. Lanciani (1891: 102 – 103) reports the discovery of several *columbaria* which were not buried until "the second century of the Christian era," as well as some humble cappuccina graves made of tiles. The archaeological evidence for tombs of both a substantial and more modest nature in the vicinity of the Esquiline Gate, in conjunction with Horace's description of "tall tombs" and the pauper's burial ground, strongly indicates that this region comprised a vast necropolis. Lanciani (1874: 46 and 1891: 64) suggests that the cemetery was divided into two separate areas, accommodating graves of differing status in each, although there is no secure evidence for this and the absence of well-documented stratigraphy and the vague nature of his reports makes it

very difficult to identify the presence of zones within the area that might signal different types of burial or status distinctions. Moreover, evidence from the later necropolis of Isola Sacra near Portus suggests that humble and monumental burials often took place in close proximity to one another, with no evidence of zoning (see Chapter 5). It is very significant that this evidence points towards the location of the *puticuli* within a *graveyard* rather than comprising part of a rubbish dump. It means that the poor who were using the cemetery for burial were not disposing of corpses in a radically different way to the rest of society. They were not abandoning them like rubbish, as descriptions of the area as a refuse dump have insinuated, but by burying them within a cemetery alongside other, wealthier and more prominent members of the community. It is, of course, possible that sectors of the cemetery were later converted into rubbish dumps, perhaps as they fell out of use, but originally the *puticuli* existed as a cemetery feature.

These observations are particularly significant for understanding the context of the *puticuli*. Legally the pits should have been designated a *locus religiosus* if they were located in a graveyard. However, as noted in Chapter 2, Varro (*LL*. V.25) refers to them as a "*locus publicus*", implying that deposition within the pits did *not* satisfy religious burial requirements. The possibility that this was ignored by the local community, who perhaps treated the burial site as if it were a *locus religiosus* regardless of its official status, has been discussed above. That Lanciani's *puticuli* may have represented a specific *locus publicus* situated *within* the *locus religiosus* of a wider cemetery also has significant implications for their interpretation. If this was the case, and the mass graves were not legally or religiously recognised burial sites, it lends considerable support to the theory (discussed further below) that they were constructed originally for a different function before being appropriated for disposal purposes once they had gone out of use or when demand for burial space rose dramatically. Furthermore, it must be asked whether the act of disposal in a pit constituted proper religious burial? Discarding a body, even into a pit, did not fulfil the requirements of religious burial, as outlined above, and the possibility that the *puticuli* remained open for a considerable length of time also suggests that the corpses were denied proper burial. It is possible that each corpse was sprinkled with earth when it was deposited in order to guarantee that the shade would not become troublesome, and the pits may have been covered with soil at regular intervals.[91] That this would have constituted only a symbolic covering is suggested by the fact that Lanciani did not observe layers of bodies separated by substantial deposits of soil. If these existed they are unlikely to have been disturbed (especially at depth) and we would therefore expect them be archaeologically visible.[92]

Lanciani's evidence

When Lanciani's account is examined from a critical perspective, it soon becomes apparent that his conclusions are based on relatively limited and uncertain evidence. When the accuracy and validity of this evidence is assessed, it becomes clear that Lanciani's conclusions are rather tenuous. There are not only

problems with his interpretation of the archaeological material but also with this material itself. Lanciani's published reports of the Esquiline excavations include only a brief description of the form of the pits, their structure and location, before providing some basic details concerning their deposits. This makes it very difficult to assess the validity of his claims. In addition, although he states that there were "many hundred *puticuli*" he also says that he only "brought to light and examined about seventy-five" (Lanciani, 1891: 64). It would therefore appear that he was merely speculating that there existed "many hundred"; he did not actually uncover them but simply assumed, probably on the basis of the size of the zone yet to be excavated, that many more existed in the surrounding area. No others appear to have been found subsequently in the region. There may indeed have been more than the 75 pits that Lanciani excavated, especially as he identified the travertine channel that surrounded the *puticuli* on one side only, although there is no positive archaeological evidence for these. The presence of several hundred, however, continues to be perpetuated in modern discussions.

Lanciani probably did not excavate all 75 pits that he reportedly saw. The logistical demands of removing around 250–500 tons of fill from each vault would have been immense. What is more, the Esquiline excavations were conducted during a time of considerable urban redevelopment that put great pressure on the members of the *Commissione Archeologica*, which was responsible for overseeing the removal and conservation of the archaeological remains, to carry out their duties quickly. The haste with which the excavations had to be conducted transformed them into emergency rescue operations and, consequently, the records of the excavations are often vague and confused.[93] It is probable, given these time constraints, that one, or possibly a handful, of the pits was emptied entirely by Lanciani's workmen. The upper levels of some of the others may have been briefly examined in order to confirm that they were essentially similar. The unexcavated pits (i.e. the majority) were possibly not filled in exactly the same way as those that Lanciani investigated in more detail, perhaps only a few held human remains. His conclusions are therefore most likely to be extrapolated from evidence derived from only a handful of the pits and consequently can not be considered as necessarily representative of the pits as a whole.

It is also worth noting here that some secondary descriptions of the *puticuli* by twentieth century scholars appear to include information not provided by Lanciani's original reports. For example, Davies (1977: 17) states that the pits contained "the remains of burned and unburned bodies together with numerous ordinary vases and lamps." Lanciani records and discusses pottery finds from the surrounding region (Lanciani 1875) but not

---

[91] This appears to have occurred in medieval Paris where mass graves had "a few handfuls of dirt thrown on top" (Ariès (1981[1977]: 56).

[92] It is also significant that the *puticuli* appear to have offered no obvious opportunity for permanent commemoration – it was impossible to mark the location of an individual burial within a mass grave and there is no evidence for the presence of a communal monument either for each individual pit or the area as a whole. This does not align with the great importance that memory preservation and commemoration held in the minds of all members of society (described in Chapter 1). It perhaps indicates that the *puticuli* were used predominantly for the burial of the truly destitute by city authorities, who were more concerned with efficient disposal than commemoration. It is also possible that the memory of these individuals was perpetuated by their family and friends in other ways (see Chapters 5 and 6 for a discussion of alternative commemorative acts amongst the lower classes).

[93] See Albertoni (1983) and Lorenzini (2004) for descriptions of the climate of urban regeneration in which the Esquiline excavations were carried out and the problems that this caused for both the recording of structures and finds, and their subsequent interpretation.

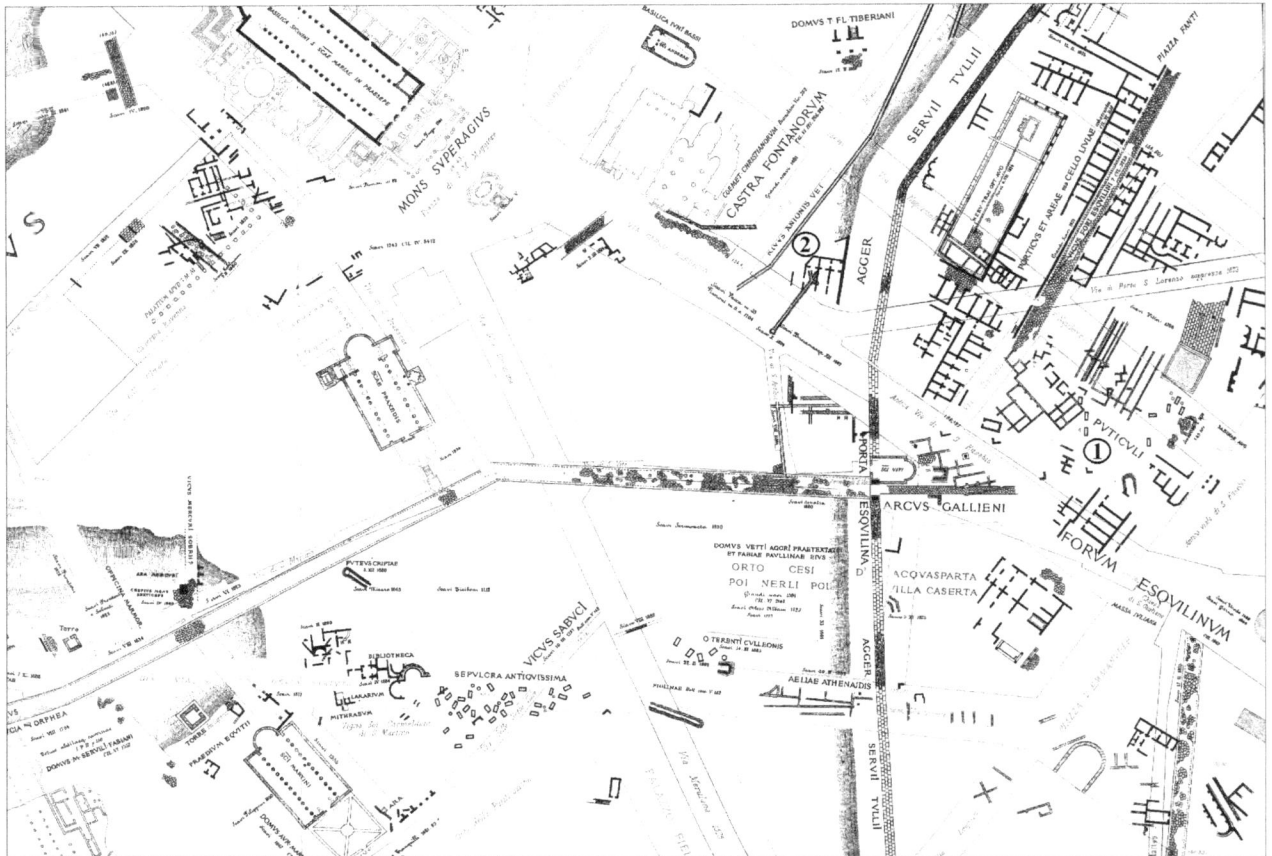

Figure 19. Section of the *Forma Urbis Romae* showing part of the Esquiline
1 the *puticuli*; 2. the ditch of the Servian *agger* filled with corpses (after Lanciani, 1893 – 1901)

specifically from *within* the pits themselves and does not comment upon the state of the bodies other than to describe the presence of some difficult to identify bones. Whittaker (1993: 13) says that the *puticuli* were "filled indiscriminately with animal carcasses, excreta, refuse and human bones (often gnawed by animals)." If the pits remained open for any length of time it is possible that remains were attacked by scavengers and rodents, but Lanciani actually makes no mention of gnawed bones in any of his reports. These two examples illustrate particularly well the way in which Lanciani's sensational accounts of the *puticuli* can, and have been, exaggerated and how easily incorrect information can be unquestioningly perpetuated.

Discrepancies can also be identified in some of the information that Lanciani does provide in his brief, and often sensationalised, publications. For example, Bodel (1994: 108 – 109, n. 163) has noted that Lanciani's observations concerning the size and lining of the *puticuli* vary. The horizontal dimensions of the pits are "variously given as four by five meters (*BCAR* 3 (1875) 43), "twelve feet square" (*Ancient Rome*, 64), and, in the revised Italian translation of the latter (*L'antica Roma*), tr. E. Staderini (1981) 67), "cinque metri quadrati"" (*ibid.*: 108, n. 163). As Bodel points out, there was doubtless some slight variation in the size of the pits, but the lack of consistent reporting throws doubt on the accuracy of Lanciani's evidence. The varied dimensions are,

however, reflected by the few plans that he did produce, on which the *puticuli* are depicted varying in size and shape (**Fig. 19** and especially **Fig. 20**) and imply that, despite his subsequent descriptions of the pits as uniform, there was a certain degree of variation amongst them. The confused nature of the archaeological evidence is further emphasised by the fact that "Lanciani identified the stone blocks lining the vaults as both *cappellaccio* (*BCAR* 2 (1874) 48; id., *The ruins and excavations of ancient Rome* (1897) 33) and *sperone* (*BCAR* 3 (1875) 43) tufa" (*ibid.*: 108 – 109, n. 163). What is more, despite his initial description of the stone lining as "an irregular mass" (1874: 48), a year later he revises this to "uniformly built with parallelepiped gabina stone, now called *sperone*, squared with remarkable perfection, their length in the middle 0.60[m], 0.30[m] high and 0.40[m] thick and ordered without cement" (1875: 43).[94] Here he describes two unmistakable extremes of construction belonging to the same feature. It is unclear exactly which is correct, or whether there was indeed some variation in the form of construction.

Bodel finds it perplexing that, despite claiming to have excavated 75 *puticuli,* only a handful are marked in a

---

[94] "… che sono tutti uniformemente costruiti con parallelepipedi di pietra gabina, detta ora *sperone*, squadrati con perfezione singolare, lunghi in media 0.60 alti 0.30 grossi 0.40, e commessi senza cemento" (Lanciani, 1875: 43).

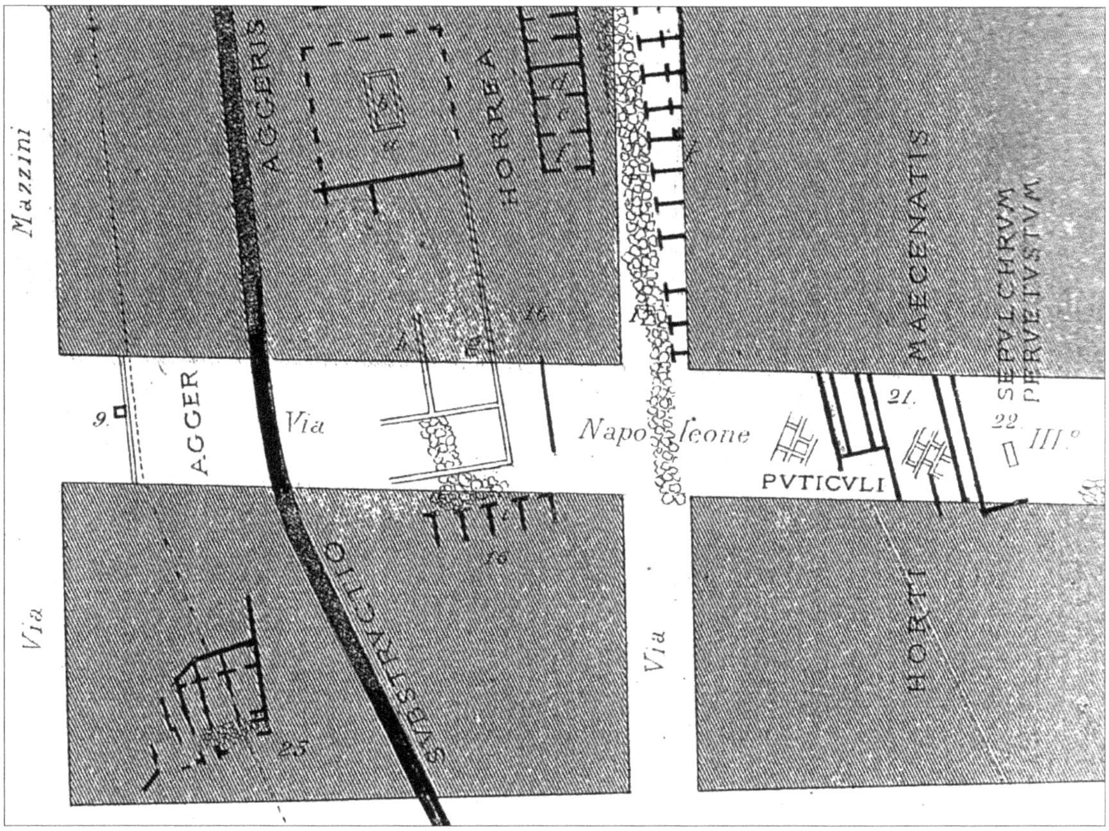

Figure 20. Section of the map accompanying Lanciani's first publication on the *puticuli* showing the location of the pits and their adjoining walls (Lanciani, 1874).

very small area on Lanciani's *Forma Urbis Romae* (**Fig. 19**). This may provide further proof of the fact that not all of them were fully investigated. Perhaps, given the time constraints imposed by encroaching construction work, he did not even have sufficient time to record the precise location of all the pits, let alone excavate each in its entirety. Furthermore, the location that Lanciani identifies as the section of the *fossa* of the *agger* that was seen to be filled with corpses, "the corner of Via Carlo-Alberto and Via Mazzini" (1891: 65), can be seen on his *Forma Urbis Romae* to be *inside* the rampart and *not* part of the ditch at all (no. 2, **Fig. 19**). This may of course be due simply to a misrepresentation of the course of the *agger* on the map or confusion about the new road layout of the region, but again emphasises the highly inaccurate nature of the evidence.[95]

The description that Lanciani provides of the *puticuli* and the region in which they were located, in addition to his conclusions regarding their identification, can also be shown to be heavily dependent on information from ancient texts. It is entirely on the basis of Varro's statement that "Outside the towns there are *puticuli* 'little

pits', named from *putei* 'pits', because there the people used to be buried in *putei* 'pits'," (*LL*. V.25) that Lanciani applies the term *puticuli* to his discoveries. He appears to have overlooked, or ignored, the fact that the vaults he excavated were not "little pits" but very deep and substantial structures. Similarly, Lanciani describes the area in which the pits were located as, "one thousand feet long, and three hundred deep" (Lanciani, 1891: 64). This appears to derive directly from Horace's *Satire* (1.8) in which he describes a pillar within the pauper burial-ground of the Esquiline which "assigned a thousand feet frontage and three hundred of depth" (*Sat.* 1.8.12). Horace's information may be accurate and these may indeed have been the dimensions of the zone designated for burial, but Lanciani, who excavated only one section of a limited area, provides no evidence to suggest that these dimensions were attested archaeologically. He uncovered no boundary stones recording the extent of the cemetery in this way (the Edict of Sentius applies to a far larger region) and found only one section of the travertine channel which he suspected marked the limit of the *puticuli*. Lanciani does not make it clear in his reports that he has appropriated Horace's description of the area. Furthermore, the accounts of Horace and Varro had led earlier scholars to posit the existence of *puticuli* (in whatever form) somewhere in the region in which Lanciani was working; so much so that a plan of ancient Rome produced by Canina between 1832 and 1850 marked the *puticuli* in the very place in which Lanciani

---

[95] The large dimensions of the chasm strongly suggest that this discovery *was* associated with the *agger*, but this provides another good example of the vague nature of much of the evidence on which all interpretations of the *puticuli*, this area of the Esquiline and the disposal of the poor have been interpreted.

reportedly found them 25 years later (Albertoni, 1983: 155, n.21). Lanciani would have been aware not only of the ancient texts that located *puticuli* in the area, but also Carina's map and may therefore have *expected* to find something that corresponded with the ancient descriptions. This must have had a significant influence on the way in which he interpreted the archaeology that he found, perhaps leading him immediately to the conclusion that the large vaults were indeed the *puticuli* that Varro described. It was only from this moment onwards that the term *puticuli* came to be used and understood in the context of mass burial, for neither Varro nor Horace specifically state that this was what they were used for. Varro's text is ambiguous on the matter of whether they were for individual or communal use.

It is difficult, on the basis of the confused evidence presented by Lanciani, to assign a specific date to the features he describes. As noted above, the presence of a *cippus* bearing the *senatus consultum de pago Montano* in the "pre-Augustan" levelling debris of the area indicates that they were probably covered prior to the rule of Augustus. Lanciani (1874: 49) observed that the pits were superimposed upon an earlier necropolis assigned to the period when Rome "was still a conglomeration of small villages" and the Esquiline pits have therefore been dated only rather vaguely to "the Republic". However, beyond the suggestion that the *puticuli* were used predominantly during the third and second centuries BC (Bodel, 1994: 50) no precise date has been established for their construction. Unfortunately, Lanciani's account of the ceramic evidence found in the region of the *puticuli* is not very helpful for refining this date since he does not identify any material derived specifically from *within* the pits, only the surrounding area in general. It is unclear exactly how he defines the composition of this area and whether or not he is referring to the layers into which the pits were dug, the contemporary surface layers or similar levels elsewhere in the excavated zone. Lanciani identified the quarry near St. Bibiana as the source of the stone lining of the *puticuli* and claimed that it was abandoned in the "first or second century of the Republican era, because the pottery found within the galleries is of a primitive workmanship, and contemporary with the pottery found within the early tombs of the Esquiline" (Lanciani, 1988: 87). If his interpretation of this relationship is correct, then the vaults must have been dug, or at least received a stone lining, during the early centuries of the Republic. Lanciani probably linked the quarry with the *puticuli* on the basis of its proximity to them, but the stone extracted from the quarry could easily have been employed elsewhere in the city without incurring serious transportation difficulties. The quarry therefore need not be directly associated with the *puticuli*. Moreover, the confusion surrounding the way in which the pits were lined either with "an irregular mass of stone" or blocks "squared with remarkable perfection," makes it difficult to assess whether the regular-sized blocks extracted from the quarry were used for this purpose. The available archaeological evidence is therefore too vague and ambiguous to be used as a reliable tool for dating the features that Lanciani discovered; compounded further by the absence of any detailed stratigraphic sections of the region that actually depict the *puticuli*.

Literary evidence for the date of the 'puticuli'

An examination of the ancient textual sources that refer to the *puticuli* helps to shed some limited light on the period in which they were in use. Horace (*Sat.* 1.8) informs us that by the time in which he was writing (the Augustan period) the vicinity of the Esquiline Gate was no longer used for burial. His silence regarding the subject of *puticuli* may indicate either that their previous existence had faded from public memory, or that they had not been in use long enough to become established as a specific characteristic of the area. As we have seen, Horace uses imagery connected with a cemetery to characterise the Esquiline. He particularly draws on the presence of disturbed shallow graves to conjure up the unpleasant nature of the area, *not* mass charnel pits, which surely would have had a more dramatic effect. Varro (*L.L.* V. 25) also uses the past tense to describe the *puticuli* and, as Richardson (1992: 323) points out, he appears to be unfamiliar with this type of burial, perhaps confusing them with the place of public execution that was located outside the Porta Esquilina. Varro, writing in the middle of the first century BC, states that, "there the people *used to be* buried in *putei* 'pits','" and "the *puticuli* are so called because the corpses which had been thrown out *putescebant* '*used to* rot' there, in the public burial-place which is beyond the Esquiline" (*L.L.* V. 25; my emphasis). The text therefore suggests that if there *were* mass graves located in this area, that they had been out of use long enough for both their origin and the manner in which they were used to become obscure. Unfortunately neither author provides direct evidence for the period in which *puticuli* were actively used. Bodel (1994: 107, n. 154) points out, however, that "Varro's reference to his master Aelius Stilo and to the playwright Afranius shows that the *puticuli* at Rome were in use already during the second century BC." Consequently, it is not possible at present to assign a more precise date to the features revealed in the nineteenth century. It can only be assumed that they were perhaps in use during the third and second century BC, although possibly originated earlier, and had ceased to be a regular part of the public consciousness by the mid first century BC. They had also ceased to be part of the urban landscape by this period.

Structure and dimensions

The dimensions recorded by Lanciani are particularly significant for understanding the Esquiline pits. Measuring *approximately* 12 feet square and dug to a depth of 30 feet, the pits represent a considerable outlay of labour and investment; a fact that sits uneasily with their interpretation as the place where the corpses of unwanted slaves and the poor were unceremoniously dumped. Examination of the economic resources available to the lower classes (Chapter 3) suggests that they probably took personal responsibility for the burial of dead friends and family. It is highly unlikely that the poor could afford, or were concerned enough about long-term problems of disposal on a large scale, to dig vast pits and to take the time to line them with stone. If the bodies dumped in the pits were simply to be left to rot, it is strange that whoever was responsible should be sufficiently concerned to dig substantial, regular and stone-lined pits. On the basis of Lanciani's accounts, each pit had a capacity of approximately 4,320 cubic feet, and he claims to have identified at least 75 (324,000 cubic feet in total, although this may be greater if, as he suggests, there were more). Such a huge undertaking can not possibly have been attempted by poverty stricken members of the community. Not only did they not have access to the economic resources that were required, but they would probably have been unable to afford the time in which to carry out such a project. What is more, such an undertaking would require a considerable degree of co-operation and organisation of manpower on a large scale. The poor members of society who Lanciani posits were thrown into the pits, were probably incapable of organising or affording construction on such a scale. In addition, permission for such a large construction project on public land would have been required and funds were needed to purchase the land in which the pits were to be dug. Suburban land at Rome was very expensive, particularly in the immediate vicinity of one of the city gates (see Champlin, 1982), and Purcell (1987: 38) cites the example of a slave who paid 120 HS for a plot just 1½ *pedes* square. The evidence reported by Lanciani therefore points more towards the construction of the pits by an authority with access to the economic resources and manpower required for such an immense undertaking.

The description provided by Lanciani of uniform cells with common walls, built as a single unit, and the map he produced to accompany his initial report (**Fig. 20**), implies that they were dug contemporaneously. This is emphasised further by the "travertine channel" which appears to delimit the area of the *puticuli* and suggests further that they were designed and built as a block. That the vaults appear to have been dug contemporaneously is very significant. Given their supposed use, one would expect them to have been created on a more *ad hoc* basis, as the need arose for new disposal space and as each pit reached capacity. That this was apparently not the case reflects a remarkable example of forward planning and may therefore be better understood not in the context of the poor creating these structures themselves but of official state involvement. It is possible that the state, recognising the need for organised disposal facilities to deal with the remains of the indigent, ordered the construction of the pits. The choice of the Esquiline for the location of these facilities may have been influenced by the regions long established history as a cemetery, continued use of the area by the poorer classes in particular for burial, and its proximity to the slums of the Subura where the majority of those who required such disposal probably resided. Furthermore, it has been observed by Patterson (2000b: 93), that noxious industries and "other activities considered hazardous or detrimental to the well-being of the citizens" were confined to the suburbs.

State involvement may also provide an explanation for the stone-lining of the pits. Bodel (1994: 103, n.119) observes that "Livy 39.44.5 mentions the lining with stone of public cesspits (rather than fountain basins, as commonly supposed) by Cato during his censorship in 184." The reasons for doing this are not stated, but could it perhaps be linked to the lining of the Esquiline pits? However, unless the stones were well mortared or covered with impervious cement or plaster – which they were not in the case of the supposed *puticuli* – the lining would not have effectively prevented the leakage of fluids. The possibility of some irregularity of the lining of the pits, the absence of cement, and the use of porous tufa thus implies that the lining of these cells was not intended to be watertight. Indeed, Lanciani (1874: 48) describes the soil surrounding the pits as blackened by the decomposition of the organic material originally deposited within them. It is perhaps more likely that the stone was intended to provide structural stability and prevent the cesspits collapsing. The same may have been true for the *puticuli*, with their considerable depth necessitating some form of structure designed to prevent a similar fate.

The extant ancient sources are silent on the matter of state involvement with disposal practices on the Esquiline, but Bodel (1994 and 2000) has observed that there was some direct involvement of the state in wider funerary activities, particularly the conduct of undertakers. He points to the *demarchoi* of fourth century Athens, who were responsible for the burial of abandoned corpses, as a possible model for the Roman system, suggesting that "at Rome the removal of dead bodies from city streets was considered a part of the *cura urbis*, a charge that normally fell to the *aediles*" (Bodel, 2000: 130).[96] Further evidence for state involvement in funerary activities is provided by a *lex locationis* from Puteoli describing the duties of public undertakers, in addition to the cost of their services and restrictions concerning their movement.[97] Kyle (1998: 163) summarises part of the text:

> "A prohibition against abandoning corpses is to be enforced with a fine of 60 HS per corpse (I, 29 – II, 2). The contracting undertaker (*manceps*) is to keep a staff of thirty-two workers, who are to be of sound body and free of marks (*neve stigmat(ibus) inscrip(tus)*). Forbidden to reside within a certain distance of town, the workers may enter the city only on official business (II, 3 – 4) and they must wear a special cap in town …."

---

[96] The abandonment of human remains was probably a common problem at Rome and is illustrated by reports in the ancient sources: Nero encountered an abandoned corpse as he attempted to escape from Rome (Suetonius, *Nero* 48), and a stray dog once deposited a human hand at the feet of Vespasian (Suetonius, *Vesp.* 5).

[97] *AE* 1971, no.88.

The Puteolan text is believed to reflect common practice at Rome and, as noted above, the Grove of Libitina where the undertakers were probably based, has been tentatively identified on the *Campus Esquilinus*. Wiseman (1998: 13 – 15) concurs with Bodel's conclusions regarding the location of the headquarters, pointing out that these were "close to those of the fluteplayers (*tibicines*), whose guild is also identified by the find-spot of a late-republican inscription ... fluteplayers, as Ovid pointed out, were much in demand at funerals" (*ibid.*: 13 – 15; Ovid, *Fasti*, VI 660, 663) (no. 4, **Fig. 16**). Bodel (2000: 130 – 131) has also suggested that the passage in which undertakers are instructed to remove the bodies of executed criminals, suicides by hanging and slaves to a place on the outskirts of the city, may imply the existence of a mass grave or disposal ground at Puteoli that can perhaps be equated with the *puticuli* of Rome. Finally, some interest on the part of the state in recording the number of deaths in the city is indicated by the suggestion that an official death register was kept at the Grove of Libitina. Originally instituted by King Servius Tullius, the register certainly may have persisted into later periods and suggests that city authorities were aware of the problems posed by mass death and the demands consequently placed on burial space.[98] Their response to this situation may have been to construct large pits on the Esquiline that were controlled by the state-employed *libitinarii* whose headquarters were nearby.

The possibility of official involvement by the city authorities, however, does not necessarily provide an instant explanation for the regularity with which the *puticuli* were constructed and lined with stone. Large unlined holes of irregular dimensions would have incurred minimal expense (both economic and in terms of time and labour) and would surely have sufficed for unceremonious dumping activities. It is unlikely that the urban authorities were concerned enough about the fate of the corpses they were responsible for the disposal of to expend resources on providing stone-lined pits in which they could be dumped; they were more concerned simply with removing them from the city and disposing of them quickly and easily.

Perhaps the Esquiline pits were created originally for some other purpose and, once they had gone out of use, or during a period of particularly high mortality, were appropriated for disposal purposes. The structure of the pits, the archaeology of the region, and ancient textual sources are not, however, very forthcoming with an explanation for what this original function might have been. Their dimensions and the regularity of their construction, in conjunction with the tufa lining of their interior, may point towards an industrial function.[99]

Livy's reference to the lining of public cesspits with stone during the early second century BC, may suggest that they acted in a similar capacity and may provide an explanation for the "travertine channel"; perhaps this was involved in draining the pits or controlling any potential overflow. Use of the vaults as cesspits might also explain the blackening of the surrounding soil described by Lanciani, which may have occurred as a result of the leaking and decomposition of the refuse deposited within them – they were, after all, not sealed with impervious cement or plaster. Unfortunately, it is unlikely that true cesspits would be located on a hill because of the need for gravity to aid flow into them. Perhaps we therefore need to interpret Livy's reference to "cesspits" in a broader sense and include general rubbish pits, into which a variety of refuse, excrement and household waste was thrown, within the remit of the regulation. Patterson (2000b: 93) points out that the *aediles* were responsible for the cleanliness of city streets and "made arrangements for the removal of all kinds of rubbish from the urban centre to the periphery; special privileges were in force to allow wagons carrying *stercus* (whether this means specifically 'excrement' or 'refuse' in a more general sense is debated) to circulate within the city during the hours of daylight (*Tabula Heracleensis* 66 – 7)." He proposes that this rubbish was deposited on the outskirts of the city where facilities may have been built to accommodate vast amounts of refuse. This would align particularly well with the location of the Esquiline pits outside one of the major city gates. However, it has been shown above that this area had, for a long time, been used as a cemetery and the presence of large rubbish pits in the centre of a thriving necropolis is difficult to explain. It may, however, be more plausible if we accept that the *libitinarii* were also involved in general disposal activities and that, for a short while, areas of the Esquiline were set apart for different disposal activities. Perhaps the area to the north of the bone-yard transformed by Maecenas was used for more general disposal activities (**Fig. 18**). This would certainly have contributed further to the unpleasant nature of the region as described by Horace.

Despite the unquestioning acceptance by modern scholars of the mixture of general rubbish, animal cadavers and human corpses in the context of the disposal of the poor, it does not naturally follow that rubbish pits were also used as mass graves. The corpses of beggars and the most destitute members of the community who died on the

---

[98] Suetonius' statement (*Nero*, 39.1) that during a plague "thirty thousand deaths came into Libitina's account" has been taken as evidence for the continued use of a death register in the city, as have other scattered references in ancient texts (Bodel, 1994: 14).

[99] It is possible that the pits were involved in the urban water supply system, perhaps acting as large reservoirs, although there is no evidence attesting the presence of such structures on the outskirts of the city during the Republican period and, most importantly, the pits were not

watertight. They may have functioned in another storage capacity, perhaps for imported grain. Although if this was the case we might expect them to be located near to the docks in order to minimise transportation. The pits may also have been used for the storage of snow, used by wealthy members of society to cool their drinks. Their remarkable depth (30 feet) would have helped to preserve the snow in its frozen state. Similar pits, dug on the outskirts of Rome during the eighteenth century, reached a depth of about 50 feet. Although this interpretation may initially appear rather fanciful, the structure and depth of the pits strongly aligns with the type of structure that would have been used for this purpose. The *puticuli* were (according to Lanciani) not covered with a vault but open to the skies and Plutarch (*Symposium* VI, *Quaest.* 6) describes how the open snow pits were covered only by straw and coarse cloth.

streets may have been thrown into these pits (the removal of their bodies being, presumably, part of the *aediles* responsibilities) but that they formed the last resting-place for *all* the lower classes seems unlikely. The *aediles* were not responsible for the disposal of *all* corpses, only those abandoned on the streets which technically constituted rubbish.

Contents

An examination of the contents of the *puticuli* and the manner in which they were filled is also essential for increasing our understanding of their use and purpose. In his first report Lanciani writes that, "the base of the cells or pits are filled with bones, ashes and organic detritus, the decomposition of which has blackened the surrounding soil" (1874: 48).[100] In a later publication he provides the following description:

> "In many cases the contents of each vault were reduced to a uniform mass of black, viscid, pestilent, unctuous matter; in a few cases the bones could in a measure be singled out and identified."
>
> (Lanciani, 1891: 64 – 65)

It is only the ditch of the *agger* which Lanciani specifically describes as "filled up with thousands upon thousands of corpses" (*ibid.*: 66), and his descriptions of the *puticuli* provide relatively little information regarding their deposits. It would appear, therefore, that he did not examine these in any detail. The absence of any comprehensive information concerning the contents of the pits can be partly explained by the period in which the excavations occurred and the haste with which they were conducted. However, it may also indicate that there were actually very few human corpses present in the pits. Lanciani refers to identifiable "corpses" when writing of the *agger*, leaving little doubt about the use of the ditch as a communal grave. However, he seems unable to identify individual corpses within the *puticuli*, only a few bones, and it is only as a result of the parallels he draws with the pits referred to by Varro that leads to the conclusion that they were communal graves. Lanciani states that only "*in a few cases*" could the bones be "singled out and identified." This may be indicative of poor osteological preservation or, more probably, that there were in reality very few human corpses and that the pits were filled largely with other refuse.[101] This, of course, cannot be verified on the basis of the available evidence, but in light of the posited use of the cells as rubbish pits, it is conceivable that there were indeed few corpses within the *puticuli* deposits. Lanciani may also have experienced difficulties distinguishing human from animal bone, and been unable to establish the proportion

of human bones present in the same way has he could for the *agger*. Only a detailed examination of the contents using modern scientific techniques can provide any insight into the actual quantity of human remains in relation to animal bones and other refuse.[102]

The capacity of the supposed *puticuli* and the manner in which they were filled also sheds light on their use. Bodel (2000) has examined the implications of the capacity of the excavated vaults for the number of human depositions that could be made in them (assuming they were actually filled predominantly with human corpses) and has drawn parallels between similar communal graves from later periods (**Table 10**). Allowing 7.5 – 8 cubic feet per corpse, Bodel postulates that Lanciani's *puticuli* could each have contained 540 – 830 bodies, although this amount may have been significantly reduced by the presence of other refuse and animal carcasses (*ibid.*: 132). He concludes that under 'normal' circumstances the pits "remained open for several weeks or even months before being filled to capacity" (*ibid.*: 132). On the basis of this, and the figures cited above for urban mortality, it is possible to calculate approximately how long the pits remained open. If it is assumed that 5 percent of the approximate eighty deaths per day in the city were those of the indigent, this would have resulted in approximately 1,500 corpses that required public disposal each year.[103] Bodel (2000: 132) distinguishes between two sizes of *puticuli* (12×12×30 feet and 13×16×30 feet) with a capacity of 4,320 and 6,240 cubic feet respectively. If 4 corpses were deposited per day in pits of this size, it would take approximately 5 to 7.5 months to fill a single pit, although this would again be affected by the amount of other refuse deposited.[104]

It is also possible to calculate approximately how long the Esquiline pits might have been in use as a whole, on the basis of the total number of corpses *theoretically* capable of being held within them. Lanciani claimed to have excavated 75 pits, each capable of holding between 540 and 830 corpses – a maximum of 40,500 – 62,250 corpses. Assuming these were deposited under 'normal' circumstances at an average of 4 per day, it would have

---

[100] "Il fondo delle celle o dei pozzi è ripieno di ossami, di ceneri, e di detriti organici, la cui decomposizione ha annerito tutto il suolo circostante."

[101] His description of the "black unctuous matter" and the organic nature of the deposits suggest that good preservation conditions were present in the pits and therefore bone should have survived sufficiently.

[102] Unfortunately it is not known whether Lanciani kept the contents of the pits or re-buried them. If any samples were retained their whereabouts is uncertain. It is very probable that they were simply re-buried *in situ* given the problems that he would have faced (ironically) in disposing of the masses of putrid organic matter.

[103] Although infants, who would have been included amongst this number (30 percent of total mortality), may not always have received normative burial rites until they reached a certain age this would have had little effect on the issues and figures discussed here. Firstly, it has been established that disposal in the *puticuli* did not constitute proper religious burial anyway and therefore there was no reason to exclude infants from them. Furthermore, if the corpses of the destitute were dumped alongside the general refuse of the city the responsible authorities are unlikely to have made a distinction between the body of an adult and that of a child since they both required removal from the city and subsequent disposal.

[104] Assuming 7.5 – 8 cubic feet per corpse the calculations for this are as follows:
12×12×30 = 540 – 575 bodies ÷ 4 corpses per day = 135 – 144 days (approx 5 months) to fill.
13×16×30 = 780 – 830 bodies ÷ 4 corpses per day = 195 – 208 days (approx 7 – 7.5 months) to fill.

Dimensions (feet)	Capacity (cubic feet)	Bodies	Cubic feet per corpse	Location (and date)
15×40×20	12,000 [8,400]	1,114	[7.5]	London (1665)
15×18×30	8,100	1,200 – 1,500	[5.4 – 6.75!]	Paris
15×18×20	5,400	600 – 700	[7.7 – 9.0]	Paris, Les Innocents (1763)
15×15×18	4,050	500	[8.1]	Paris, Rue de Bagneux (1746)
12×12×30	4,320	[540 – 575]	(7.5 – 8)	Rome, Lanciani's *puticuli*
13×16× (30)	6,240	[780 – 830]	(7.5 – 8)	Rome, Lanciani's *puticuli*

Table 10. Size and capacity of mass burial pits in London, Paris and ancient Rome
(Figures in square brackets are deduced; those in parentheses are hypothetical)
(after Bodel, 2000: 132, Table 10.1)

taken 30 – 46 years to fill 75 pits (if *only* human corpses were deposited, probably quicker if other refuse was dumped there too). This data is, of course, only approximate and would have been affected significantly by other factors, including the use of the *puticuli* for the disposal of other rubbish and animal carcasses.[105] However, they provide an indication of the relative speed with which the 75 pits uncovered by Lanciani could have been filled, given the fact that they are believed to have been in use for centuries. The calculations assume that only the destitute were deposited within the pits but they would have been filled even more rapidly if *all* lower class burials were made in this way. These calculations consequently imply that the pits could only have been a relatively short-lived response to the burial demands of the city and at least three, if not four, times as many would have been required in order to have been in constant use for two centuries as Bodel has suggested (1994: 50).

It has been proposed (Bodel, 1994: 50) that the authorities were compelled to use a section of the nearby ditch of the Servian *agger* as an "overflow" burial space. Similar calculations to those outlined above can be made for this feature. Lanciani (1891: 66) estimates that there were 24,000 corpses within this space but his allowance of 20 cubic feet per corpse is, as he himself admits, "more than sufficient." Bodel (2000: 150, n.3) suggests a figure closer to 60,000 – 64,000

corpses for an area with a maximum capacity of 480,000 cubic feet. If the ditch was filled at the same rate as the pits, it would have taken approximately 45 – 48 years to fill the ditch to capacity (the approximate equivalent of 75 individual pits). The ditch may not, of course, have been filled to capacity, but notwithstanding this possibility and the presence of other refuse, 48 years represents a considerable length of time for a single mass grave to have been left open. Bodel (2000: 132) observes that even a few weeks or months would have been sufficient for putrefaction to have set in and "the unpleasant symptoms of decay (stench and putrid air) would have emanated into the environs." In addition, the involvement of the *aediles*, state funds and the official control of the site implied by the structure of the pits would have made it possible to create new pits once the existing ones reached their limits. This suggests that not only was the ditch probably filled under 'abnormal' circumstances, but that the *puticuli* do *not* represent the normal method of disposal for the lowly members of society. It is unlikely that the "ordinary poor," even if they were unable to afford a substantial funerary monument, would have found their way into these pits if they had family and friends to take care of their remains. The "four corpses per day" represent the "truly destitute" and thus the minority.

The real 'puticuli'?

Before examining other suggested explanations for the function of the *puticuli*, it is important to consider strong evidence that suggests the pits discovered by Lanciani are not *puticuli* at all. Lanciani himself provides the most convincing evidence for this proposal. In a letter to *The Athenaeum* (November 10th, 1877) he reports the

---

[105] If the bodies were buried in coffins the capacity of the pits would also have been considerably reduced. However, the use of coffins seems unlikely given the fact that the bodies seem to have been discarded and not buried. Coffins would have represented an additional and unnecessary expense.

discovery of a "new type of tomb" (Lanciani, 1988: 44) and provides the following details:

> "Their position *within* the walls of Servius Tullius testifies of their extreme antiquity. They are built in the shape of a well, 0.8m in diameter, and from ten to twenty feet deep. The 'cappellaccio' through which they are sunk being very soft and porous, the shaft is coated with slabs of Gabinian stone. This was done before the construction of the walls by Servius Tullius, when the ground surface of the ground was level with the mouth of the pits. Afterwards, when the ground was raised the shafts were prolonged also by the addition of colossal cylinders of terracotta, nearly three feet in diameter, on which the names of the deceased is scratched with a sharp point. Many ex-votos or funeral offerings were picked up in the neighbourhood of the wells, some in the shape of an ear, some like half-pyramids, all bearing archaic inscriptions."

The editor of his letters, Anthony Cubberley, suggests that these vaults might be "more appropriately called *puticuli* than those which generally go under that name" (*ibid.*: 45, n. 7). This conclusion is reached also by Coarelli (1999: 174), who compares the wells of the Esquiline with similar structures at Fregellae.[106] According to Varro (*L.L.* V.25) the term *puticuli* came from *putei* 'wells' or 'pits'; a derivation that certainly aligns more closely with the early graves described as "wells". The location of these within the Servian wall dates them to a period prior to the construction of the embankment in the fourth century BC; a fact that again aligns with Varro's use of the past tense and his lack of detailed understanding concerning their function and origin. Bodel (1994: 41) agrees with the parallels drawn between the wells of the Esquiline, Fregellae and the text of Varro but points out that these appear to have "contained only individual burials (if any) and one of which (from the Esquiline) was capped by an inscribed terracotta disc, [and] are not easily reconciled with Varro's description of a place where corpses were casually abandoned and left to rot (*cadavera proiecta ... putescebant*) or with Horace's evocative allusion to an expanse of ground strewn with whitening bones." However, as we have seen, Horace was probably referring to a graveyard outside the Esquiline Gate that was comprised largely of the shallow, modest and easily disturbed burials of the humble classes of Roman society. He makes *no* direct reference to "mass graves" or *puticuli*. Bodel's (1994: 31 – 32) explanation of the use of the term *proicere* in conjunction with words for corpses, meaning "to abandon" or "to leave unburied" during the time in which Varro was writing is convincing. However, when first referring to the *puticuli* Varro suggests they were so named "because there the people used to be *buried* in *putei* 'pits'" (*L.L.* V. 25, my italics) and only when referring to the interpretation provided by Aelius does he speak of "*cadavera proiecta*". It is therefore highly probable that the early wells found at

Rome were *puticuli* in the true sense of the term. It must be remembered, however, that this true meaning of the term does not necessarily also equate to mass burial. The use of the term to describe a communal grave is brought about only by Lanciani's adoption of it to interpret his discoveries.

* * * * *

Several conclusions can be drawn concerning the so-called *puticuli* of the *Campus Esquilinus* on the basis of the above discussion. Evidence for the use of these vast pits is obscure but it is unlikely that they represent the last resting-place of the majority of the urban poor. This is particularly important because many modern scholars continue to refer to Lanciani's *puticuli* as the most common means of disposal for the lower classes as a whole. Not only were the pits evidently open for a relatively short period of time but they were also incapable of meeting the demands imposed by high mortality, even in the short-term. Although it remains a possibility that the truly destitute were discarded in pits or disposal areas such as these if the disposal of their remains fell to the city authorities, there were also vast numbers of "ordinary poor" residing in the city. If Lanciani's *puticuli* were designed to accommodate the remains of *all* these individuals this would have necessitated many more pits than the 75 he said he excavated, or even the hundreds he predicted.

Other explanations

Victims of the arena

Kyle (1998) investigated the possibility that the Esquiline pits were used for the disposal of the many corpses that were produced by arena spectacles. These spectacles involved two groups of people: gladiators and criminals/condemned individuals (*noxii*). Gladiators often received individual burial, and Kyle (*ibid.*: 160) points out that "inscribed tombstones, many with carved reliefs, show that professional gladiators were generally allowed and sometimes provided with decent burial. Corpses could be claimed and buried by owners or editors, relatives, burial clubs, or fellow gladiators." Hope (1998) has also demonstrated how proper burial and the erection of a funerary monument allowed these socially stigmatised individuals to negotiate their place within society and assert their identity (see Chapter 1). Given the superstitious character of many gladiators and the imminence of their death it is probable that they were eager to make arrangements for suitable burial in advance and it is unlikely that large numbers ever found their way into mass graves. This contrasts greatly with the fate of the *noxii*. These victims of the arena were criminals, often condemned for treason, a crime which brought "infamy, ignominy and denial of even the most basic rites" (Kyle, 1998.: 162). The corpses of *noxii* were unlikely to be claimed, leaving their disposal either in the hands of the spectacle organisers or city undertakers. Given their lack of status and contaminated nature, it is highly unlikely

---

[106] See also Coarelli and Monti (1998).

that they were the recipients of proper religious burial. Disposal of these corpses in mass graves may have been one solution to the problem of what to do with them but, as Kyle notes (*ibid.*: 163), there were others, including burning and use as food for animals employed in the spectacles. Alternatively, Kyle (*ibid.*: 213) observes that, "Roman history and religion point to the Tiber River, more than to pits, beasts, and fire, as a traditional means of ultimate disposal (and of denial of burial) for victims. Examination of early executions and later spectacles, often taking place close to the river, indicates that the Tiber was repeatedly used to dispose of corpses." Moreover, "neither ancient texts nor Lanciani connect the Esquiline to arena spectacles" (*ibid.*: 168).

The number of corpses produced each year by spectacles is difficult to calculate but was probably large and continued to rise as spectacles grew ever more lavish. The supposed *puticuli* would have been very quickly overwhelmed if this was the usual means of disposal for arena corpses. As Kyle (*ibid.*: 168) observes, "the Esquiline and the suburbs had enough problems without the addition of arena victims." Furthermore, the Esquiline pits were closed before the huge arenas of Imperial Rome had been established. Although gladiatorial bouts associated with aristocratic funerals began at Rome during the third century BC and became a form of popular entertainment in their own right after the contest organised by the consuls P. Rutilius Rufus and C. Manlius Maximus in 105 BC (Jacobelli, 2003: 6), the lavish spectacles witnessed by audiences in the Colosseum were not seen until the first century AD, at which time mass disposal on the Esquiline was no longer possible. The remains of some arena victims probably did find their way to the Esquiline, but it is not possible to suggest that Lanciani's *puticuli* were specifically created, or frequently used for, this purpose.[107]

War victims and executions

The Esquiline had a long established association with the execution of criminals and captives. Its location on the outskirts of the Republican city made it ideal for such activities, which appear to have continued even after the redevelopment of the area. Kyle (1998: 165 – 166) outlines the textual evidence for execution on the Esquiline:

> "Tacitus (*Ann.* 2.32.3, Loeb) ties the Esquiline to traditional forms of execution: under Tiberius the senate expelled astrologers and magicians from Italy; one was thrown from the Rock, another was executed 'by the consuls outside the Esquiline Gate according to ancient usage (*more prisco*) and at the sound of the trumpet.' Under

Claudius foreigners who usurped the rights of citizens were to be executed in *campo Esquilino*, and Nero ordered the execution of a consul-elect in 'a place set apart for the execution of slaves (*locus servilibus poenis sepositus*),' which Hinard takes as the Esquiline."[108]

The remains of execution victims were probably disposed of nearby, and because of their condemned status this is unlikely to have involved proper burial. Denial of burial entailed a further punishment and mass graves offered a simple solution to the demand for rapid disposal. However, how many criminals were executed each year on the Esquiline rather than in the arena? The *puticuli* and the ditch of the *agger* could potentially accommodate thousands of corpses and it is unlikely that sufficient numbers to fill them were executed before the closure of the area during the late Republic. Moreover, the victims of executions which took place after the reclamation of the Esquiline could not have been buried in the immediate vicinity which now lay within the city limits. This suggests that it was not necessary, even if it was certainly more practical, to dispose of corpses at the site of execution. Hinard (1987, cited in Kyle, 1998: 179, n.69) links several textual references describing denial of burial and exposure with the Esquiline, but, as Kyle asserts, it is neither necessary nor possible, to associate every unspecific reference to such activities with this area of the city. Execution probably occurred in other suburban areas where visibility was high and the punishment could be witnessed by large numbers of people. The executed followers of Spartacus, for example, were crucified and exposed along the road from Capua to Rome.

The presence of large numbers of corpses in an area traditionally associated with execution may be explained in the context of a mass grave of the victims of war – either captives or those killed in battle. It is unlikely, however, that there were ever so many captives awaiting execution in Rome at any one time. It is also difficult to link the corpses to any specific historical battle. According to Kyle (*ibid.*: 179, n.69) Hinard suggests that "the rebel soldiers executed in 270 BC in the Forum and exposed 'outside the city' were dumped on the Esquiline, but this seems logistically unlikely. Again, Hinard, 113–14, feels that those executed and denied burial on the return of Marius in 87 (App. *B. Civ.* 1.73) ended up on the Esquiline." However, despite its association with execution and exposure, it can not be assumed that the Esquiline was the only site used for such purposes. The Tiber may have been used for the disposal of criminals and prisoners of war, allowing for both convenient disposal and denial of burial.

Epidemic/plague victims

During pestilential periods mortality in the city soared, resulting in an increased need for fast and efficient disposal of large numbers of corpses. It has been

---

[107] In addition, mass graves have not been identified at other cities known to have frequently staged gladiatorial games, such as Pompeii. Other disposal mechanisms must consequently have been in place in these cities and therefore probably also at Rome. The reasons stated above for why it is unlikely that substantial, stone-lined pits would be created in order to receive the remains of abandoned bodies, also apply here.

[108] Claudius: Suet. *Claud.* 25.3; Nero: Tac. *Ann.* 15.60.2.

proposed (Kyle, 1998: 178 – 179, n.69) that communal graves may have been integral to the disposal process: "Hopkins (1983), 208–9, discusses the practicality of using pits during epidemics, and notes that, 'In such circumstances, cremation was too costly, because it consumed expensive fuel'...[and] mass graves were space- and labour-efficient; they were a common response in Europe in times of mass death when normal methods of disposal were insufficient." It is possible, therefore, that pits were dug in order to facilitate the disposal of those affected by an outbreak of plague. Preparations may have been made in advance of such an outbreak, and at state expense, thus perhaps also explaining the regularity and structure of the pits. [109] The structural support offered by the stone lining of the pits possibly implies that they were prepared and left open for some time before they were filled. Perhaps on one occasion these purpose-built pits were filled too rapidly, or not dug at all, leading to the appropriation of the nearby Servian *fossa* as an overflow or alternative. However, although mass graves were time- and labour-efficient, and epidemics, although unpredictable were inevitable, ancient accounts regularly emphasise the inability of city authorities to cope with high levels of mortality and refer to desperate measures, rather than planned disposal systems:

> "Dionysius writes of the corpses of the very poor being thrown into the Tiber in the plague of 463 BC, and again in 451, when corpses were thrown into the sewers as well. Diodorus describes corpses being left unburied for fear of contamination during the plague in Sicily in 396 BC ... Orosius claimed that the plague of 142 BC killed so many undertakers that corpses had to be left to rot in their beds, eventually making Rome uninhabitable ... Procopius describes corpses being thrown down pell-mell inside fortifications during the plague at Constantinople in AD 542."[110]

(Duncan-Jones, 1996: 113)

The Constantinople example is reminiscent of the many corpses deposited in the ditch of the Servian *agger,* and may therefore indicate that this was an extreme measure taken during a period of very high mortality. In addition, the frequency of epidemic outbreaks at Rome would have required many more than the 75 pits uncovered by Lanciani.

If the Esquiline pits *were* created as a response to an epidemic it is difficult to establish when this occurred. Why similar pits were not used more often, particularly in later periods, as a response to the disposal difficulties caused by disease is also curious. What happened to the victims of previous and later epidemics? Are there other

mass graves lying undiscovered on the outskirts of Rome? The "greatest" plagues of Rome, such as those which ravaged the population under Nero and Commodus, took place when the limits of the city had been extended beyond the Esquiline Gate and do not seem to have led to the creation of state organised mass graves.

André (1980) charts the progress of ancient concepts of epidemic disease and Roman ideas of pestilence, recording an increased awareness of their association with public hygiene and sanitary conditions. As a result it is difficult to believe that the pits would have been left totally uncovered for any great length of time. It must therefore be assumed that if they were used for the bodies of epidemic deaths that they were linked to a single plague event, but none of the ancient sources refer to such organised measures being taken. Furthermore, the pits were not impervious and the stone-lining can therefore not be linked to a desire to contain and control contamination. In addition, Varro, Horace and other ancient sources make no reference to the specific use of the Esquiline for the disposal of plague victims or official mass graves. It is therefore probable that during an outbreak of plague the space offered by the ditch of the *agger* was used to receive the vast number of corpses, but the *puticuli*, were not created as a response to such a situation.

Unwanted slaves

Other explanations have also been proposed, including the disposal of deceased household slaves to whom the owner felt little or no attachment and therefore no desire to provide them with decent burial, or who had been punished and deemed unworthy of proper burial rites. It is again, however, difficult to understand the structure of the pits in such a context. Why go to such monumental lengths simply to dispose of the body of an unwanted or condemned slave?

A new theory?

Substantial tombs once existed in the vicinity of the Esquiline Gate. The poorest classes of Roman society who used the necropolis were unlikely to have been in a position to afford such structures and were probably buried in humble shallow graves like those to which Horace appears to allude. The archaeological evidence for such practice forms the subject of Chapter 5. For the purposes of the present discussion it is sufficient to note that modest burials marked only by an amphora, ceramic fragment, wooden marker or row of tiles were probably scattered amongst the more substantial tombs of the Esquiline cemetery. When the *Campus Esquilinus* was reclaimed, the authorities responsible would have faced the task of clearing all structures from the site, including the most humble of grave-markers, and re-landscaping the area. Eradication of the visible signs of burial, however, represented only superficial clearance. *Total* reclamation of the land may have been required by those responsible for its reorganisation and would have necessitated the removal

---

[109] Land was certainly set aside for mass graves in advance of the Black Death in England (1348 – 50). See Hawkins (1990).
[110] Dion. Hal. 9.67 and 10.53; Diodorus 14.70 – 71; Orosius 5.4.8 – 9; Procop. *Wars* 2.22 – 23.

of any burials deposited within it in order to negate its status as a *locus religiosus*. A similar process seems to have occurred outside the Colline Gate when the site was to be used for the Temple of Honour, with the Pontiffs declaring that burials must be removed: "for the college decided that a place which was public property could not receive a sacred character through rites performed by private citizens" (Cicero, *de Leg.* 2.23.58). Although the context of this example is very different, this incident provides a precedent for the removal of interred remains in order to reclaim a site and change its legal status. According to Robinson (1992: 126) "Marcian quotes a decree of the *divi fratres* forbidding disturbance of a corpse, but permitting the transfer of a coffin with its contents to some more convenient place if circumstances required." Although this belongs to a later period, together with the example provided by Cicero it suggests that such activities may have occurred in Republican Rome. A similar incident took place during the construction of the Basilica of St. Peter on the Vatican where it was necessary to level the cemetery on which the church was to be constructed. Toynbee and Ward Perkins (1956: 13) describe how "Constantine's builders took care to respect the dead themselves, carefully stacking in sarcophagi bones from those burials which they could not avoid disturbing." They suggest (*ibid.*: 12 – 13) that Constantine's position as *Pontifex Maximus* may have allowed him to circumvent the laws on *violatio sepulchri*, although the fact that the cemetery was largely pagan may also have been significant. However, a precedent for such action had been set several centuries earlier outside the Colline Gate and possibly also at the burial ground between the old and new Via Salaria which was probably covered by earth removed during the creation of Trajan's Forum (Robinson, 1992: 125).

If the authorities proceeded with a similar course of action on the Esquiline, either out of a desire to release it from its current legal status or in order to re-landscape the area, they may have completely emptied the land of burials. They would therefore have faced the problem of what to do with the disinterred remains and were probably faced with three options:

- rebury, burn or dump the remains elsewhere;
- rebury the remains using the ditch of the *agger*;
- rebury the remains in purpose-built/newly dug pits.

The regularity of the dimensions and structure of the *puticuli* may be explained by this process of clearance and reburial. Maecenas or the senate would certainly have had access to sufficient funds and labour to create these pits, in which the removed remains could have been reburied – rich alongside poor.

Other parallels

It is also important to note, in a critical discussion of the *puticuli* such as this, the existence of early modern

parallels for the use of communal graves in other periods and different parts of Europe and the ways in which this can aid interpretation of the Roman pits. For example, Ariès (1981) describes the communal graves of late-medieval France. The dimensions of these pits (**Table 10**) bear a striking similarity to those discovered by Lanciani, although appear to have been dug directly into the ground without any form of lining or support. Ariès (*ibid.*: 56 – 57) suggests that the use of these pits "... became habitual during the epidemics of plague that ravaged the towns," citing an occasion in October 1418:

> "according to the *Bourgeois de Paris*, 'so many people died in such a short space of time that it was necessary to dig pits, in each of which were placed thirty or forty persons, piled like bacon, with a few handfuls of dirt thrown on top.' It also speaks of big graves in which about six hundred persons were placed: 'They had to dig some more big pits, five at Les Innocents, four at la Trinité, and in other places.'"

These pits were clearly created as an emergency measure designed to cope with a sudden high demand for disposal, rather than an established type of burial. However, Ariès (*ibid.*: 64) suggests that eventually the pits, which seem to have been left open until filled to capacity, were "no longer reserved for times of high mortality. After the fifteenth century, and until the end of the eighteenth century, they were the usual place of burial for the poor and for those who died in modest circumstances" (*ibid.*: 57). This, however, cannot have been the case at Rome for the number of pits required to accommodate the dead of many centuries and such a vast population would have been enormous. There is also no suggestion that the French pits were ever constructed in the same complex manner as those of Rome, but appear to have been formed on the *ad hoc* basis that would be expected for such facilities.

Large communal burial pits existed in other early modern European cities, including London and Hamburg. The pit from London included within **Table 10** and dated to 1665, can be directly associated with the burial of plague victims, but non-epidemic related communal graves also existed in English urban churchyards. Gittings (1984: 61) has suggested that prior to the early eighteenth century, even the most miserable pauper, condemned criminal and epidemic victim could expect to be buried in accordance with the customary religious rituals, receiving a Christian burial often at the expense of the local parish. However, a population explosion during the early eighteenth century appears to have enforced a change of practice, with communal graves being increasingly employed in urban contexts. Gittings (*ibid.*: 63 – 64) provides the following quotation from a text written in 1721:

> "It is well known that several out-parishes ... are very much straitened for room to bury their dead; and that to remedy in part that inconvenience, they dig in their church yards or other annexed burial ground, large holes or pits in which they

put many of the bodies of those whose friends are not able to pay for better graves, and then those pits or holes (called the poor's holes) once opened are not covered till filled with dead bodies."

The creation of pits appears to have occurred primarily due to lack of space rather than an excessively large number of corpses, a situation that was largely due to the requirements of Christian burial within consecrated ground. Burial at Rome took place outside the city and was therefore comparatively free from such constraints, with space at less of a premium than in the crowded churchyards of early modern London. Gittings (*ibid.*: 64) also provides an account from 1774 which describes the burial of the poor in a churchyard in central London:

"The greatest evil is what is called parish or poor's graves: these are pits capable of holding three or four coffins abreast and about seven in depth; are always kept open till they are full, then the tops are covered over with earth; and another pit about the same size is dug on the side of it, leaving the sides of the former coffins always open."

Although the "poor's graves" could be extended, their individual capacity of approximately 28 coffins was considerably less than the 830 of the Roman *puticuli*, perhaps a reflection of a situation in which individual parishes were responsible for burial rather than the city as a whole. That these pits were commonly referred to as "poor's graves" indicates an association primarily with urban paupers rather than plague victims. However, it was noted in Chapter 1 that even the poorest members of early-modern society were anxious to provide decent burial for themselves and their family, often putting aside what little money they possessed for burial expenses, and Gittings (*ibid.*: 65) notes the existence of burial clubs designed to aid this process. As a result, even the "poor's graves" of eighteenth and nineteenth century London cannot be viewed as the last resting-place of *all* the humble members of society. They were probably used for the corpses of the desperately poor who were unable to provide burial for themselves.

This situation is paralleled in seventeenth and eighteenth century Hamburg, where an increase in population and consequent overcrowding of churchyards eventually led to the removal of burial to new cemeteries outside the city (Whaley, 1981: 104). Funerals in Hamburg during this period were lavish social affairs displaying the wealth and popularity of the deceased – not dissimilar to those of ancient Rome. Whaley (*ibid.*: 91) points out, however, that the really indigent were excluded from such social rituals: "the 'Nose-squeezer', a plain cramped box, deposited without ceremony in a communal grave, marked the end of many a miserable life on the margins of subsistence." However, he also observes that "the emphasis was on real indigence rather than mere poverty. The *Leichenbitter* often boasted that they provided their services free to the poorer sort" (*ibid.*: 91). A difference

can again be detected between levels of poverty, with only the corpses of the truly destitute finding their way into the anonymous common graves. During times of epidemic in London and Hamburg, other lowly members of society were probably also disposed of in this way, but in both cities it is evident that not all of the poor were regularly buried in mass graves.

These early modern parallels shed useful light on the situation in ancient Rome, especially given the perceived importance of decent burial and the social opportunities offered by the funerary ritual in both societies. The scale of the pits at Rome was evidently much greater – something that cannot simply be explained by the size of the urban population, but perhaps suggests that they were not designed to function primarily as mass graves. Smaller, more rapidly filled and sealed pits were clearly more suited to the purpose from both a practical and hygienic perspective. The processes surrounding communal graves are evidently more complex than has been assumed and the presence of a large pit should not necessarily be taken as indicative of indiscriminate dumping of all the poor members of society.

After the *puticuli*

In order to comprehensively assess the position of the Esquiline pits in the disposal practices of the Roman urban poor it is important to investigate the manner in which these remains might have been disposed of subsequent to the closure of the area during the late Republic. Bodel (2000: 133) notes the absence of references in the ancient sources to mass burial pits elsewhere in Rome during the early Imperial period,[111] an absence that is paralleled by a dearth of archaeological evidence for such pits, and he points out that not until the Christian period can similar features be identified (*ibid.*: 149, n. 4). Shaw (1996: 102) describes a series of pits (*pozzi*) in the Christian cemetery of Commodilla, each capable of containing approximately 50 corpses. It is unclear, however, whether these late Imperial *pozzi* represent the graves of the lower classes or those of plague victims. Either way, they were not constructed on the scale of the *puticuli* and were incapable of accommodating the vast number of poor corpses produced each year by the city.[112] There is no other archaeological or textual reference to communal graves in the vicinity of Rome, which points strongly towards the suggestion that the pits of the Esquiline fulfilled a specific role during a short period of time and were not established as the "normal" method of disposal for the lower classes of the urban community.

---

[111] It could be suggested that there is a lack of reference *anywhere*, for even Varro does not specifically mention "mass graves" and there is no current archaeological evidence for similar pits elsewhere in the Roman suburbs.

[112] The rise of Christianity and its resultant change of attitude towards burial may also be partly responsible for changing burial practices but the mechanisms for disposal of the indigent are unlikely to have altered significantly.

Bodel (2000: 133) postulates a shift from mass inhumation to mass cremation at public crematoria, where corpses were burnt on a communal pyre. He cites ancient literary texts as evidence for the use of public crematoria, including the remark of Martial (8.75.9 – 10), after his description of *vespillones* bearing a pauper's bier, that "the unlucky pyre receives a thousand such." He also draws attention to Plutarch's comment (*Quaest. Conv.* 3.4.2) that it was common practice to stack one female corpse with every ten male bodies on the pyre (Bodel, 2000: 133). He rejects the suggestion that such crematoria would be inefficient, pointing out that once burning the pyre would have reached a higher temperature and burned much faster than a single pyre (*ibid.*: 133). Kyle (1998: 169 – 170) disputes the claim, pointing out that although Martial refers to a *rogus* (funeral pyre) he may have been using the term figuratively. He also observes that the evidence for mass cremation of the poor is very limited (*ibid.*: 170). No site has been identified archaeologically that can be associated with cremation on a scale required to replace the *puticuli*. Cremation on such a large-scale would have required vast amounts of fuel at great expense in addition to a considerable degree of regulation to prevent the spread of fire. It is therefore unlikely that these services would have been provided free of charge as has been assumed for the *puticuli*. It is also interesting to note that the switch to cremation that this entailed would have occurred shortly before a more widespread change *from* cremation to inhumation. The absence of any direct replacement may be interpreted as evidence for the relative *unimportance* of the so-called *puticuli* within the wider burial practices of the urban poor at Rome.

The development and establishment of *columbaria* has also been attributed to the closure of the Esquiline pits (Davies, 1977: 17; Hopkins, 1983: 211 – 212). These tombs, capable of containing large numbers of cremated remains, began to emerge in the early Imperial period, indeed one of the first, dated probably between 55 and 35 BC, was constructed in the Esquiline cemetery itself. However, as Tupman (2002: 33) points out, such tombs are unlikely to have provided a solution to the problem of where to bury large numbers of the Roman lower classes. She notes the relatively small numbers of free men recorded on inscriptions from within *columbaria* in comparison to the large numbers of slaves and freedmen, and concludes that they do *not* represent the new resting-place for the free poor previously interred within communal graves (*ibid.*: 33). Furthermore, Purcell (1987: 39) suggests that "there are simply not enough *columbaria*, even though their chances of survival are excellent," and Heinzelmann (2001: 184) points out that most of the *columbaria* of Rome were erected by individuals for themselves and their dependants, with only a few built by *collegia* or other, freeborn, groups. If the *puticuli* were the burial places of members of society unable to afford proper burial, it is highly improbable that these same people would have been buried within *columbaria* within which they would have to purchase a burial niche *and* pay for cremation. If the Roman authorities did provide public crematoria where the indigent were cremated free of charge it is highly improbable that they would also have constructed substantial *columbaria* to receive the burnt remains when they could be disposed of with minimal expense and ceremony elsewhere, such as in simple graves or even the Tiber. *Columbaria* can therefore not be linked directly to the closure of the Esquiline pits.

Conclusions: mass graves?

It has been demonstrated here that the evidence for regular burial of the urban poor in large pits on the Esquiline is not as definitive as scholars have assumed. The data provided by Lanciani is not only limited by the manner in which it was collected and reported, but the heavy reliance on an ambiguous passage of Varro also renders his initial conclusions untenable. The Esquiline pits were incapable of coping with the long-term burial demands imposed by high levels of mortality at Rome, and can thus no longer be directly associated with the normal disposal practices of the lower classes. They also cannot be directly linked with the disposal of arena victims, executed criminals or large numbers of slaves as has often been suggested. The structure and dimensions of the *puticuli* allow various proposals to be made with regards to their intended function, including the possibility that they were constructed for industrial purposes or as part of a wider urban sanitary system that was supervised by the *aediles*. Alternatively, the need to reclaim the area of the Esquiline in order to create the *Horti Maecenati* during the late first century BC, may have forced the removal and subsequent symbolic reburial of any human remains (of all social classes) that had been interred within the region. It remains possible that the pits uncovered by Lanciani were closely associated with one of the many significant epidemics that ravaged the urban population during the late Republic, although it is currently not possible to assign them to a specific event.

All of these possibilities require further investigation in order for us to comprehensively understand the function and origin of the pits uncovered by Lanciani and the role that they placed within the wider disposal practices of the ancient city. However, for now, and for the purposes of this study, it is possible to conclude that although the corpses of the truly destitute who lived and died on the streets of Rome may have found their way into these vast pits alongside the general refuse of the city, it is highly unlikely that large numbers of the "ordinary poor" were buried in this way. There is no evidence to suggest that the urban poor regularly made use of mass burial pits and consequently the *puticuli* should no longer be described as the communal graves of the lower class inhabitants of Rome. However, in light of this conclusion, how, and where, were the remains of these people actually buried and what does the archaeological evidence for their disposal tell us about common attitudes to commemoration and proper burial?

CHAPTER FIVE

IDENTIFYING LOWER CLASS BURIAL PRACTICES IN ITALY

"Let the bawd's tomb be an old wine-jar with broken neck, and upon it, wild fig-tree, exert your might."

(Propertius, *Elegies* IV. 5. 75 - 76)

Continued interpretation of the *puticuli* as the common burial place of the urban poor is largely a result of the absence of alternative textual or archaeological evidence for the funerary practices of the lower classes, or at least few attempts to integrate the little evidence that does exist into existing dialogues. However, it has been shown here that the Esquiline pits were not designed as mass graves for the remains of the humble members of the urban community, and that these people were probably as eager to bury and commemorate the deceased as the more privileged members of society. Equally, features that might be comparable to the *puticuli* have not been identified at other Italian urban centres – a fact that implies the existence of other disposal mechanisms that were used by the poor. If, therefore, the *puticuli* were not regularly used for such purposes, it remains to be asked exactly where and how were the bodies of the poor buried, and what were the implications of these practices for the observance of commemorative and burial traditions?

Locating the poor in the cemeteries of Italy

Given the relatively limited evidence for these activities at Rome itself it becomes necessary to look a little further afield and examine this evidence in conjunction with the data that has been provided by various sites within the immediate vicinity of Rome and other urban areas in Italy **(Fig. 21)**. It is, of course, not possible to assume that cemeteries far from Rome necessarily reflect the type of activity that occurred at the capital. However, as we shall see, there are certain grave typologies, commemorative customs and burial activities that appear consistently at these sites that have also been attested at Rome. These provide us with an insight into the *type* of practices that were being employed by the urban poor. The sites that have been selected for discussion in this chapter are designed largely to provide as wide a range of well-excavated examples of these as possible. Clearly there was no other urban site in ancient Italy that was comparable to Rome in terms of size, demography, wealth or political importance (all of which probably played a big role in influencing burial practices) and it is therefore only natural that some differences will exist between locations. Nevertheless, there does appear to be

a remarkable degree of 'standardisation' across the sites examined. The first three sites discussed here are found at, or near, Rome itself and represent the evidence (often rather limited) that is currently available for poor burial in the capital.[113] The discussion which follows then turns to sites a little further afield, in both the immediate hinterland of Rome and northern-central Italy. These sites have been selected partly because they are representative of urban centres in Italy but also because they have been suitably excavated and published. Until recently many archaeological excavations tended to focus on the larger monumental structures of cemeteries but these examples, many from more recent excavations, provide enough information to allow us to comment on the funerary activities of the more humble city-dweller.[114]

The discussion which follows is far from comprehensive and is not intended to provide a detailed survey of *all* the Italian evidence for poor burial. It is designed, rather, to provide an insight into the types of burial and commemorative activity that was carried out by the urban poor; to identify common practices and highlight the relationship of these to the pressures, demands and fears that were examined in Chapters 1, 2 and 3. If, as I would suggest, the *puticuli* were not used for disposal, it is important that we investigate the evidence for alternative practices and suggest where we might start to look for this socio-economic group in the ancient cemetery.

The necropolis of Isola Sacra, Portus

The site and its excavation history

One of the sites that provides us with the most comprehensive range of data concerning lower class

---

[113] The term "available" is used here to mean published site reports and articles. The purpose of this study was not to scour the records of the Soprintendenza di Roma for all examples of poor burial, rather to provide a contrast to the *puticuli*. There are undoubtedly many unpublished examples of poor burials in the archives, particularly hidden in the notebooks of the excavators of the eighteenth and nineteenth centuries.

[114] See, for example, Floriani Squarciapino (1958) – a very detailed survey of the tomb architecture of the Ostian cemeteries that rarely mentions the *people* buried within them. Perhaps there were no humble burials within these cemeteries, or perhaps they were not actively looked for.

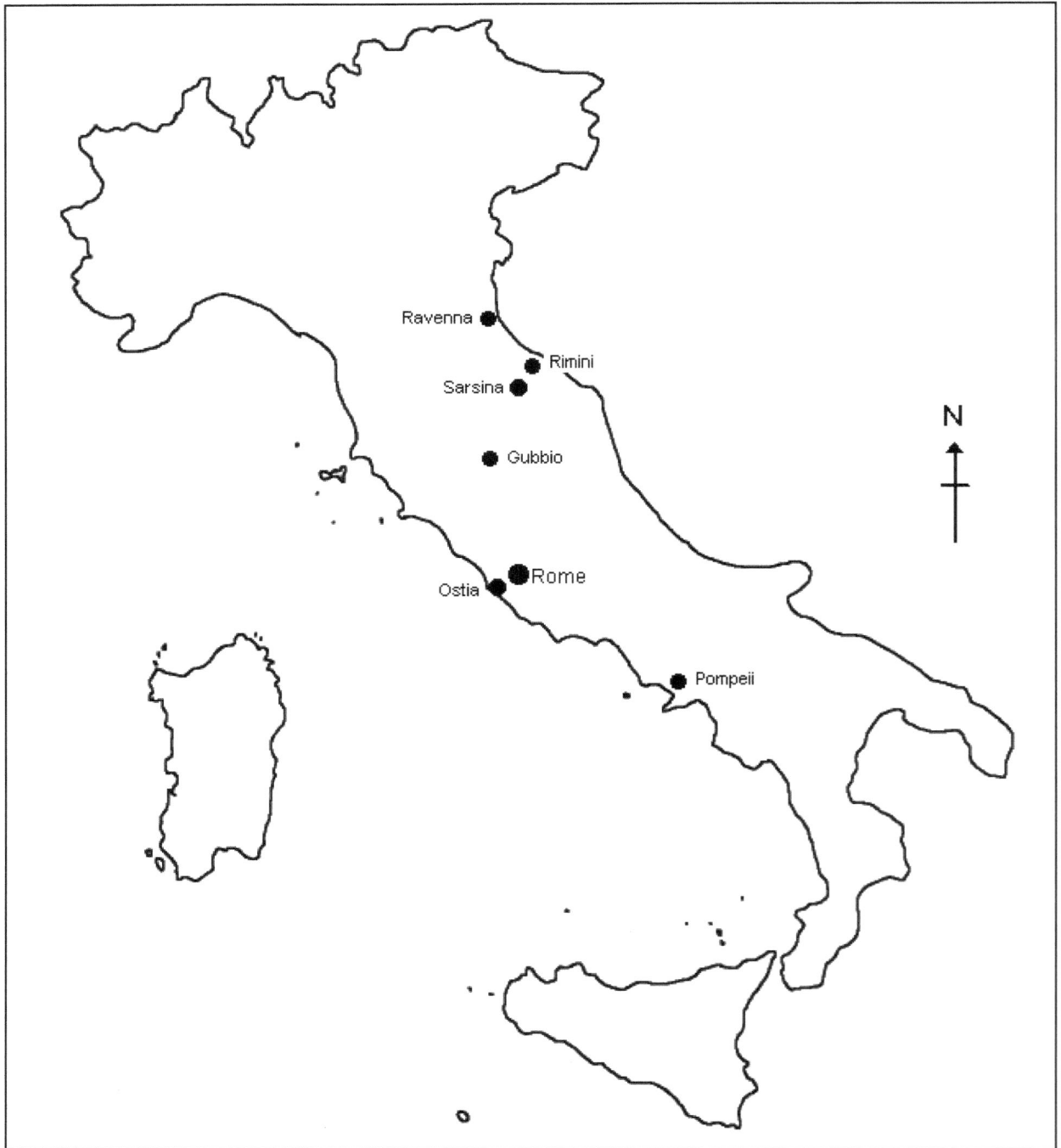

Figure 21. Map of Italy, showing the location of the main sites mentioned in the text.

Figure 22. House tombs at Isola Sacra (photo: author).

burial is Isola Sacra, near Portus and Ostia, the port towns of Rome. The necropolis of Isola Sacra, situated approximately 23km from Rome, can perhaps be considered representative of the type of urban cemetery that existed in the suburbs of the capital during the Imperial period.[115] In AD 103 a canal (the *Fossa Traiana*) was created in order to directly link the harbour town of *Portus Romae* with the Tiber and thus provide a direct communication and transport link with Rome. The new canal created an island between Portus and the other major port of Ostia, which was bounded to the north by the *fossa*, to the east and south by the Tiber and the sea to the west. Across this island, first referred to as 'Isola Sacra' by Procopius in the sixth century AD (*de bello gothico* 1. 26), ran a busy highway that linked Portus with Ostia, and along which was situated an extensive cemetery. The excavated section of this cemetery stretches for approximately 250m, although the discovery of outlying tombs suggests that it originally may have extended for at least 1.5km. Composed largely of tombs dated to AD 100 – 250, the site appears to have remained actively used until the fourth century.

The densest concentration of structures occupies the western side of the highway where tombs arise in rows that are roughly aligned with the main thoroughfare (**Fig. 23**). The mausolea take the form of brick-built barrel-

vaulted house tombs; their facades commonly crowned with a triangular pediment (**Fig. 22**). Above the low doorways an inscribed plaque was often inserted into the facade, occasionally flanked by two narrow slit windows. Some of the tombs are located within enclosures, many of which were apparently added subsequent to the construction of the main tomb structure, and others have masonry *biclinia* which flank the doorway and are associated with ovens and wells. The walls of the decorated tomb interiors are lined with niches for cremation urns, and *arcosolia* recesses, designed to accommodate inhumations, were later cut into the lower walls (see Baldassarre, 1987: 136 – 137). Similarly, *formae* were dug beneath the floors of existing tombs in order to receive inhumations as the latter became the more popular rite during the second and third centuries AD. In many instances this involved lifting and then replacing the mosaic floor of the tomb each time a deposition was made below. Libation conduits have also been identified in the floors of the tombs.

The epigraphic evidence associated with the monumental tombs reveals that they were built predominantly by freedmen for their families, friends, and their own freed slaves. Occupational reliefs, which were mounted on some of the tomb facades, depict these individuals participating in various occupations (**Fig. 24**). Unusually, the oldest tombs, dating from the late first century AD and the Hadrianic and Trajanic periods, were built furthest from the road with later structures occupying the spaces in front of them. Excavation has revealed however, that the tombs of the cemetery overlie earlier burials (see

---

[115] Obviously this cannot be stated with absolutely certainty but, as will be seen, other cemeteries at and around Rome contain the same type of features that are illustrated so well by the excellent preservation conditions at Isola Sacra.

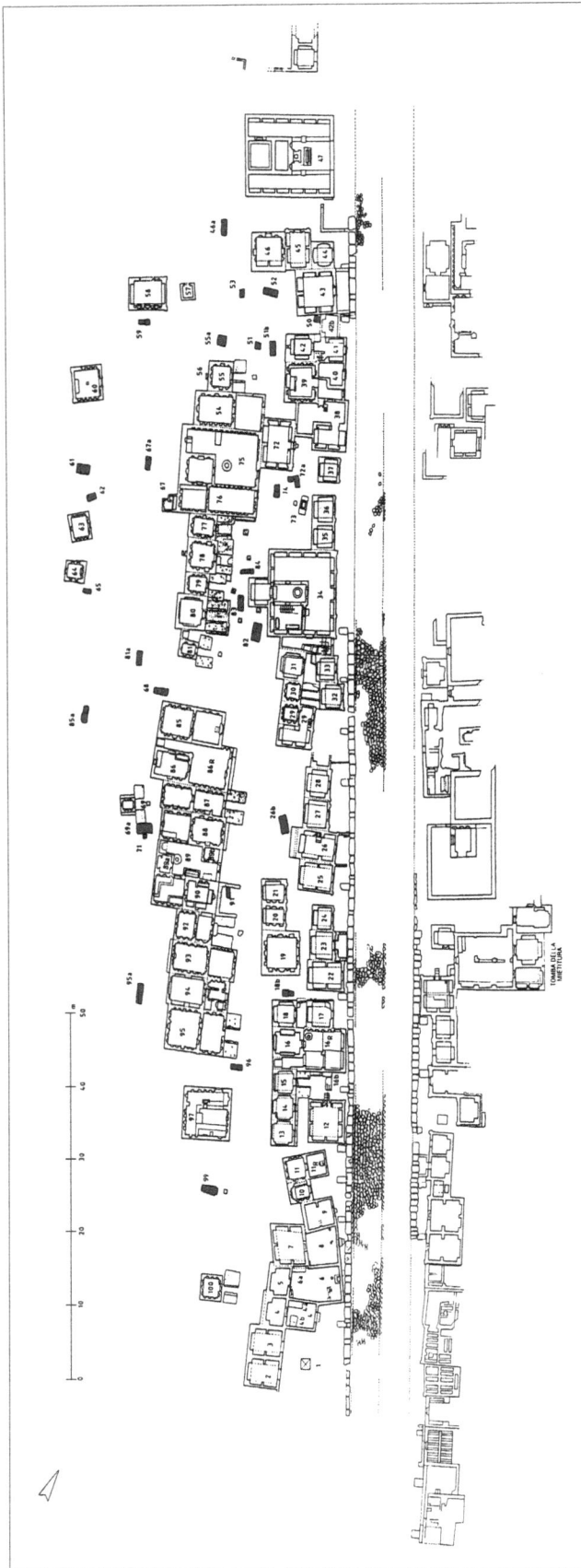

Figure 23. Plan of the necropolis of Isola Sacra. The cassone are shaded. (after Baldassarre *et al.*, 1996)

Figure 24. Tomb 78 with occupational reliefs mounted on the façade, Isola Sacra (photo: author).

Baldassarre *et al.*, 1985) and it is therefore possible to suggest that the site was in use for some time before the construction of the existing tombs. The Via Severiana existed as early as the beginning of the first century AD and may well have been used as a burial site from the start.

Evidence for poor burial

The cemetery of Isola Sacra was initially excavated between 1925 and 1940 by Guido Calza during which the majority of the extant monumental house tombs were uncovered. Calza described an area behind the main rows of house tombs, away from the road and free of monumental structures, as the "field of the poor" due to the presence of several more modest burials signalled by small masonry chests (cassone), tiles (cappuccina) and amphorae (Calza, 1940: 80). Calza (*ibid.*: 80) concluded that these "have to be considered as burials of the very poor" and the area in which they were found a space that had been specifically set apart for the lower classes (*ibid.*: 44 and 55). Further excavations at the site were conducted during the 1970s and 1980s by the Istituto di Archeologia dell'Università di Roma. The first of two major projects focused on the chronological development and structure of the monumental tombs. The second (1988 – 89) instead comprised an intensive investigation of the open spaces between and in front of the house tombs.

These extensive excavations revealed that the seemingly empty areas between the house tombs were also occupied by non-monumental burials, and they brought to light a further 627 examples (Angelucci, *et al.*, 1990) (**Fig. 25**). Investigation of these spaces has demonstrated conclusively that there was no segregation between social, legal or economic classes within the Isola Sacra

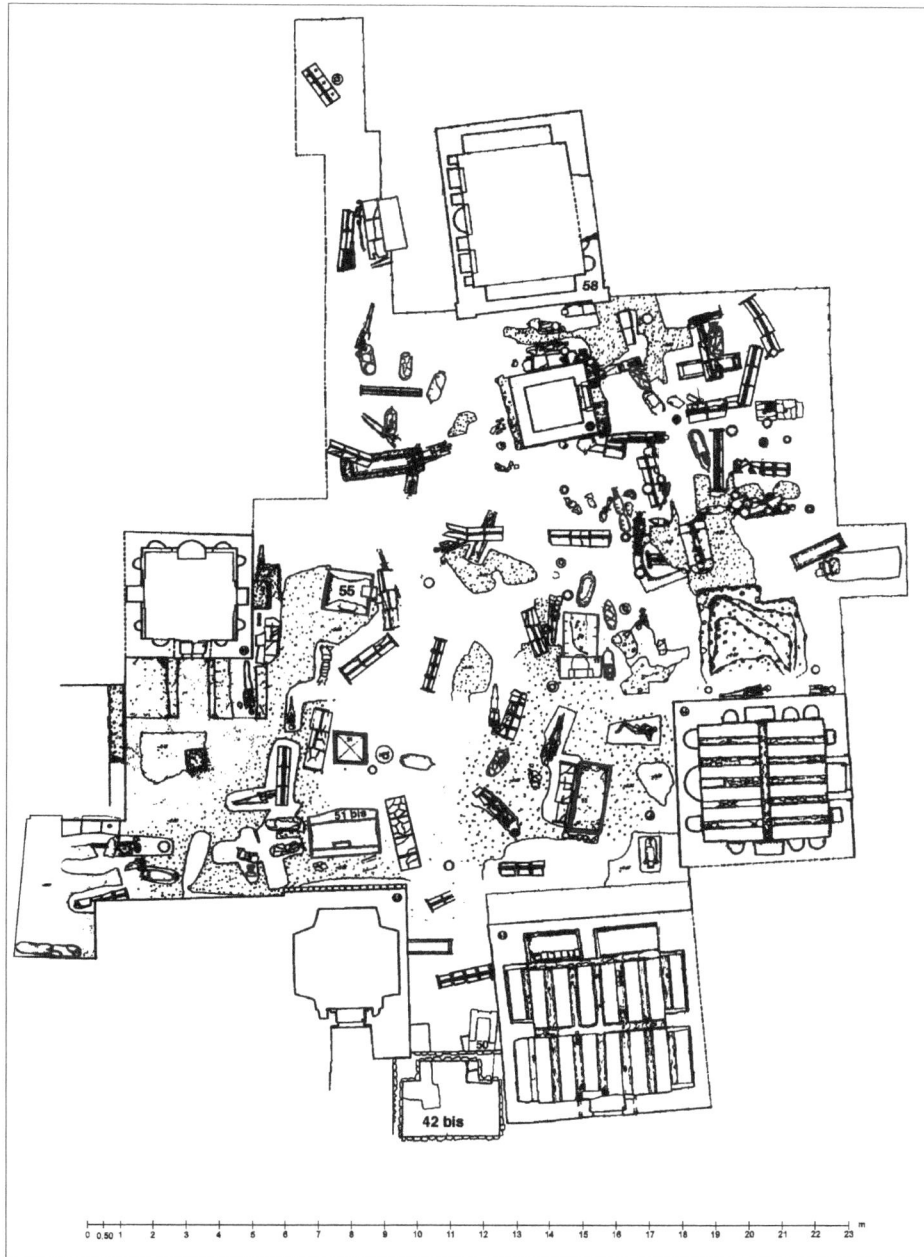

Figure 25. Plan showing some of the non-monumental burials recovered during the 1988 – 89 excavations of Isola Sacra, in the area outside Tombs 57, 58, 46, 43, 42 and 55
(after Baldassarre *et al.*, 1996 fig. 46).

cemetery. The 627 burials are not confined to specific areas, as Calza suggested, and they actually occupy *all* the free areas around the larger tombs. As a result, the common suggestion that the poor were separated in death from other members of the community in a so-called "potter's field" appears unfounded.[116] Amongst the most recently discovered burials there were 580

instances of inhumation. This may reflect the widespread dominance of the rite during the second century AD, perhaps also attested by the scarcity of *ustrinae* within the necropolis but may also reflect the continuing use of the less expensive rite of inhumation amongst the less wealthy members of society. Cremations are, however, also present amongst these humble graves, although only three take the form of *busta*. An examination of these graves and the form they take is particularly useful for understanding the burial activities of those at the lower end of the economic scale and allows us to investigate their responses to death and the desire to commemorate.

---

[116] Morris (1992: 45), for example, even goes as far as to suggest that "[t]he poor probably had separate cemeteries." Quite how this would have worked is unknown, as is why there would be a need to bury the poor elsewhere, away from the visible, busy cemeteries of the rest of the community. The price of burial plots may, however, have been a factor.

(a)

(b)

(c)

Figure 26. Cassone at Isola Sacra:
(a). Tomb 91 (b). Tomb 99 (c). Tomb 71
(photos: author).

Cassone

Within the Isola Sacra necropolis 43 examples of cassone (chest burials) have been identified. Measuring up to 1 metre in height and generally between 2.40 × 1.25m and 1.50 × 0.80m in size (Calza, 1940: 78), these take the form of semi-cylindrical masonry chests that were constructed directly on the ground above a deposition (**Fig. 26**). The depositions consist primarily of inhumations, although cremation urns have been found in association with some cassone (Angelucci *et al.*, 1990: 75 – 77). A thick layer of red plaster originally covered the cassone, which were also occasionally painted with green vegetation (Calza, 1940: 76; Baldassarre *et al.*, 1996: 21). Baldassarre *et al.* (1996: 21) propose that the painted vegetation was intended to evoke the image of a tumulus of earth covered with plants. Some of the cassone also appear to emulate the architecture of the larger red brick mausolea amongst which they are located. The barrel vaults of the cassone parallel those of their neighbours and the placement of an inscribed plaque on one of the shorter sides also mirrors the design of the house tombs. Furthermore, structures with a small triangular pediment and inscription are occasionally attached to the end of the cassone, often with a niche located below (*ibid.*: 21; Calza, 1940: 78) (**Fig. 26**). Such forms have led to the suggestion (Angelucci *et al.*, 1990: 71) that the cassone reflect abbreviated forms of house tombs and thus a shared ideology of display. This should not be surprising, for as we have seen already, the importance of commemoration and communication with the living was important to all members of the urban community, regardless of their wealth or status. However, despite structural similarities, the cassone were designed to accommodate only single depositions with the introduction of further remains necessitating significant modification of their structure.[117] They were therefore designed primarily as individual monuments, rather than as collective family tombs that were popular at the time. They perhaps, as a result, reflect a continuation of the ideals and practices of an earlier period when the individual was stressed rather than the group. Economic factors may also, however, have been influential.

---

[117] It is possible that some cassone were occasionally reopened, with the thick plaster reapplied to the exterior in order to conceal damage inflicted on the main structure in the process. In instances of cassone with small additional niches, original depositions could be made beneath the cassone with the niche providing the location for a future deposition.

The inscriptions which belong to these small monuments provide a small amount of information concerning the people with whom they were associated. Taglietti (2001: 155) observes that freedmen, slaves and a small number of freeborn individuals are documented among the dedicants of the cassone. This is relatively unsurprising given the predominance of freedmen within the inscriptions of the house tombs and aligns with the general belief that the population of Portus was composed largely of former slaves who were eager to capitalise on the commercial opportunities on offer in the port city (Prowse, et al., 2004: 260).

However, although the cassone are generally regarded as monuments related to the lower classes, it is evident that a degree of economic investment was involved in their construction and the term "the lower classes" may again be too broad. The cassone should therefore perhaps be considered indicative of the funerary monuments of the slightly less successful freedmen, slaves and freeborn individuals who occupied an economic level below that of those who owned the large house tombs; perhaps those that Garnsey (1998: 227; see Chapter 3) would define as the "temporary poor". These people were clearly incapable of affording the probably considerable expense of a house tomb but evidently wished to display their identity and success to other members of the community in a similar manner. They therefore drew on the iconography of the larger tombs in order to assert their place in the community of the cemetery. It is also possible that the designs painted on their surfaces were similar to those found in the interiors of the house tombs which are known to include floral motifs. These images would have acted to attract attention to the cassone, as well as to communicate certain information to onlookers. Indeed, it has been observed (Baldassarre, et al., 1996: 22; Angelucci et al., 1990: 82) that the cassone were primarily directed towards communication with the living rather than the protection of the remains of the dead, with the latter task often entrusted to other below ground structures such as terracotta sarcophagi and cappuccino which were buried below the cassone. The cassone then, despite their appearance, were not burial containers or a type of masonry sarcophagus, but they were commemorative monuments that were concerned with communication, display and social negotiation. The commemorative function of the cassone is further attested by the presence of libation conduits in the form of pipes or amphorae which indicate that those responsible for constructing the tombs intended to return regularly to the site in order to fulfil their ritual obligations.

Structures that are of similar form to the cassone of Isola Sacra have been found commonly in other coastal regions of the Mediterranean, including North Africa and Spain,[118] and examples have also been identified elsewhere in Italy (Angelucci, et al., 1990: 77; see also

the sites below). The presence of cassone at Isola Sacra is therefore fully coherent with the cosmopolitan nature of the community of Portus and Ostia which was in regular commercial contact with these other regions (ibid.: 77). The epigraphic data does not, however, indicate any direct association of these monuments with particular ethnic groups from any of these regions or elsewhere (ibid.: 77). The construction of the cassone appears to be more closely linked to social and economic factors, thus indicating that they perhaps represent the less commercially successful free population of Portus or Ostia.

Cappuccina

The cappuccina burials of Isola Sacra take the form of depositions covered by pairs of large tiles (tegulae) that were arranged gable-wise over the interred remains. The burials, sometimes placed on an artificial platform built of bricks or tiles, include both inhumations and cremations (Angelucci, et al., 1990: 83 – 84). Depositions were also sometimes placed within additional containers, including wooden coffins and terracotta sarcophagi, and the joints between the tiles were occasionally covered by pieces of cut pipe (ibid.: 84). The excavation photographs of Calza suggest that these simple structures originally stood above ground but it seems more likely that they were buried either completely or partially. Cappuccina burials occupy all of the spaces between the major tombs throughout the cemetery (**Fig. 25**) and on occasion a semicappuccina was constructed with tiles that were leant against one wall (usually the back or side) of a house tomb. The individuals who were buried within the semicappuccina may have been affiliated with the owner of the adjoining mausoleum, possibly as a slave or former slave. By physically joining their own tomb to that of their patron or master these people could claim association with that family. This may have been important for their sense of identity but may also have been linked to process of commemoration. When commemorative rituals, such as the pouring of libations, were carried out at the tomb on behalf of the *familia* who were buried there, the individuals whose remains were interred beneath the semicappuccina may have been included within the scope of these acts by virtue of the position of their graves. Libation pipes sunk into the floor of the house tombs seem to have served the needs of all those who were interred within the tomb itself, including those occupying niches or *arcosolia* in the walls which were not reached directly by the liquid offerings. It is therefore possible that these ritual activities also extended to external burials that made contact with the tomb structure. Angelucci *et al.* (1990: 66) suggest a more functional explanation, pointing out that burial in this way offered greater physical protection for the remains which were deposited below and reduced the chance that the tiles would be damaged or disturbed. Perhaps both factors were influential. The attitudes of the house tomb owners to encroachment upon their property remain unknown. They may have overlooked the presence of these burials given the positive effect it may have had on their public image

91

to have large numbers of people who wished to be associated with them.

The relative simplicity and inexpensive nature of the cappuccina and the materials used to create them seems to point towards an association with the lower classes. Tiles are unlikely to have been expensive in such small numbers and could probably have been salvaged quite easily from old or demolished buildings. The cappuccina clearly reflect a wish to protect the interred remains; something which is emphasised further by the use of coffins and other subterranean structures in conjunction with the cappuccina. These represent some additional expense and the use of terracotta sarcophagi, for example, may reflect a higher economic status. Despite this, however, there appears to have been little incentive or desire to externally advertise this economic status and the subterranean receptacles were directed primarily towards ensuring greater protection for the remains and were invisible on the surface. The cappuccina are completely devoid of inscriptions and thus communicate no direct information concerning those either interred or responsible for their construction. If they were originally buried beneath a mound however, their existence would have been made clear on the surface. The mound may have been adorned with some form of grave marker or other means of identification that no longer survives. The presence of grave markers in the necropolis is discussed further below.

These graves probably represent an economic and social level below that occupied by those who constructed cassone; perhaps those who were less able to secure regular employment. This therefore appears to reinforce the concept of varying levels of poverty that was outlined in Chapter 3. However, they also indicate a significant interest in the protection of the remains of the deceased and thus a degree of concern about the provision of proper burial.

Amphora burials

Two types of amphora burial have been identified at Isola Sacra. The first involved the direct deposition of the (usually cremated) remains of the deceased below an amphora, with its base cut or pierced, that was sunk vertically into the soil above it (Calza, 1940: 54) (**Fig. 27**). It is unclear from Calza's description whether the remains he uncovered below these amphorae were contained within urns, other receptacles such as bags, or deposited directly into the ground. The amphora itself served a double function, marking the position of the interred remains and acting as a libation conduit. The external body of the amphora may have been painted originally with the names of the deceased and other biographical information, although no evidence for this survives.

The vertical amphora burials again reflect an investment in burial and a concern for the welfare of the dead. The amphorae allow, and indeed are designed specifically to facilitate, the pouring of libations, and consequently

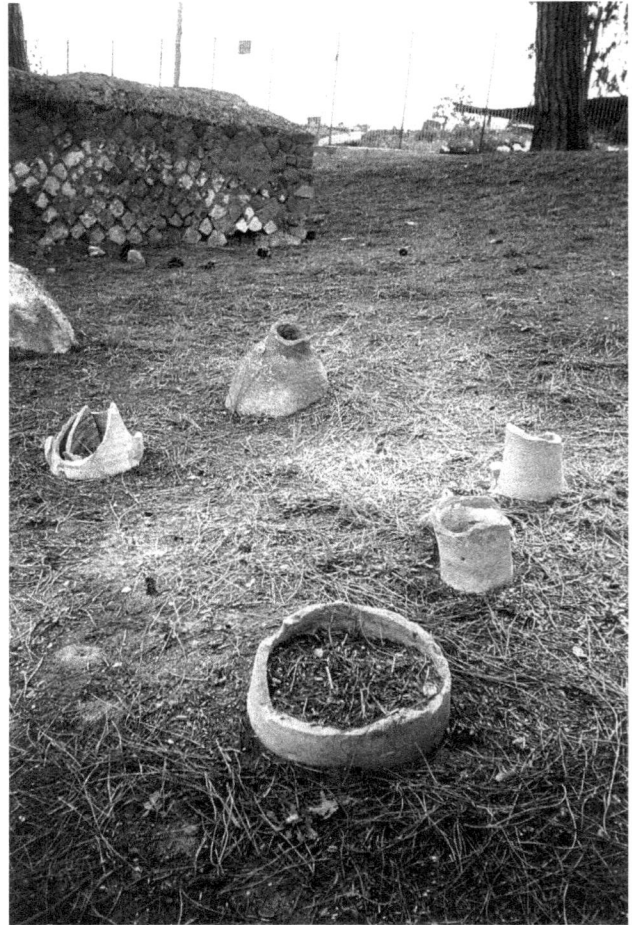

Figure 27. Vertical amphorae burials at Isola Sacra (photo: author).

indicate an intention on behalf of the mourners to return to the grave and perform ritual activities. In these cases the desire to protect the interred remains is often reduced to an above-ground signal of their presence with little evidence for subterranean physical protection, although it is possible that the remains were placed in receptacles. In economic terms these vertical amphora burials represent minimal investment since they required only an amphora that did not necessarily have to be completely intact and perhaps a simple container for the cremated remains.

The second type of amphora burial documented at Isola Sacra is more commonly associated with inhumation. For the burial of infants an amphora was split vertically into two sections and served as a receptacle for the body (Angelucci, *et al.*, 1990: 85). For adult burials several amphorae were required, often broken into several large fragments that allowed greater manipulation of the cover (*ibid*: 85). These ceramic covers were occasionally supplemented with fragments of brick, tile, stone and other pottery (*ibid*.: 86), indicating that any material that was available at the time of the burial was used in order to construct the grave. The horizontal amphora burials bear many similarities to the cappuccina in terms of providing a protective cover for the inhumed remains, but the use of old and broken amphorae and other

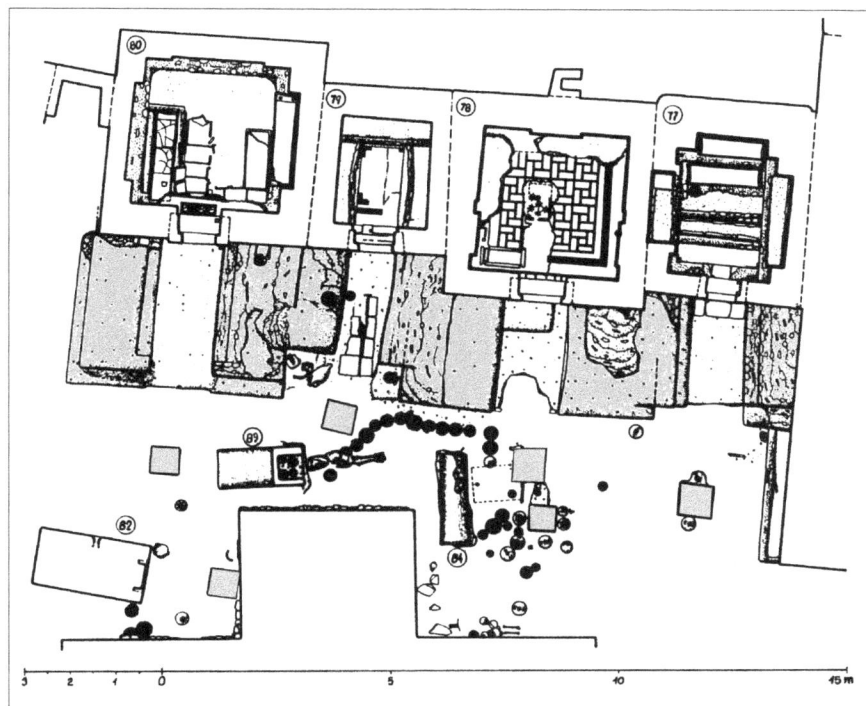

Figure 28. Plan of Tombs 80 – 77, Isola Sacra showing the clustering of amphorae burials around the permanent dining facilities of the tombs (shaded) (after Baldassarre *et al.*, 1996, fig. 31).

fragmentary material suggests that they were possibly less expensive. They were certainly less elaborate structures that were probably not intended to be seen. Toynbee (1971: 102) suggested that the amphora fragments projected above the surface, although this remains doubtful given that the various fragments were not cemented in position and could therefore be easily disturbed. Like the cappuccina, these burials were primarily concerned with the protection of the remains of the deceased rather than signalling the presence of a grave. Nevertheless, if they were fully buried as suggested for the cappuccina, a mound would have been formed on the surface which would have served to mark the location of the grave.

Excavations have revealed the presence of both types of amphora burial throughout the necropolis and identified an occasional clustering around the larger mausolea and their associated structures. For example, the small masonry blocks and dining facilities placed outside the tombs 80 – 77 are surrounded by amphora burials (Baldassarre *et al.*, 1985: 288) (**Fig. 28**).

Examination of the vessels used for both types of amphora burial has indicated that they do not correspond to a specific commercial activity but appear to have been selected largely on the basis of their physical properties. Thick-walled vessels were especially favoured (*ibid.*: 85); this again emphasises the existence of considerable concern for the protection of the body. Portus and Ostia were major commercial centres where complete and fragmentary vessels were probably available in large numbers. The artificial mound of Monte Testaccio, near the Aventine in Rome, illustrates the extent to which amphorae were discarded once they had fulfilled their original function. Reaching a maximum height of 35m and covering an area of 20,000 square metres Monte Testaccio is composed mainly of broken olive oil amphorae discarded between *c.* AD 140 and 250 (Mattingly and Aldrete, 2000: 148). Similar dumps of unwanted amphorae undoubtedly existed at other urban centres and access to these broken vessels may have been relatively straightforward. Mattingly and Aldrete (*ibid.*: 148) note that the inner surface of oil amphorae tended to absorb the oil, subsequently becoming rancid, and were thus often broken up and discarded once their contents had been removed. Although many of these fragments were probably abandoned at sites such as Monte Testaccio, others were certainly reused. Fragmentary amphorae were employed, for example, in the construction of the Castra Praetoria at Rome where they were placed one on top of the other separated by a layer of earth in order to form a damp-course, and in various other construction contexts throughout the Empire (Callender, 1965: 34 – 35). Intact oil amphorae may have been unsuitable for further storage or transportation of foodstuffs but they were occasionally employed in other contexts, for instance within the architecture of the Circus of Maxentius at Rome (Mattingly and Aldrete, 2000: 148). Other types of intact amphorae were used for secondary purposes elsewhere and Callender (1965: 30) observes that "[i]t appears to have been a fairly common and widespread practice to use empty amphorae as *pissoirs*. Their employment as such at Rome is mentioned by Macrobius (*Sat.* iii.16.5); at

Pompeii they were placed at street-corners and then removed full of urine for use by the fullers of the city." Amphorae employed in this capacity have been identified on Hadrian's Wall where they were also used to construct hearths (ibid.: 34). In addition, amphorae were used as planting pots at Pompeii, water-butts in Britain, and Seneca (Quaest. Nat. vi.19) speaks of their role as acoustic devices (ibid.: 36). Amphorae have also been found in burial contexts at Rome, for example in the Via Triumphalis necropolis that is discussed below.

The processes that were involved in acquiring previously used amphorae are largely unknown. It is likely that vessels which were broken and discarded, like those which form Monte Testaccio, could either be purchased at minimal expense or collected free from the place in which they had been abandoned. Complete amphorae, such as those required for vertical amphora burials, could be reused for a variety of purposes, including further storage or transportation, and were therefore probably sold second-hand at a reduced price by the merchants responsible for importing their original contents. Prices probably varied according to their condition and perhaps also their shape, with different forms and sizes being required for different purposes. The fact that approximately 53 million vessels could be accumulated at Monte Testaccio over a period of only 110 years (Mattingly and Aldrete, 2000: 148) throws some light on the vast number of amphorae that were in circulation throughout the Roman world. These vast quantities make it likely that second-hand fragments or intact containers could be obtained relatively easily and with little expense. The amphora graves of Isola Sacra therefore probably do not represent a major economic investment and may consequently belong to poorer members of the lower classes, perhaps those who occupied an economic level below that of those buried within cappuccina, or who, at the time of the burial found themselves in a precarious economic position and were unable to afford any other form of burial. It must be stressed, however, that even though these burials were of a less elaborate or impressive form than some of the others at Isola Sacra, such as the cassone, they were no less significant to the people who created them. They signify that they had performed their pious duty as mourners to provide the deceased with proper burial and show that they were concerned to mark the place where this had occurred in order to return to it and remember them. They certainly do not reflect a lesser degree of concern simply because they are less elaborate or expensive.

Other burials

According to Toynbee (1971: 101), "[t]he simplest tombs of the Roman world were holes in the ground, unadorned by any form of structure, in which were placed either the receptacle containing the deceased's burnt bones and ashes or his or her unburnt skeleton." Many burials of this type were uncovered during the course of the 1988 – 89 excavations at Isola Sacra (**Fig. 25**) and many more were probably removed or destroyed in the course of earliest investigations of the site (see Taglietti, 2001:

157). Amongst these graves were found examples of cremations and inhumations that had been placed directly into the ground without a receptacle, in terracotta sarcophagi typical of the mid-Imperial period and at least 6 wooden coffins (Angelucci, et al., 1990: 85). Nails and dark stains in the sand suggest the presence of further wooden receptacles. The recovery of coffins, preserved by the waterlogged conditions, is particularly significant given their rarity in other urban centres. They were evidently modest forms, especially compared with the sarcophagi, and the simplicity of their construction indicates a lack of specialist production (ibid.: 85).

Grave goods

During the investigation of the house tombs of the necropolis a widespread absence of grave goods was recorded and attributed to a general indifference toward the individual in the afterlife, and the transfer of the symbolic content of grave goods to the tomb as a whole (ibid.: 74). However, the phenomenon has been subsequently shown to be more widespread within the cemetery, with the newly discovered humble graves also lacking significant quantities of grave goods. Single coins were the most commonly attested item and were usually placed inside the mouth of the corpse, although one was identified in an orbital cavity and another in the hand of the deceased (ibid.: 74). These coins, ideologically associated with the need to pay a fare to cross the River Styx in the afterlife, further signal concerns for the fate of the deceased and a desire to provide them with an appropriate religious burial. Oil lamps were also deposited within graves, with one deposition accompanied by 5 individual lamps (ibid.: 74), but generally they contained few items. This parallels the situation recorded within the larger tombs and should therefore *not* be considered a sign of poverty but a conscious decision on the part of those responsible for burial and part of a wider societal trend.

Grave markers

Although a few stone stelae have been recovered from Isola Sacra the general absence of these elements does not indicate a lack of concern for commemoration. As noted above in Chapter 1, gravestones in the form of stelae are generally rare at Rome and in the surrounding area. The cassone certainly embody a strong desire for commemoration with the above ground structure concerned primarily with communication. In addition, the vertical amphora served a double function as both libation conduit and grave marker. Similar grave markers made of amphorae possibly existed above many of the other graves but may have been damaged, destroyed, or removed in order to improve access routes, since the open spaces in which they were located also functioned as pathways.[119] The same may be true of other, more

---

[119] The fragility of these markers is illustrated by the fact that although several vertical amphorae remained *in situ* after Calza excavated the site, many have subsequently been damaged or removed and continue to be damaged by visitors to the cemetery and the weather (see **Fig. 27**).

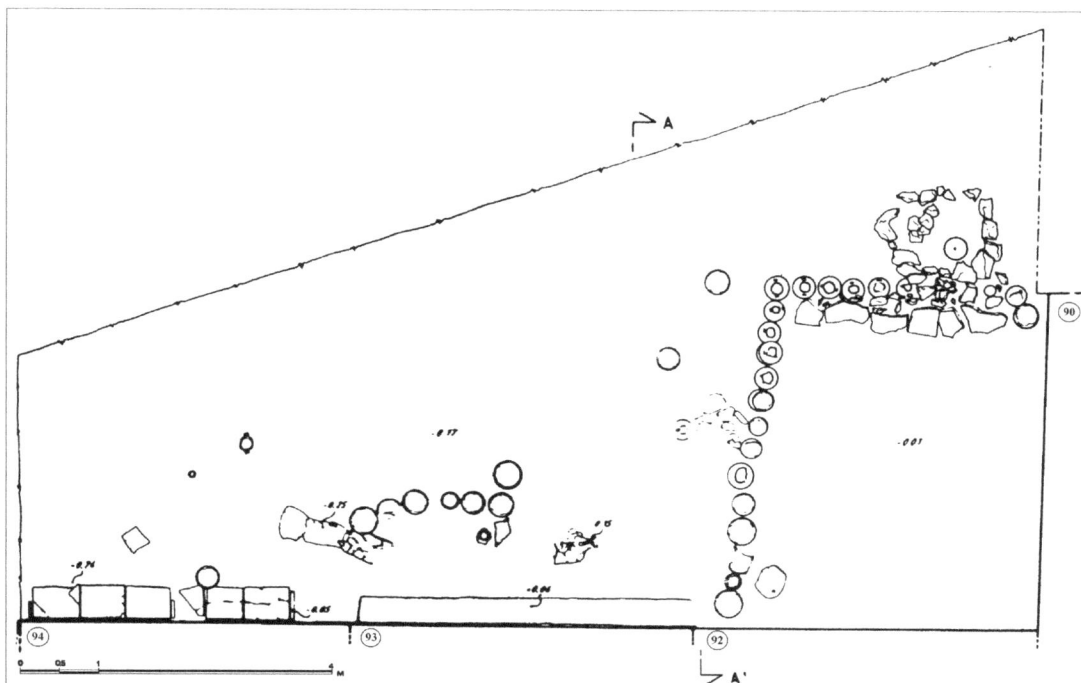

Figure 29. Plan of the area behind Tomb 92, Isola Sacra showing an area clearly delimited by vertical amphorae with an adjacent enclosure of flint flakes (after Angelucci *et al.,* 1990 fig. 6).

perishable, markers that may have taken the form of low tumuli, pots, urns, wooden markers, hedges or other plants.

One further indication that the most humble graves were probably marked on the surface is the remarkable absence of intercutting and disturbance within the cemetery, despite a large number of depositions within a restricted area (Angelucci, *et al.*, 1990: 57). **Figure 25** clearly illustrates the intensive occupation of space within the cemetery and strongly suggests that graves were distinguishable on the surface. It has been proposed (*ibid.*: 57) that perishable wooden enclosures or hedges may have defined specific areas, and formed 'family' groups or plots. Calza (1940: 80) also recorded the presence of vertical amphorae that had been arranged in groups of 4, 6 and 8 (**Fig. 28**). These may have defined a specific group of burials or an area belonging to a particular group of people. More permanent enclosures also existed, including that located behind Tombs 92 and 90, which comprised a continuous series of amphorae driven into the ground, supported by slivers of flint, that delimited an area that was approximately square (*ibid.*: 55 – 57) (**Fig. 29**). A total of 8 depositions were excavated within this enclosure, including 3 simple graves, 3 cappuccina, 1 semicappuccina and 1 terracotta sarcophagus. The enclosure, constructed from readily available, inexpensive materials, represents the intentional reservation of an area for use by a particular group of people. Unfortunately there is no epigraphic evidence associated with the enclosure to indicate who belonged to this distinct group. Was it perhaps a family, a group of friends, or slaves who were associated with one

of the adjacent tombs? There is no indication of who was considered eligible for burial within it and whether or not this was regulated in any way. It is possible that the land enclosed within it had been actually purchased by a group of people or donated to them as a distinct plot, although it may equally have been appropriated independently. It can be proposed, on the basis of the form of the enclosure and the burials within it, that these people were probably members of the poorer levels of society. The typology of the burials varies, perhaps indicating changing fortunes or the availability of different materials. This may also indicate that grave typology was unrelated to identity groups or ideological factors.

Adjacent to this enclosure was a second, within which an apparently unmarked cappuccina was signalled on the surface by an enclosure of large pieces of flint, within which was also located the cut base of an amphora (*ibid.*: 57) (**Fig. 29**). Similarly, a continuous line of 15 vertical amphorae emerges in front of the *biclinium* of tomb 78 and between tombs 83 and 84 (Baldassarre *et al.*, 1985: 288) (see **Fig. 28**). Taglietti (2001: 157) has suggested that these groupings, seemingly associated with the monumental structures, represent the graves of individuals with a relationship to the owners of the larger mausolea, possibly slaves, clients or friends. However, the extant house tomb inscriptions indicate that freedmen and slaves were usually granted permission to be buried within the tomb. Perhaps, for some unknown reason, these individuals were excluded from the family mausoleum and yet their sense of identity made them want to continue their association with the household after death. Perhaps there was simply no longer any space in the main tomb to accommodate new burials? Taglietti (*ibid.*: 157) also points out that these groups imply that the *locus religiosus* of the tomb was extended to include the area immediately outside the built structure itself. Perhaps these burials should be viewed instead as further attempts to benefit from the religious activities that occurred in and around the mausolea; something which was possibly influenced additionally by the extra physical protection offered by their proximity to the latter.

Discussion

The community who used the cemetery of Isola Sacra evidently employed a variety of different burial and commemorative methods, the form of which was perhaps closely linked to their economic status. There was a strong desire to protect the remains of the deceased and to ensure that they received the appropriate religious rites subsequent to the burial itself. Precise identification of these individuals is not possible given the absence of epigraphic data but these humble graves probably represent members of the free poor of Portus.[120]

At this point it is perhaps worth commenting upon the connections that have been made so far in this chapter between simple graves and the poor. It goes without saying that this is a dangerous connection to make. As Cannon (1989) has shown, commemorative practices appear to operate within cycles of emulation, with the increasingly elaborate customs of the elite being emulated by the less privileged members of society. As differences between the practices of the different classes begin to become less marked the commemorative activities of the elite gradually become less elaborate and increasingly internalised in order to set themselves apart once more. The assumption that 'simple = poor' is therefore not necessarily valid. These observations are important for understanding Roman burial and commemorative practice. Changing levels of exterior display and increased internalisation can be seen in the emergence of family tombs such as the house tombs of Isola Sacra, which are relatively uniform in terms of their exterior appearance. However, despite this, it must not be forgotten that economic status will still have played a major role in the choice of monument. To put it simply, not everyone could afford to a construct a tomb for themselves, their family and dependants. However, this does not mean that they did not want to and wouldn't if they had the opportunity.[121] As Chapter 3 has demonstrated, poverty is primarily an economic condition, not just a social and legal one. The urban poor of Rome and the cities of ancient Italy, and indeed the wider Empire, were restricted in the ways in which they could provide burial and a memorial for their dead family

and friends. It is therefore to be expected that some people were buried with simple, cheap materials. Many of us may feel uncomfortable making such a direct assumption that the simple graves of Isola Sacra represent the lower class population of Portus and Ostia, but when we look at what those with access to greater resources were doing at the same time, and the general trends that can be identified within society, it perhaps does not seem so dangerous a conclusion to make. These people were still burying their dead in the best way that they could – they were clearly concerned that the dead should receive a proper burial, should benefit from the appropriate ceremonial rites at different times of the year, and that the place where their remains lay be marked and remembered. Obviously if there remained any extant epigraphic information in conjunction with these burials it might be possible to examine more closely whether they were associated with different ethnic, social, legal or religious groups, although given the fact that enclosures such as that constructed behind Tombs 92 and 90 contained a variety of different grave typologies, it currently seems safe to conclude that economic factors were more significant. This group defined itself by the place of burial and association with other graves within that group, rather than the exterior appearance of their graves. This also appears to support the discussion of Chapter 3 where it became clear that the fortunes of members of the urban community rose and fell at different points in their lifetime and that access to financial resources was very unpredictable. The most important thing to note here is that these poor city-dwellers were actively choosing to bury their dead properly and to observe the appropriate religious and commemorative activities that were performed by the rest of the community. They certainly were not just abandoning the corpse to rot.

Despite the fact that burial at Isola Sacra occurred from the late first century AD onwards, the evidence that it offers concerning the burial of the poor may be relevant to a discussion of late Republican and early Imperial Rome. The harbour towns of Portus and Ostia offered cosmopolitan environments not dissimilar to that of Rome, and the necropolis therefore probably developed in a similar, if somewhat demographically reduced, context. Furthermore, the burials at Isola Sacra appear to represent well-established typologies since later tombs are found constructed over cappuccina, cassone and other graves that date to the early phases of the cemetery's use, perhaps even associated with the first harbour created by Claudius. Although the interior arrangement of the house tombs was altered to accommodate changing customs of burial, there does not appear to be any obvious change in custom amongst the poorer graves. The various forms of humble burial may reflect chronological changes or different ethnic or religious groups, although there is little evidence to support this, and the provisions for ceremonial activity appear to suggest close adherence to traditional Roman religious beliefs concerning burial rather than foreign influence. The predominance of amphorae within the cemetery may be partly explained by the association of the cemetery with the harbours of

---

[120] Some slaves may also have been included among their number, although this is impossible to verify.

[121] Of course, some individuals may have 'opted out' of traditional practices and chosen to be buried in a different manner. However, the large number of cappuccina, amphorae, cassone and other simple burials at Isola Sacra seems to suggest that these were considered 'normal' practice and were not representative of a different religious or philosophical outlook on life, death and commemoration.

Claudius and Trajan where such vessels would have been very readily available. But how does the evidence from Isola Sacra compare with other urban cemeteries at Rome itself? Two cemeteries on the Vatican hill provide comparative evidence.

The Vatican necropolis, Rome

The site and its excavation history

Ancient and modern development of the Roman suburbs has obliterated many of the cemeteries that once lay within them. Scattered individual tombs have been identified throughout the city suburbs but there exists little evidence for concentrated cemetery areas such as that of Isola Sacra or those immediately outside the city gates of Ostia and Pompeii. However, the construction of the Basilica of St. Peter on the Vatican has preserved a section of one such cemetery. Toynbee and Ward Perkins (1956: 5) describe the Vatican, in the northern part of the transtiberine region, as a "thoroughly suburban, not to say rural, district, noted for its clay, from which earthenware vessels and bricks were made…." Despite its almost rural character, the Vatican retained important links with the urban centre by virtue of the presence of several major monuments and parks in the region in addition to three major highways which passed through it: the Via Triumphalis, the Via Cornelia and the Via Aurelia (Basso, 1986: 7) .

Excavations beneath the Basilica of Saint Peter during the 1940s revealed part of a necropolis running for approximately 70m from east to west in alignment with the Via Cornelia which passed to the south (Zander, 2003: 3) (**Fig. 30**). Other tombs have subsequently been located further downhill in the area of the abandoned Circus of Nero. The cemetery, again composed primarily of house tombs, was constructed between AD 125 and the end of the second century, although it remained in use throughout the third and early fourth centuries (Toynbee and Ward Perkins, 1956: 28 - 33). Two rows of tombs have been identified but others, possibly built behind or in front of these, may have been destroyed during the construction of the Basilica or remain undiscovered beneath its foundations. The tombs are comparable to those of Isola Sacra and accommodate both inhumations and cremations, although those of the Vatican lack large enclosures and external *biclinia*, tending to have upper storeys instead - perhaps a result of the higher price of land at Rome (*ibid*.: 70). The interior of the Vatican tombs are more elaborately decorated than those of Isola Sacra and there is a distinct absence of occupational reliefs and few epigraphical references to the daily lives of the deceased. Based on the extant epigraphy however, Toynbee and Ward-Perkins (*ibid*.: 106) have suggested that "in the Vatican cemetery we are moving less in commercial and manufacturing circles than among the lower clerical and administrative grades of the public services." The community who erected these tombs was, however, composed largely of freedmen and freedwomen, and was very similar to that frequenting

Isola Sacra in terms of social, legal and economic status. What is more, this statement refers to the owners of the remaining house tombs, not necessarily to the other individuals and groups who used the necropolis.

Evidence for poor burial

Although Toynbee and Ward Perkins (*ibid*.: 36 – 37) suggest that most of the smaller and simpler burials of the cemetery were destroyed during the construction of the Basilica or by modern excavations which were focused on the more substantial tombs, the Vatican cemetery provides some evidence for the burial of the poor.

Cassone

The term cassone is not used directly by the excavators of the Vatican to describe any of the burials in the cemetery, but tombs of this type were certainly present. Toynbee and Ward Perkins (*ibid*.: 36) describe a "bench-like tomb of masonry with a semicircular coping which once spanned the corridor between [tombs] L and V, and another similar tomb at right-angles to it" (**Fig. 30**). These tombs appear to be of the cassone type and similar structures have been recorded elsewhere in the cemetery. The area known as Field P, for example, where Saint Peter is believed to have been interred in a simple poor grave (Zander, 2003: 58), appears to have remained largely free of substantial structures (**Fig. 31**). Several simple burials were recovered from this area including the grave of a child (Grave γ) which appears to have taken the form of a cassone:

"The terra-cotta coffin was protected above by pairs of large flat tiles, laid gable-wise, and for some two-thirds of its length, towards the head, it was encased within a rectangular mass of masonry, which housed a vertical tube for the pouring of libations to the dead beneath. The upper part of this masonry mass, which was faced in brick as a basis for marble veneer … was originally visible above ground …."

(Ibid.: 145)

Not only does this grave include a cappuccina structure comparable with those found at Isola Sacra, but the structure of Grave γ is also reminiscent of the cassone and is indicative of a desire to both protect and commemorate the deceased. It is quite possible that the terracotta coffin that was protected by the tile covering represents the initial burial with the cassone structure being built at a later date, perhaps when the family could afford the additional expense that it entailed. The sarcophagus was stamped and provides a date of AD 115 - 123 (Zander, 2003: 59). Grave η, also in Field P, consisted of "a chest, built up of tiles, which was protected above by a layer of mortared brick and rubble and the whole covered by a marble slab" (Toynbee and Ward Perkins, 1956: 146). This again appears to be a type of cassone, or at least a masonry structure designed to protect, cover and mark the interment.

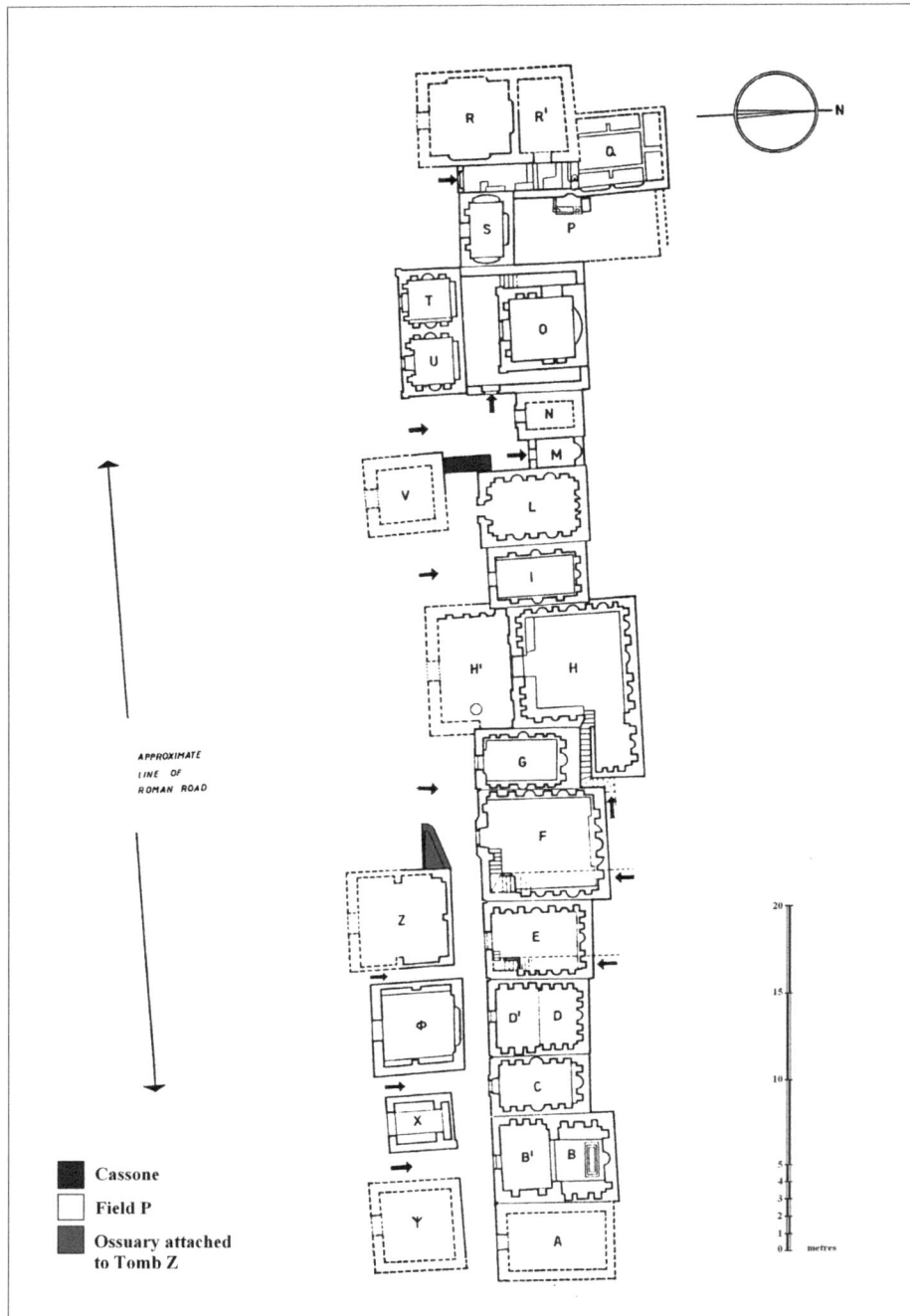

Figure 30. Plan of the Vatican necropolis, Rome
(after Toynbee and Ward Perkins, 1956 fig. 3).

Although the structure of these tombs varies they evidently correspond to the same general typology as those of Isola Sacra and they display a concern for protecting and commemorating the deceased – the presence of libation tubes indicates the performance of post-funeral activities. The absence of inscriptions, however, prevents further speculation on the nature of the social, legal or economic status of the deceased and their family.[122]

Cappuccina

In addition to the presence of cappuccina used in conjunction with cassone, graves of this type have also been identified within Field P. For example, in Grave θ, which lies slightly to the north-east of Grave γ, the body was deposited directly into the ground before being covered by pairs of tiles set gable-wise (*ibid.*: 146). One tile, which bears a makers stamp, indicates that the burial

---

[122] In the case of Grave γ it is probable that the family, rather than any form of burial association, was responsible for the burial because the

deceased was still a child. As noted above, only fully paid-up members of *collegia* were entitled to burial privileges.

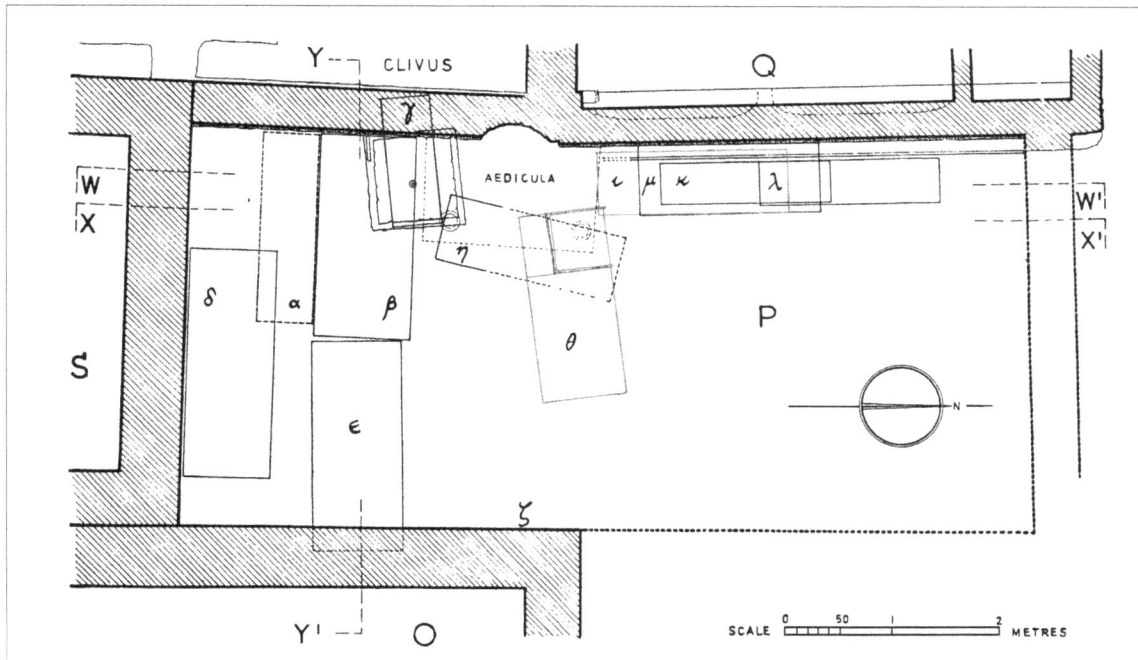

Figure 31. Field P, the Vatican necropolis (after Toynbee and Ward Perkins, 1956 fig. 11).

was not made before the reign of Vespasian (AD 69 – 79) (*ibid.*: 146). Burials ζ and ι, can also be identified as cappuccina graves of approximately the same date (*ibid.*: 146 – 147). The number of cappuccina is much reduced in comparison with those at Isola Sacra, although this can be partly explained by the limited extent of excavation within the open spaces of the cemetery and the restrictions that are imposed on further investigation by its location beneath the present basilica. The comparatively small area of Field P was nevertheless used quite intensively for simple burials and therefore suggests that other parts of the necropolis, including access routes, may have been used in the same way regardless of their size.

Other burials

Further non-monumental burials are attested in the cemetery within a small structure associated with Tomb Z (**Fig. 30**). Attached to the eastern side of the tomb is an irregular-shaped chest-like masonry structure which is contemporary with the building of the mausoleum and was filled with human bones (*ibid.*: 53). The structure appears to be pre-Constantinian in date, a fact that prevents any association with the clearance of the site immediately prior to the construction of the Basilica. As a result, "the probable inference is that these are the remains of earlier burials, found and carefully reburied when the tomb was built" (*ibid.*: 53). This discovery has consequently led to the proposal that the early Vatican cemetery was composed primarily of very modest burials that were gradually replaced by more substantial tombs (*ibid.*: 145); perhaps not dissimilar to the situation proposed for Isola Sacra. However, simple inhumation (and possibly cremation) burials probably continued to

occur within the cemetery subsequent to its development as attested in Field P.

Discussion

Several explanations can be offered for the notable absence of amphora burials within the Vatican necropolis. It is possible that grave markers or other above-ground indicators of the presence of burials, such as libation conduits, were removed during the construction of the Constantinian Basilica in order to provide or improve access to the site, or were simply destroyed during the process. It is also possible that relatively few amphora burials existed within the cemetery at any time. This might be a reflection of local taste and tradition or the availability of material. Cappuccina, and burials that incorporate bricks and tiles into their structure, seem to be more common within the cemetery than amphorae. This may reflect the nature of the environment in which it was located, since the Vatican was established as one of the major brick and ceramic production areas of Rome. Such noisy and noxious industrial activities were confined to the suburbs along with cemeteries. As a result, tiles and bricks may have been more readily available to the community who were making use of this necropolis than amphorae, which may have been more easily obtained in areas associated more closely with trade than industry. It is clear, however, that regardless of the details of their form, modest burials occupied the spaces between the tombs that were built on the Vatican and again represent varying social and economic levels. Indeed, Toynbee and Ward Perkins (*ibid.*: 145) suggest that this mixture of tombs and humble burials is "what one might expect to find on excavating any early-imperial Roman roadside cemetery."

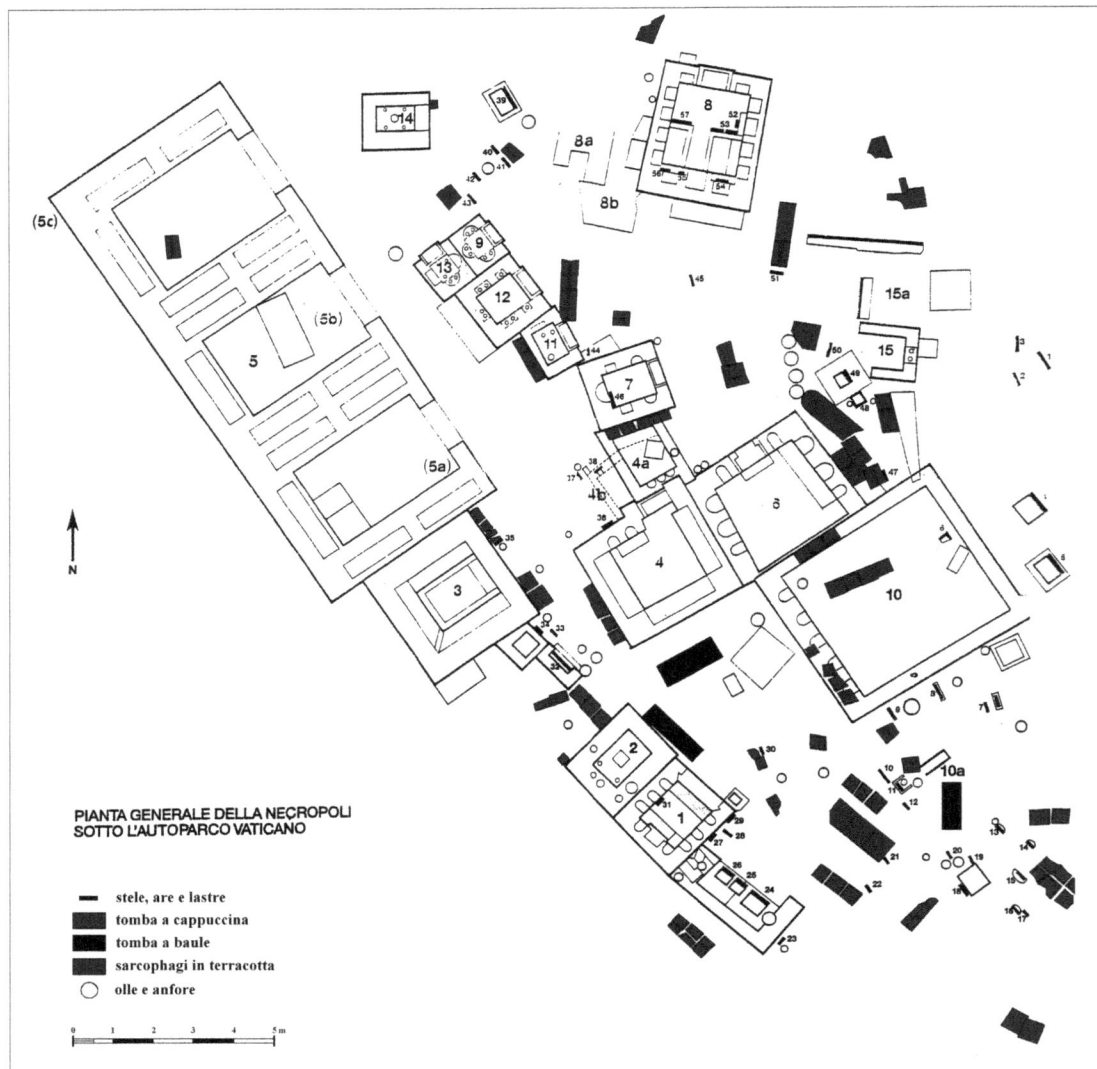

Figure 32. Plan of the Via Triumphalis cemetery, Rome (after Steinby, 1987 plan 1).

The Via Triumphalis, Rome

The site and excavation history

Another of the ancient highways which crossed the Vatican region was the Via Triumphalis, along the length of which have been identified several scattered tombs, *columbaria* and individual burials. During the construction of a new car park for the Vatican in 1956 part of a more concentrated necropolis was uncovered. Approximately 240m² of the cemetery was excavated under the direction of F. Magi in 1956 – 58 but it has never been comprehensively published (Steinby, 1987: 92).[123] The monumental tombs of the cemetery are

arranged in relation to two pathways which pass through the necropolis and which run parallel to the Via Triumphalis itself, but open areas also exist between them (**Fig. 32**). The tombs generally take the form of family *columbaria* and enclosures of the Neronian or Flavian periods. The architecture of these tombs is noticeably more modest than those of Isola Sacra or the Vatican. Freedmen and freedwomen are named in large numbers within the inscriptions recovered from the cemetery, as are slaves: a demography which is reminiscent of both Isola Sacra and the Vatican. The cemetery was primarily in use from the mid-first century AD to the early third century, during which time frequent landslides appear to have significantly altered its topography (*ibid.*: 104 – 105). Libation tubes are very much in evidence within the cemetery and although there are no *biclinia* or other permanent provisions for funerary dining rituals, these

---

[123] Steinby (1987: 92, n.47) points out that the documentation concerning these excavations consists only of a 59 page excavation journal and 453 accompanying photographs. Her discussion of the site is therefore based on an attempt to interpret these preliminary observations in conjunction with the photographic record. It is also observed (*ibid.*: 92, n. 47) that the excavation was not conducted stratigraphically, which can make it difficult to establish the

chronological relationships between the various elements of the cemetery.

presumably took place with the use of portable furniture and equipment in the open spaces around the tombs.

Evidence for poor burial

Cappuccina

Large numbers of cappuccina burials were excavated within the cemetery, in addition to several semicappuccina, such as those that were attached to Tombs 4 and 11 (**Fig. 32**). Steinby (*ibid.*: 95) proposes that these burials belong to the later phases of the cemetery (the late second century AD), when the mausolea had gone out of use. However, the same phenomenon is seen at Isola Sacra, where the tombs appear to have remained in use despite the presence of these graves. It is therefore possible that the semicappuccina of the Via Triumphalis reflect the same concerns proposed for those at Isola Sacra – greater protection, a relationship with the owner, or the extension of ritual activity.

Steinby (*ibid.*: 95; 108) observes that several stone stelae were found in direct association with cappuccina burials, pointing, for example, to stele NA 51 in the north eastern sector of the cemetery which was aligned with the end of a cappuccina (see **Fig. 32**). The dimensions of the burial plot provided by the inscribed text correspond to the dimensions of the cappuccina (*ibid.*: 95). This evidently signals access to greater financial resources than the structure of the cappuccina might suggest and indicates that there was a desire for permanent commemoration. What is more, it demonstrates that plots could probably be purchased on an individual basis. The cost of burial plots no doubt corresponded directly to their size, and one has to wonder if that on which a semicappuccina was built was cheaper still. Exactly who was responsible for the sale of plots is, however, unknown. Perhaps the owners of larger tombs sold land that was adjacent to them to individuals who wished to build a cappuccina or semicappuccina?

Amphora burials

Vertical amphorae have also been identified in the cemetery and Steinby (*ibid.*: 95) has suggested that these served as protective containers for the urns which held the cremated remains of the deceased, although only one urn containing ashes was recovered. Several of these amphorae were placed in front of, or clustered behind, free-standing stelae (*ibid.*: 96). For example, stele NA 50, erected by *Ti. Claudius Aug. L.* and his freeborn son to his wife (a freedwoman), can possibly be associated with the 5 amphorae aligned behind it (plus a sixth that was partially visible in the embankment) (*ibid.*: 94). This may represent a family group, with the amphorae protecting (in addition to marking, and facilitating libations) the cremated remains of the three named individuals in addition to other family members, slaves or freedmen. These 'family' plots are reminiscent of those postulated for the amphorae clusters found at Isola Sacra. Perhaps these too were once marked in some way, even if not

with inscribed stelae. Not all of the amphorae in the Via Triumphalis cemetery were associated with inscribed stone markers; a situation that Steinby (*ibid.*: 108) explains as the result of destruction or a lack of attention to proper documentation during the initial excavations. Alternatively, the amphorae themselves may have provided the only visible indication of the presence of a grave, again highlighting the presence of individuals with access to differing economic resources within the same necropolis.

Discussion

Cassone have not been specifically identified within the cemetery, although the "tomba a baule" shown on the plan (**Fig. 32**) may correspond to this type of burial.[124] The quantity of inscribed stelae within the Via Triumphalis cemetery indicates that many of those buried within it had greater access to the economic resources required for permanent commemoration than those of the other cemeteries discussed above. However, these resources evidently did not allow for the construction of a more substantial family mausoleum and the stelae may therefore signal the upper limit of their resources. Individuals buried within cappuccina or amphorae which were marked by stone stelae may have exhausted their financial resources on the purchase of a substantial marker, perhaps not erecting it for some considerable time after the burial. The stelae would have provided a 'permanent' memorial for the family even if not all of those buried in the associated plot were named on it – not unlike the inscriptions affixed to house tombs which perhaps named the owner and his immediate family but not all of the freedmen and slaves who were also entitled to burial within it. These people may have been named on the individual niches within the tomb and so perhaps the separate amphorae were also marked with personal information. The two types of burial therefore reflect the same ideals and practices. The presence of stelae in the Via Triumphalis necropolis may also be indicative of the slightly earlier date of the use of the site for burial than the other sites discussed here. The stelae, some of which contain portrait busts, seem to reflect the late Republican tradition amongst freedmen for funerary portrait reliefs and were no doubt viewed as rather outmoded and old fashioned by the period in which the Via Triumphalis seems to have been in use, beginning perhaps in the Neronian period. They do provide a good example, however, of the way in which freedmen were eager to associate themselves with traditional practices and perhaps continued these for longer than other members of society in order to exhibit their status and identity.

Steinby (*ibid.*: 109) proposes that the necropolis had "an air of poverty;" something that was emphasised particularly by the absence of a regular layout or

---

[124] Steinby does not provide specific details concerning this feature, although its designation as a "trunk tomb" (*tomba a baule*) hints at a relationship with cassone (chest tombs). The dimensions of these structures certainly seem comparable to those of Isola Sacra and the Vatican.

organised plan, the high number of small tombs and the modest artistic quality of their decoration and design. The cappuccina and amphora burials should also be included within this, for although some were associated with inscribed stelae, there remain many more that were unmarked by such elements (although may have originally has some form of perishable marker). Given the circumstances surrounding the original excavation, it is possible that many other non-monumental burials also once existed within the cemetery. However, despite the lack of more evidence, it is clear that the Via Triumphalis necropolis again illustrates the varying levels of poverty that existed within urban society and the various burial options that were available.[125]

* * * * *

Lower class burial in Italy

In order to place the data discussed above within its widest context and to investigate the extent of the evidence for humble burials and the grave typologies already identified, it is necessary to examine the evidence for poor burial that has been found at various other sites in Italy (see also **Table 11**). The nature and availability of the evidence for lower class funerary practices at the sites examined above has made it possible for them to be discussed in terms of grave typology, but due to limited evidence the following summary focuses on each site as a whole.

The Via Nomentana, near Rome

Immediately to the north-east of Rome, a short distance from the course of the Via Nomentana, lie three suburban cemeteries.[126] Dating to the Imperial period, the northern and southern cemeteries of the estate of Boccone D'Aste and one located a short distance along the road of Vigne Nouve, comprise approximately 137 individual graves (Filippis, 2001: 55). Included amongst these were isolated examples of *busta sepulchra* (4 in the southern cemetery), terracotta sarcophagi (3 in the northern

cemetery) and a single marble sarcophagus (northern cemetery), although the majority of burials were simple inhumations which were covered by a protective layer of tiles or bricks (*ibid*.: 58). De Filippis (*ibid*.: 58) has identified two types of tile cover amongst these – those which were raised up into cappuccina and others which were placed level with the top of the grave, noting that varying numbers of tiles (between 2 and 8) were employed in each case. Almost all of the materials used in the construction of the grave covers within these cemeteries, including the variety of broken ceramic vessels used to seal the covers, show traces of previous use, except for a handful of cappuccina in the southern cemetery which may have employed material that was purchased specifically for the purpose (*ibid*.: 58), or were perhaps yet to be used elsewhere. De Filippis (*ibid*.: 59) notes, for example, that 14 graves dated to the second century AD make use of ceramics and tiles that can be attributed to the Republic and that the 30 stamps found on tiles and bricks within the southern cemetery imply that material was recovered from a nearby villa originally built during the late Republic or early Imperial period. The reuse of readily available second-hand building material in this way parallels similar activity identified at Isola Sacra and suggests that grave cover typologies were dictated more by the availability of material than religious, ethnic or traditional customs.

It has also been observed (*ibid*.: 58) that although wooden coffins and other receptacles are rare in these cemeteries, the depositions were still made with considerable care. De Filippis (*ibid*.: 58) has identified at least two examples of graves that were furnished with small tufa 'pillows' and 15 instances in which the grave was cut in order to carefully accommodate the head of the deceased. He has also proposed (*ibid*.: 55) that the spatial organisation of the southern cemetery, the most densely occupied of the three (80 graves), and the use of similar grave typologies and materials, indicates the existence of distinguishable family groups; something that has also been observed at Rome and Isola Sacra. Agricultural activity has largely destroyed any above-ground grave markers that were present in the cemeteries although traces have been found of terracotta libation pipes that were positioned vertically above the head of the deceased in both the southern and northern cemeteries (*ibid*.: 60). Similarly, damage to the graves themselves has tended to destroy evidence for grave goods, although these appear to have been nevertheless generally scarce. Ceramic vessels were occasionally deposited within the graves, in addition to lamps, glass perfume vials, coins and nails. Despite the absence of grave goods within the burials, ceramic vessels have been found placed outside or on top of the tile cover of the grave, which provide further strong evidence for continued ritual activity once the grave had been sealed (*ibid*.: 60). De Filippis (*ibid*.: 60 – 61) concludes that the individuals who were interred within these cemeteries belonged to a relatively low socio-economic level, perhaps slaves or farmers, who were dedicated to the agricultural exploitation of the land on which they resided. The isolated examples of *busta* and terracotta or marble sarcophagi may represent members

---

[125] It is interesting to note here a short article by Sophie Arie published in *The Guardian* (Tuesday March 11th, 2003) in which it was reported that in the process of clearing space for a *new* car park for the Vatican, tombs and graves dating to the reign of Nero were discovered. Amongst these was "the tombstone of Nero's secretary, along with well-preserved urns and amphorae." This perhaps indicates that a particularly large area of the Vatican hill was used in Antiquity as a burial site and that there may have been more amphora burials than excavations in the region have previously recorded. I have been unable to locate any further details concerning the location or nature of these discoveries. Publication of these excavations will allow us to further our understanding of the burial activities that took place on the ancient Vatican before its transformation by Constantine.

[126] It might be argued that these sites, and several of the others discussed here, actually represent *rural* cemeteries as opposed to the obviously urban ones already discussed. However, they all lie within the immediate sphere of significant urban areas and can therefore be expected to reflect similar patterns of behaviour. These cemeteries, as we shall see, exhibit the same burial typologies and concerns for burial and commemoration as those more closely associated with Rome itself. It has already been noted that there existed no urban centre that was directly comparable with Rome and therefore we must examine smaller cities.

of the community who possessed a higher economic status or position within it (*ibid.*: 60).

Malafede-Fralana

A similar cemetery has been located in the area of Malafede-Fralana in the locality of Ostia. Believed to be associated with the late Republican-early Imperial villa of Fabius Cilo, this necropolis consists of 30 burials dating from the second to fourth century AD (Falzone, *et al.*, 2001: 129). Inhumation was clearly the dominant burial rite within this cemetery, although at least 9 cremation burials were present, including 3 *busta sepulchra* with clay-lined pits (*ibid.*: 129). The cremated remains of the latter were each protected by a cappuccina and provided with libation conduits made of various materials. At least 2 other cremation graves had cappuccina erected above them and a further 2 had tiles placed flat across of the top of the grave (*ibid.*: 129). Similar flat grave covers were employed for inhumation burials and several variants of cappuccina have also been identified, including those making use of *bipedales* and amphora fragments to cover and seal the joints between tiles (*ibid.*: 130). Only 3 instances of horizontal amphora burials have been located, each using fragments taken from different amphorae which were then placed side by side (*ibid.*: 130). This perhaps indicates that they were taken from a group of discarded and broken vessels. Although these burials have no grave goods, they have been dated to the second century AD onwards on the basis of the amphora types. The presence of African vessels of the third to fifth century AD indicates that these burials were amongst the last to made in the necropolis (*ibid.*: 313). Grave goods are scarce in general within the cemetery, with only 13 objects recovered, including oil lamps and small jugs containing coins or nails, which were usually placed at the feet of the deceased but sometimes deposited outside the cappuccina (*ibid.*: 131). The grave goods exhibit traces of use, thus indicating that they were not made specifically for funerary purposes. The cemetery was used primarily during the second century AD and sporadically during the third, by a community that appears to have been socially modest, probably the inhabitants of the nearby villa and other neighbouring residences (*ibid.*: 133).

Pianabella

The site of Pianabella also lies near to Ostia. Located to the south-east of the city, this region was employed as a necropolis for a considerable period of time, at least up to the fifth century AD (Carbonara, *et al.*, 2001: 139). Unlike the previous two examples however, this area was very closely connected with the urban centre itself, and lies close to the excavated cemetery of the Via Laurentina (see Floriani Squarciapino, 1958). The composition of the necropolis bears many similarities to the other cemeteries of Ostia (and, to an extent, Isola Sacra), and it contains several substantial structures. These are generally of the *columbarium*-type or open enclosures similar to those in the Via Laurentina and Porta Romana cemeteries at Ostia (Carbonara, *et al.*, 2001: 141).

Carbonara *et al.*, have examined two cemetery areas within this region, the first of which lies to the south-west of the modern cemetery of Pianabella and consists of at least 6 structures that were aligned with both a major road and an internal cemetery access route (*ibid.*: 140). Between the simple unroofed enclosures, which were built during the first century AD, were located isolated cassone, one of which contained the body of a child inhumed at the end of the first century AD and accompanied by 2 small common ware jugs and a libation conduit (*ibid.*: 141). Other cremation and inhumation graves have been identified within the open enclosures, including a cinerary urn fitted with a libation tube, a cremated neonate placed within an amphora and a cappuccina built above an adult inhumation (*ibid.*: 141). During the Imperial period the free spaces between the mausolea also become increasingly occupied by burials in earthen graves, semicappuccina, cappuccina and amphorae (*ibid.*: 141). In the second area of investigation, near to the Christian basilica of Pianabella, 15 structures of variable size were aligned with the edge of an ancient road. Behind these structures were built two plastered cassone with libation devices, each built over a cappuccina which protected the remains (1 inhumation, 1 cremation) (*ibid.*: 143 – 144).

It has been concluded that, although only partially excavated, the two burial areas reflect a community of mid or low social status (probably slaves and freedmen) where the rites of cremation and inhumation were used contemporaneously (*ibid.*: 148). This conclusion is based largely on the paucity of grave goods – a situation reflected by all the cemeteries discussed in this chapter. It can, however, be supported further by the grave typologies found within it.

Gubbio, Umbria

Similar cemeteries and grave typologies have also been identified further north of Rome. Cipollone (2002: 5) reports the discovery of two distinct burial sites (one of Republican date, the other Imperial) comprising 237 graves at Gubbio (Perugia) in Umbria. The graves were, "arranged in a regular manner and at times grouped inside an enclosure or marked by inscribed stelae and markers. There is evidence of both cremation – in pots and other vases or in pits – and burial – in graves, in "tombe alla cappuccina," in amphorae and in jars" (*ibid.*: 5). The arrangement of these graves, which respect the orientation of one another, suggests that many were originally recognisable on the surface, perhaps by the presence of a grave marker or libation device. This is also further suggested by the absence of intercutting or grave superimposition within the cemeteries, a fact that has led Cipollone (*ibid.*: 8) to propose that perishable materials such as fences or hedges may have once delimited burial plots.

The Imperial-period graves have been attributed to the first and second century AD, particularly between the Claudian and Antonine periods (*ibid.*: 10). Discovered amongst these graves were several cremation urns that

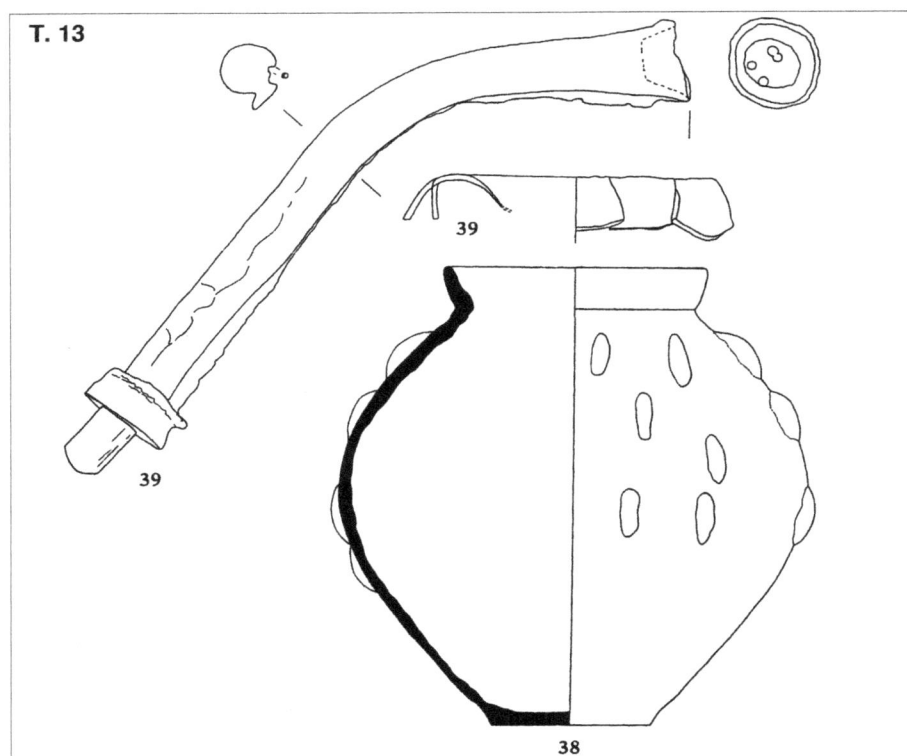

Figure 33. Cremation urn (38) and lead libation pipe and cover (39) of Tomb 13, Gubbio (after Cipollone, 2002, fig. 26).

had been deposited within stone-lined pits, occasionally also covered with fragments of tile. Examples were also identified of cremation urns that were sealed with lead that had been moulded around the rim of the vessel, often with an accompanying lead libation conduit (up to 50cm in length) inserted at the centre of the lid (**Fig. 33**). The cremation burials have been dated predominantly to the first and second centuries AD and the inhumation graves largely from the second century AD onwards. These were often made using wooden coffins or funerary stretchers (attested by a linear arrangement of nails on the base of the grave) that were placed directly into the grave and covered with a tile cappuccina. For example, three flat tiles, covered with a fine layer of soil, were arranged on the base of Tomb 89 prior to the deposition of the body, contained within a coffin or placed on a stretcher, which was in turn protected by a cappuccina of 5 fragmentary tiles and a re-used urn lid, with 2 further tiles used to seal the open ends of the structure (*ibid.*: 118). A significant amount of care to protect the body and to provide it with a proper burial that was unlikely to be disturbed, is evident in this example.[127] There was a limited range of grave goods within the cemetery, often restricted to a single deposit of an oil lamp, coin, glass vessel or ceramic cup.

Substantial mausolea are absent within the confines of this site but the cemetery nevertheless displays a considerable degree of variety amongst its simple graves. Libation conduits indicate that continued ritual activity was considered very important, and the design of the devices ensured that the offerings reached the remains of the deceased. The use of cappuccina, and in some cases the reinforcement of graves with tiles or stones, testifies to the care with which the dead were buried and a desire to protect the interred remains.

Emilia Romagna

Similar grave typologies are encountered in the modern Emilia Romagna region in the north-east of Italy, including both direct (*bustum*) and indirect cremations and inhumations that have been dated to the Imperial period (Ortalli, 2001: 228 – 229). Ortalli (*ibid.*: 229) has observed that protective structures were frequently built into the graves once the remains had been deposited. These often consist of inverted amphorae, bricks, cappuccina or tiles that were laid flat across the grave. Clear evidence for preparations for continued ritual activity again takes the form of libation devices. Ortalli (*ibid.*: 231 – 232) notes the use of vertical amphorae that were employed for this purpose and proposes that instances in which the base of the vessel was not pierced suggest that the custom of giving offerings may occasionally have assumed a purely symbolic nature. Examples of true libation devices in the form of cut amphorae inserted into the cappuccina or brick cover of graves have been recorded at Sarsina, Riccione and

---

[12] The presence of a thin layer of soil on the tiles at the bottom of the grave is intriguing. Does this perhaps reflect a desire to secure the structural stability of the grave whilst still ensuring that the body was entirely encased in earth? Or does it indicate that the grave was dug and left open for a short time before the burial was made?

Identifying Lower Class Burial Practices in Italy

Rimini, and lead pipes were fixed either into the tomb structure or directly into the ground in the Via Flaminia cemetery at Rimini (*ibid.*: 232). Traces of funerary meals (including animal bones) have also been identified in conjunction with graves, in addition to offerings of lamps and ceramic or glass vessels made after the grave was sealed (*ibid.*: 230 – 231), all of which demonstrates ongoing activity at the site of burial itself.

At Sarsina (ancient Sassina), within the Emilia Romagna region, two small burial areas have been identified immediately outside the hypothesised line of the city walls to the south and east of the urban area (Ortalli, 1987: 155). Both areas have been documented only by occasional discoveries but appear to have been composed largely of Imperial-period cappuccina without any significant monumental structures (*ibid.*: 155). Although it has been suggested that the location of these graves appears to exclude the presence of a *pomerium* (*ibid.*: 156), the same situation occurs at Pompeii where Mau (1899: 421) suggested that space in the public strip of land around the town might have been granted to the poor for burial purposes (see below). The main concentration of tombs at Sarsina, however, lies approximately 1km from the city at Pian di Bezzo, the flat plain bordering the river at the bottom of the valley, where an inscribed cippus of the mid first century BC was discovered (Ortalli, 1987: 157). The text of the cippus reports a donation made by Orations Balbus to the less well-off citizens of Sarsina providing each person with an area of land 10 feet square within which they were not permitted to raise monuments until the death of the addressee (CIL 1² 2123) (*ibid.*: 157). Ortalli (*ibid.*: 157) notes that this not only presupposes the existence and official recognition of a significant and definitive under-privileged class within the population of Sarsina during the late Republic, but also that wealthier members of the community carried out acts of benefaction. However, it is unlikely that *every* member of the city community was granted a burial plot,[128] and ancient concepts of 'poverty' and those worthy of charitable acts probably excluded those most in need of assistance. Furthermore, the dimensions and time restrictions imposed on the use of these plots indicate that they were intended to contain monuments of significant size and expense. The cappuccina adjacent to the city walls suggest that even when burial space was provided free of charge not everyone was capable of affording the construction of a substantial memorial within it. It is therefore likely that the "less well-off" intended by the inscription corresponded to ancient concepts of 'the poor' rather than socio-economic reality, and referred to the "less rich" members of the urban community at Sarsina.

Discussion

This brief examination of evidence for lower class burial activities elsewhere in Italy has highlighted the following:

	Cassone	Cappuccina	Vertical amphorae	Horizontal amphorae	Terracotta sarcophagi	Wooden coffins	Urns	Earthen graves	Busta sepulchra
Isola Sacra	•	•	•	•	•	•	•	•	•
Vatican	•	•			•				
Via Triumphalis		•	•		•		•		
Via Nomentana		•			•				•
Malafede-Fralana		•		•					•
Pianabella	•	•			•		•	•	
Gubbio		•			•	•	•	•	
Emilia Romagna		•	•	•				•	•
Sarsina		•							

Table 11. Summary of the grave typologies identified at the sites discussed in the text.

- Similar grave typologies were in use in all areas of Italy and do not appear to correspond to local customs[129] (see **Table 11**).
- The availability, accessibility and cost of materials seem to have often been the dominant factors in determining the typology of the grave's protective cover.
- Cremation and inhumation often coexisted without apparent religious or ethnic associations.
- Provision for ritual activities and offerings to the deceased were highly important and even once buried the deceased were not forgotten by their surviving friends and family.
- Protection of the remains of the dead and the provision of a proper burial were highly significant.

Although many of these sites were not purely urban in nature, they were all associated with local urban centres (Rome, Ostia, Gubbio, and Sarsina) and it is unlikely that considerable differences existed in terms of attitudes and burial traditions between the inhabitants of a city and its suburbs. The only real difference that existed between these sites and Rome itself was one of scale and the number of individuals who required disposal.

---

[128] We have to ask, for example, how long such a donation may have continued or whether it was a unique event, and exactly how eligibility for the grant was defined.

[129] Possibly with the exception of cassone, which are largely confined to the area of Rome and Ostia – although this can be explained largely by the fact that they appear to be a Mediterranean phenomenon and these port cities had more direct contact with North Africa and Spain than cities further from the coast.

Figure 34. Two of the small vessels with rough inscriptions from the San Cesareo vineyard that have been associated with the rite of *os resectum*, Rome (Museo Nazionale Romano) (photo: author).

Other poor burials?

The problems inherent in the archaeological identification of lower class burial activity can be illustrated by two further examples. Both instances involve apparently simple or modest burial and commemorative activities which on closer examination prove to be unrepresentative of the funerary practices of the lower classes.

San Cesareo and the Via Salaria, Rome[130]

In 1732 approximately 300 small ceramic pots were discovered in the vineyard of San Cesareo on the Via Appia, close to the ancient Porta Capena (**Fig. 34**). These vessels, which take the form of small single-handled pitchers (approximately 6-8cm in height), contained pieces of burnt bone. The body of each jug was inscribed or painted with a name and a specific date. These

inscriptions were generally made with a stylus and were very simple in form, for example:

A(ulus) A(elius) a(nte) d(iem) IV non(as) / Martias[131]

(CIL VI² 8217)

The commonware pots probably date to the second or first century BC and common interpretations of their contents and texts has focused on a probable connection with *os resectum*, also known as *os exceptum*. The rite of *os resectum* is generally believed to be closely linked with religious beliefs concerning proper burial, allowing the deceased to receive symbolic inhumation in instances where their remains were cremated. Varro (*L.L.* V. 23), Cicero (*De Leg.* II.xxii. 53 – 56), and Festus (*Frag. ex apogr.* LXII) refer (briefly) to the practice, which appears to have involved the severing of a bone, usually a finger, of the deceased prior to cremation for separate burial. Possible examples of this rite have been identified in Imperial Gaul, including at Civeux where an entire unburnt right foot and the toes of the left were deposited alongside an urn holding the cremated remains of the same individual (Simon-Hiernard, 1987: 93). Messineo (2001: 35) also reports the discovery of several small vessels in the cemetery on the Via Salaria at Rome. The lids and bodies of these vessels also bore inscribed names, accompanied occasionally by reference to a *cohors*. Carbonara *et al.* (2001: 147) note the presence of a single bone within an urn at Pianabella near Ostia.

---

[130] Since writing this section I have conducted extensive re-analysis of the literary texts and archaeological evidence for *os resectum* at Rome, including the remaining San Cesareo material, and it has become apparent that the custom was probably not linked to ideas about proper burial at all. It seems more likely, given the fact that Varro refers to the re-aining of bone in order to "purify the household" and the fact that the osteological remains from San Cesareo were burnt, that the rite was more closely associated with rituals of purification (during the *suffitio* ceremonies that followed the funeral) and the symbolic ending of the unclean mourning period. For details of this new interpretation see Graham (forthcoming a and b). However, despite this, the decision was made to include the original discussion of *os resectum* in this chapter in order to highlight the problems with its current interpretation and because it demonstrates particularly well how difficult it is to identify specific lower class practices and how we can not always assume that size is everything. See Becker (1988) for a rather inaccurate discussion of the San Cesareo vessels and their relationship to the rite of *os resectum*. Also Friggeri (2001), Messineo (1995, 1999 and 2001), and Simon-Hiernard (1987).

---

[131] Aulus Aetius, 4th March.

Varro (*L.L.* V. 23) explains that the process of *os resectum* was carried out in order to purify the family who otherwise must remain in mourning. It remains unclear, however, at which point of the funerary ceremony either the cutting or burial of the bone took place. Simon-Hiernard (1987: 93) has suggested that this took place on the day of the funeral as part of a single ceremony. However, Messineo (2001: 36) points out that Tibullus (I, III, 15 – 22), in his description of the collection of cremated remains and their subsequent interment, makes no reference to the specific selection of individual bones or a double burial involving the burnt and unburnt remains. What is more, the XII Tables expressly forbade the secondary burial of remains. In addition, the San Cesareo vessels are reported to have contained *burnt* bone, which perhaps implies that the severing of the bone occurred after or during the incineration process. The frequency with which this rite took place is also unknown, Messineo (2001: 36) has suggested that the few archaeological attestations and the scarcity of textual references to the process indicate that it was not very common, although in certain periods and perhaps under specific circumstances it may not have been unusual. He also proposes a link between the vessels of the Via Salaria and individuals who died away from home, pointing out that references to *cohors* may indicate a military context (*ibid.*: 37). However, as he subsequently notes, both these vessels and those from San Cesareo often bear female names and therefore cannot be exclusively connected with the military (*ibid.*: 37; see also Carroll, 2006). Moreover, the remains may have belonged to individuals who died in foreign lands and were returned to their families for burial, but this does not satisfactorily explain why they were all buried together, unless they had some form of personal or official relationship with one another during life. The names recorded on both sets of vessels recall those of the lower classes, including freedmen, slaves and freeborn individuals but it is unlikely that the remains of slaves would be regularly returned to Rome should they die elsewhere.

The frequency of these names has led to the association of the pots with lower class funerary practices (Friggeri, 2001: 67), but this assumption can be questioned on the grounds that cremation was an expensive activity, made considerably more complex by the need to remove a piece of bone at some point during the proceedings. It is possible that the individual bone was selected from amongst the least destroyed cremated remains once the pyre had been extinguished, although the frequency of finger bones in the San Cesareo pots certainly points towards the selection of a specific part of the body. The fate of the other cremated remains of the deceased is also unknown; Messineo (2001: 36) has observed that Plutarch (*Rom.* 79) explicitly states that the rite of double burial was reserved for heroes of the state. Furthermore, the scarcity of archaeological attestations of *os resectum* implies that it was not a regular part of every cremation and that burial of the ashes was usually considered sufficient guarantee of proper religious burial. Both the vessels of the cemetery on the Via Salaria and San

Cesareo were discovered amongst the remains of larger tombs, in the case of the former a first century AD *columbarium* (Messineo, 2001: 35). The relationship between the pots and the tombs is difficult to establish and it is unclear whether they originally occupied niches within them or were interred in the ground outside. If the vessels were directly associated with the tombs they may therefore represent the remains of members of an early *collegium* or large household with the rite of *os resectum* being specific to that particular group.

Although these pots evidently belong to ex-slaves, slaves and other members of the lower classes it cannot be concluded that this practice was restricted to the more humble levels of the urban community (see Graham forthcoming a and b). What is important to note here, is that the simplicity of the containers and their inscriptions mask what may have been a particularly complex, and possibly expensive, process.

Pompeii, Campania

Despite the excellent preservation of several Pompeian cemeteries,[132] there exists a surprising lack of evidence from the city for the presence of lower class burials. However, in the late nineteenth century, Mau (1899: 421) made the following observation:

> "No part of the highway leading from the Nola Gate has yet been excavated. In the year 1854, however, excavations were made for a short distance along the city wall near this gate, and thirty-six cinerary urns were found buried in the earth. In or near them were perfume vials of terra cotta with a few of glass. Here in the pomerium, the strip of land along the outside of the walls, which was left vacant for religious as well as practical reasons, the poor were permitted to bury the ashes of their dead without cost. In some cases the place of the urn was indicated by a bust stone; often the spot was kept in memory merely by cutting upon the outside of the city walls the name of the person whose ashes rested here."

Mau's claim that the poor were buried free of charge within the *pomerium* is interesting, especially given the parallels that can be drawn with the simple cappuccina graves located adjacent to the city walls at Sarsina. Maiuri (1929: 107) claimed that regulations concerning the use of the *pomerium* at Pompeii were greatly relaxed during the Imperial period and that houses and gardens were constructed within its limits. That this was, however, considered problematic is attested by a series of inscribed regulations erected outside several of the gates of the city (Porta Nocera, Porta Ercolana, Porta Vesuvio, Porta Marina), that bear the following text:

---

[132] For a variety of descriptions of these cemeteries and their monuments see Brion (1960), D'Ambrosio and De Caro (1987), Dyer (1875), Kockel (1983), and Maiuri (1929).

'By the authority of the Imperator Caesar Vespasian Augustus, Titus Suedius Clemens, tribune, made an inquiry into public lands appropriated by private individuals, carried out a survey, and restored then to the Pompeian state.'

(CIL X 1018)

One of these inscriptions remains *in situ* 29.35m outside the Porta Nocera (see Sertà, 2001 – 2002, and Cooley and Cooley, 2004), and its location at the furthest limit of the *pomerium* indicates that it was this strip of public land in particular that concerned the authorities. The area within the *pomerium* was evidently not intended to be used for private purposes but people had obviously begun to disregard this in order to construct houses and gardens in the empty spaces at the edge of the city. Tombs were probably also excluded from this area since burial of human remains rendered the ground no longer public but religious, although exceptions could presumably be made in instances where burial space within the *pomerium* was granted to individuals by the city authorities. The inscribed regulations cannot, however, have been in force for more than ten years (the survey was conducted under the authority of Vespasian and the city was destroyed in 79 AD) and it is therefore difficult to assess their true impact on activities within the *pomerium*.

Mau's observation also remains important as an illustration of the desire to record the name and existence of the deceased regardless of their status, as well as the transient nature of some forms of commemoration. The names inscribed upon the city wall seem to have been erased by exposure to the elements, something that would have occurred far earlier had the eruption of Vesuvius not preserved them.[133] This perhaps reflects the fate of other forms of "permanent" commemoration that were employed by the lower classes – their perishable nature rendering them vulnerable to destruction or decay. It also further illustrates the widespread exploitation of diverse materials for funerary purposes.

Since Mau's initial observations, the "bust stones" have been re-examined and reinterpreted. Known as *columellae*, these take the form of small stelae which resemble a human head, neck and upper torso (**Fig. 35**). Male and female *columellae* were often differentiated on the back of the head which was left smooth for males but often carved with various stylised hairstyles to represent females. Made of limestone, lava, local tufa and, in later periods, marble (De'Spagnolis, 2001: 176), the face, or more rarely the trunk, is often inscribed with a name although many were also anepigraphic. These *columellae* are found within a very restricted geographical region, comprising Pompeii, Nocera, Stabiae, Sorrento, Herculaneum and Sarno, and date from the second century BC to the time of the eruption in AD 79 (*ibid.*: 176).

Figure 35. *Columella* at Pompeii, Campania (photo: author).

Mau (1899: 421) interpreted these simple stelae as the commemorative monuments of the poor, given the simplicity of their design and inscription. However, recent excavations suggest that his interpretation is incorrect. Excavating the Porta Nocera cemetery, D'Ambrosio and De Caro (1987) uncovered several enclosure tombs containing *columellae*. Often the enclosures were defined only by the arrangement of *columellae* in an angular inverted U-shape (*ibid.*: 215)[134] and have been interpreted as belonging to family or household groups. The *columellae* record the names of both the enclosure owners and their freedmen and slaves (*ibid.*: 218). A further group of 11 *columellae* was revealed in the locality of Calcarella at Castellammare di Stabia, all but one (anepigraphic) of which bear inscriptions relating to freedmen/women and slaves of the *gens Poppaea* (Magalhaes, 1999: 224). The majority of the cippi were accompanied by simple burials (generally cremations) which were either contained within, or protected or marked by amphorae and other ceramic vessels, or small cappuccina. Libation conduits linked several of the burials with the surface and provide evidence for continued ritual activity. To the south-east of

[133] A search of the city walls immediately outside the Porta Nola failed to find any trace of these inscriptions and the bust stones have been removed.

[134] These may, of course, have been once bounded by a fence or hedge that no longer survives.

the main concentration of *columellae* lay a circle of limestone containing evidence of burning, interpreted as the remains of an *ustrinum* (*ibid*.: 231). These *columellae* clearly represent a distinct group of slaves and former slaves from a single *familia*. In addition, *columellae* were incorporated into the façades of the more elaborate tombs of Pompeii (Hope, 1997: 82) where they represent various significant members of the household and the family. It is therefore impossible to regard the *columellae* as grave markers that belonged exclusively to the lower classes. They formed part of a local commemorative tradition with strict geographical limits and Hope (*ibid*.: 83) states that "[a]s these stelae are generally of uniform size and shape, it seems unlikely that status and identity were stressed through design." This highlights the difficulties inherent in the identification of lower class burial activity and demonstrates that simple graves and grave markers do not necessarily reflect a low social, legal or economic status.

The relative absence of large numbers of lower class burials at Pompeii is intriguing. Although this lack of evidence may be attributable to the context in which many of the cemeteries of the city were excavated, it is unlikely that this is entirely responsible. Pompeii was a large, thriving city with a not inconsiderable population (estimates vary between 8,000 and 12,000 at the time of the eruption (Lazer, 1997)), not all of whom are represented within its cemeteries. It is possible that many of those who worked within Pompeii resided outside the city and were perhaps buried closer to their place of residence or traditional family home. There is little evidence for lower class housing at Pompeii, for example, and although it is probable that much of this existed in the upper storeys of buildings destroyed during the eruption there were evidently no major apartment blocks such as those of Ostia and Rome (see Robinson, 1997). Equally, it is conceivable that urban centres such as Pompeii simply did not have a considerable population of poverty stricken individuals. It is likely that the population density of the city was determined by its economy, with a limited number of opportunities for employment beyond established limits. Unemployment levels were probably low, and, although beggars and those at the lowest end of the economic scale undoubtedly existed, they may have been in the minority. Individuals finding themselves out of work may have moved elsewhere, possibly to Rome were there were believed to be greater and more varied employment opportunities. Rome was therefore likely to have had a larger population of unemployed individuals and casual or temporary workers than a smaller city such as Pompeii and thus greater levels of poverty. However, other small cities, such as Sarsina and Ostia, discussed above, *do* demonstrate evidence for the existence of a large lower class population, and it therefore seems unlikely that Pompeii would be any different. Perhaps the absence of burial evidence for this socio-economic group at Pompeii is more closely related to changing attitudes towards the use of cemetery space after its destruction and the absence of proper scientific excavation in the areas where we might expect to find these graves.

Conclusions

In Chapter 3 it was suggested that varying unstable levels of economic poverty, and consequently social status, existed within the urban lower classes. To an extent these differing degrees can be detected within the modest burials that have been discussed here. The diverse types of graves encountered (including cassone, cappuccina, vertical and horizontal amphorae, sarcophagi, earthen graves and *busta*) cannot, however, be directly equated with specific groups within the lower classes due to the absence of epigraphic data. The grave typologies appear to have been largely dictated by the availability of inexpensive building materials, and the characteristics of the grave may not necessarily be a direct reflection of the economic, legal or social status of the deceased. The cassone do, however, reflect a considerably greater financial investment and, as a result, can possibly be loosely associated with the "temporary poor", described by Garnsey (1998: 227) as "small shopkeepers and artisans, who enjoyed a somewhat higher social and economic status, but were liable to slip into poverty in times of shortage or at difficult points in their life cycles." This might explain their ability to afford a more substantial above-ground structure.

One of the most significant details to emerge from this discussion is the attention that was paid to the protection of buried remains, seen in the use of multiple containers, terracotta sarcophagi interred below cappuccina or cassone, and cremation urns placed within amphorae. This wish to ensure that the remains of the deceased were not disturbed may have been influenced, in part, by the location of these graves in highly frequented areas of the cemetery, but it also implies the existence of strongly held beliefs concerning proper religious burial. The poor were evidently affected by social and religious pressures, and their consequent demands for proper burial and commemoration, to the same extent as the rest of the urban population. The emphasis that has been placed on the *puticuli* in modern scholarly literature has created of an image of the poor as unconcerned with the fate of the body but the burials discussed here indicate that this was certainly not the case. These concerns extended also to ritual activities designed to care for the shade in the afterlife, and libation conduits are a common feature within all the cemeteries examined. The living evidently intended to return regularly to the grave and ensured that facilities were in place in order to assist the efficient observance of rituals. Permanent, or inscribing, forms of commemoration were also important, although substantial evidence for this does not often survive. Modest graves were probably signalled by above-ground markers of varying elaboration and different materials, including vertical amphorae which may have been painted with personal information. Perhaps most significantly, commemoration also occurred through the process of ritual activity and the regular visits made to the grave by surviving family and friends to make offerings.

CHAPTER SIX

CONCLUSION: REMEMBERING THE ANCIENT URBAN POOR

This study of the burial practices of the urban lower classes at Rome during the late Republic and the early Empire has attempted to examine this often neglected socio-economic group in the widest possible context, taking into account as many of the factors as possible that may have influenced their reactions to the demands posed by death. During the course of the discussion it has become clear that the poor were generally not unlike most other members of the urban community and that their attitudes to death were, unsurprisingly, also much the same. It was only their limited access to reliable and predictable economic resources that set this heterogeneous group of individuals apart and forced their material responses to the need for disposal and commemoration to take a different form. Even these, however, have been shown not to be radically different – the cassone of Isola Sacra for example, seem to reflect the same ideologies of display, protection and commemoration as the monumental house tombs which surround them. This final chapter summarises the conclusions that have been reached throughout the text and examines the implications that these may have on future studies of burial practices, cemetery topography and the lives and deaths of the urban lower classes.

Burying and remembering the urban poor

Most members of the Roman urban community, regardless of their wealth, rank or identity, evidently considered post-mortem commemoration to be an essential part of the funerary process and, particularly during the late Republic, acted on this belief in increasingly elaborate ways. Acts of commemoration, in any form, not only provided the deceased with immortality by preserving their memory in the face of the potential annihilation of the soul in the afterlife, but also operated amongst the living to establish, promote and negotiate the social position and identity of the dead and their surviving family. Through the public display of identity (and the so often related issue of wealth) the funerary monument acted to create and legitimise the identity of the deceased, whoever they were. The inherent instability of urban society during this period heightened the significance of these processes even further in the minds of individuals who possessed an uncertain or relatively new socio-legal status that might be vulnerable to challenge or change. It was the funerary monument that allowed these individuals or families to make public statements that affirmed their identity in a permanent and socially acceptable format. Of course, in reality these monuments, in whatever form they took, were not all permanent, as the ruined remains and fragments of tombs and monuments attest. Nevertheless, they were *believed* to represent lasting statements, and that was what was considered important.

The significance of these commemorative processes was certainly not confined to the wealthy but encompassed the entire socio-economic spectrum. Poorer members of the urban community were also affected by fears about the afterlife (or lack thereof) and experienced an equal desire for immortality as a consequence. They too wished to publicly display their identity and affirm their existence in the memories of the community. Although identity was frequently linked closely to related issues of social status and wealth, an absence of either did not decrease the desire of people to be seen to be a part of respectable Roman society and to have that fact publicly recognised and acknowledged. Occupational reliefs mounted on tomb facades and the frequent references that are made to occupation and commercial success in funerary inscriptions, for example, clearly demonstrate a powerful urge to display an identity that was centred on economic roles and success. Equally, commemoration and the desire to preserve memory were influenced by strong emotional forces which, although difficult to define, affected the lives of all members of the community and were particularly powerful on the occasion of death. Economic constraints may have compelled poorer members of society to express these emotions through more modest forms of memorial and funerary activities, but a simple memorial was not indicative of an absence of emotion, affection or grief. The act of memorialising itself signalled a significant amount of emotional investment.

The need to provide the remains of the dead with proper religious burial and the appropriate ceremonial rites was also highly influential in shaping the funerary activities of all social groups and became entangled with the already complex commemorative process. Religious beliefs concerning legitimate burial were based on traditional and firmly established customs and practices. The strength of these beliefs is illustrated by the persistence of the same ideas through time and the role that these played within established legal contexts. They were evidently taken very seriously. Members of the lower classes did not have radically different beliefs to those of the wealthy elite; this can be seen particularly well in the care and attention that was paid to burial and commemorative activities in the ancient cemeteries of Rome and Italy.

The funeral was also essential to the maintenance of an individual's social position and the expression of their identity, allowing direct communication with the populace. Although the funerary ceremonies of the poor were undoubtedly more modest than those of the aristocracy, the desire to partake in such activities and recognition that these occasions offered opportunities for personal advancement, legitimacy and immortality, was not diminished. The simplest funerary procession could provide the deceased with a degree of immortality, even if the image they created in the minds of onlookers was only fleeting, and could make public statements about their identity and the important relationships of their life.

Who were 'the poor'?

Contemporary views and opinions on the issue of 'poverty' and 'the poor' were varied and our knowledge of them is based primarily on literary stereotypes. Many have unfortunately been perpetuated by modern studies of Roman urban society, which tend to treat the lower classes as a relatively inconsequential part of the community whose attitudes and activities had little bearing on the direction of wider social trends and customs. The subject of poverty is fundamentally economic in nature, essentially involving the definition of a group of people on the basis of differences in wealth, and the extent to which our limited sources allow us to differentiate between these has been discussed at length in Chapter 3. Social status and identity are also integral to determining the composition of this social group, particularly in terms of their sense of individual and collective identity, but the basis of any definition of 'the poor' must focus primarily on economic resources and constraints.

The term 'poor', as it stands, has been shown to be too ambiguous to be of value to a study of urban society and an attempt has therefore been made here to provide a more comprehensive economic breakdown of what it meant to be 'poor' in ancient Rome. Analysis of the economic situation that was faced by the lower levels of society has shown that there existed varying fluid degrees of poverty that were subject to diverse financial pressures. The 'poor' were certainly not a single homogenous entity and can no longer be treated as such in discussions of the social strata of the Roman city. The absence of accurate evidence for income and expenses renders this investigation of the economic resources of the lower class population of Rome rather speculative, but it serves to adequately illustrate the precarious and varied nature of life at the lower end of the social scale. It also demonstrates that the fortunes, identities and status of these people were liable to unpredictable change (for better or worse) and that the opportunities that funerary activities offered for stability, expression and negotiation are therefore likely to have been considered important. Few other opportunities for public display were available to the poor that allowed them to register their existence in the communal consciousness. Death allowed them to take an active part in the same activities that were being performed by the more privileged members of the community and to do so in the same physical and religious environment. Although life was undoubtedly

hard and fortunes very uncertain, the desire to commemorate and, more importantly, to provide the remains of the deceased with a decent religious burial, remained very strong. Familiarity with death did not necessarily result in indifference; indeed this fact may have increased their awareness of the significance of funerary activities.

Was mass burial the answer?

The general absence of sepulchral monuments which commemorate members of the lower classes has often been equated with a lack of concern for the dead and consequently been used to interpret the *puticuli*. However, the evidence for the *puticuli* has been critically re-examined here and placed within its relevant social, legal, religious and economic context. During the course of this re-assessment, it has become evident that Lanciani's original conclusions concerning the purpose of the now infamous pits are seriously flawed. The evidence on which these were based has been shown to be inaccurate and heavily reliant on a rather ambiguous textual reference by Varro, which does not specifically state that *puticuli* were mass graves nor satisfactorily explain the mechanisms of disposal with which they may have been associated. New examination of the chronology, structure, dimensions, location, number and contents of the *puticuli* has also suggested that the long-standing interpretation of the pits as mass graves is incorrect. The corpses of the destitute, abandoned on the streets, may indeed have been thrown into these pits by the *aediles* (or more likely their 'staff') as part of their responsibilities for keeping the city streets free from refuse, but the *puticuli* do *not* represent the 'normal' graves of the urban poor as a whole. The pits uncovered by Lanciani may have been employed as a response to a unique event, perhaps a period of particularly high mortality brought on by one of the many epidemics that periodically struck the city. It is difficult, at present, to state unequivocally why, how and by whom the *puticuli* were created and used, but this re-assessment of the evidence for these features has highlighted the problems that exist with current interpretations. It is, however, possible to conclude that they were *not* employed as a regular form of disposal by the poor, as evidenced by, amongst other things, the rapidity with which they would have been filled and the absence of any direct replacement once the Esquiline was closed and re-landscaped.

Incorporating the poor within Roman cemeteries

It is evident from sites such as Isola Sacra and the other urban cemeteries examined in Chapter 5 that modest burials occurred within regular city cemeteries. Inexpensive and readily obtainable materials were used as grave markers as well as to form a variety of grave typologies, and close attention was paid to the physical protection and careful deposition of the remains. It is very likely that the majority of these graves represent the final resting places of the poorer city inhabitants. The urban poor were undeniably concerned with the provision of proper burial for their relatives and friends and, through repeated ritual activities including particularly the pouring of libations and the observance of specific funeral festivals, the commemorative process was actively continued after the funeral.[135]

It would therefore appear that the 'incorporating practices' of commemoration, defined by Connerton (1939) and discussed here in Chapter 1, took on a particular significance for the poorer members of the urban community. This is not to say, of course, that they were not also important to other members of that community, but for those who were unable to afford the considerable expense of the more traditional material accoutrements of commemoration, such as tombs and funerary monuments, repeated ritual activity provided a means by which they could actively participate in the same processes and celebrate the lives of their ancestors. Williams (2004: 52) has argued that "both during the funeral itself and in post-funerary rituals, remembrance can be manifest through the transformation, fragmentation, destruction and disposal of artefacts and the orientation and movement of the human body." It was therefore possible, through repeated ceremonial activities, to recall the rites that were performed during the original funeral and thus also the memory of the deceased, in order to celebrate their existence, identity and personal relationships. It was the process of experiencing these ritual acts on a regular basis that allowed the living to commemorate the dead and negotiate their own relationships with one another and society as a whole. As Barrett (1993: 237) suggested, "the material world makes sense when memories are recalled through experience."

Hope (2003: 117) has questioned the extent of "real remembering" that occurred during these graveside rituals, suggesting that they were "more about the present than the past; they brought people together and celebrated the ties between the living as much as ties between the living and the dead." However, this was an equally significant part of the commemorative process and the repeated observance of funerary rituals allowed the living relatives and friends of the deceased to negotiate and affirm their own identities within society and in relation to one another, whilst actively remembering the deceased. The funerary dining events that took place outside the tombs at Isola Sacra, for example, allowed individuals, families and other groups to make public statements about themselves, their relationships, their identity and status, and provide an opportunity for them to (re)negotiate their position within both the urban community and that of the cemetery itself (see Graham 2005b). These processes occurred amongst the families and friends of those who were buried within the more elaborate monuments of the cemetery, but may have also held particular significance to groups who did not possess substantial visual reminders of the identity of the deceased. It is therefore not possible to differentiate

between the activities and attitudes of the lower and upper classes; the latter were simply able to produce more elaborate, substantial and, importantly, lasting memorials to their existence. These monuments were, however, only one of the many ways in which the dead could be commemorated and their memory perpetuated. Cicero himself commented on this fact when he wrote: "what do the procreation of children, the propagation of the name, the adoption of sons, the care taken about wills, the very burial monuments and epitaphs mean, if not that we also think about the future?" (*Tusc. Disp.* 1.31). There were evidently a great many ways in which to remember and celebrate the dead, and such remembrance was a continuous, everyday process. We should not view the funerary monument as the pinnacle of the commemorative process, but simply as one means amongst many by which the living maintained the memory of the dead. Doing so allows us to include the poor city-dweller in our dialogues on life and death in the ancient city and to make our discussions of these activities more comprehensive in their scope.

A missing community

One issue, however, requires further explanation. The humble burials discussed in Chapter 5 belong predominantly to the Imperial period, particularly from the late first century AD onwards. Furthermore, many of these relatively late graves were dug in cemeteries in which the monumental structures had been established much earlier. For example, at Sarsina, the anonymous cappuccina burials of both the Pian di Bezzo cemetery and the small concentrations of graves immediately outside the city walls date to the first century AD, despite the fact that construction of monumental tombs began in the area during the late Republic (Ortalli, 1987: 161 – 163). It is important that we investigate briefly some of the potential reasons for this chronological delay. Since the *puticuli* have been shown to be unconnected with normal disposal practices amongst the lower classes, it is unnecessary to attempt to explain the time gap that existed between the pits and the emergence of cappuccina, amphora burials and other modest grave types. As Chapter 4 has demonstrated, there was no response to the closure of the pits because they were not established as part of normal practice. However, the reasons for the absence of these humble graves in the urban cemeteries of Italy during the late Republic and the sudden visibility of such features during the Imperial period must be examined in order for us to understand their significance within wider lower class funerary practices. In simple terms, where were the lower classes buried during these earlier periods and why do we only find evidence for them, albeit limited, in later cemeteries?

A possible explanation for the comparatively late emergence of these graves may lie within wider burial trends. Heinzelmann (2001: 181 – 182), examining the place of the *familia* within funerary practices, observes that during the late Republic competition between wealthy members of urban society led to the creation of increasingly elaborate tombs that emphasised the

---

[135] Although it remains possible that other activities also occurred without leaving physical evidence in the form of related equipment and permanent facilities.

individuality of the owner (see discussion in Chapter 1). These structures, such as the pyramid of Cestius or the tomb of Eurysaces the baker, were designed to be used on a single occasion and were sealed once the remains of the owner had been interred within them. Few facilities appear to have been provided for libations or other funerary rituals in this period (*ibid.*: 182).[136] Heinzelmann (*ibid.*: 183 – 186) has noted that this situation altered during the Augustan period when new tombs were built in order to accommodate members of the *familia*. Although several tombs of earlier periods had provided burial space for these individuals, for example those at Porta Romana (Ostia) where simple burials were made inside family enclosures, these graves remained anonymous (*ibid.*: 183). The new tombs, in the form of *columbarium*-type mausolea, provided burial for all members of the *familia* in ash urn niches accompanied by inscriptions or name plaques which rendered the dead identifiable (*ibid.*: 187). Heinzelmann (*ibid.*: 186) suggests that these tombs adopted a new quality as places for social interaction where funerary rituals, banquets and other activities took place. *Triclinia*, wells and hearths were installed to facilitate these events and libation conduits were provided in order to make offerings directly to the dead (*ibid.*: 185). The tomb owners retained their position of importance within the "grave community" by virtue of the location of their remains in the most elaborate niche of the tomb, usually in direct alignment with the doorway (see also Eck, 1987) but group activities had now assumed considerable importance.

Several aspects of this model can contribute towards our understanding of the emergence of visible poor burials during the Imperial period and the form that these took. During the late Republic funerary practices appear to have been largely dictated by social competition, the large tombs of Cestius and Eurysaces attesting to the desire for individuality and display. The majority of the urban population, unable to produce such elaborate structures, were probably all buried without any form of substantial grave monument or tomb, or perhaps only with a perishable marker to communicate basic biographical information and to signal the presence of human remains. Minimal commemoration was therefore probably the norm for all but the *very* wealthy. To put it simply, there are just not enough extant tombs, monuments or inscriptions to account for every member of the urban population during this, or indeed any other period, of Roman history. This does not necessarily indicate, however, that religious concerns for proper burial were not of great significance and undoubtedly the appropriate rituals were always closely observed. There was thus perhaps little external social differentiation between socio-economic levels below that of the elite/wealthy, with different status probably signalled through the presence of grave goods of varying quality and quantity and the activities of the funeral itself. The

pyre provided an ideal opportunity for elaborate display, along with the eulogy and funerary procession that preceded it.

Furthermore, the large individual tombs of the aristocracy and wealthy dictated the topography of urban cemeteries. These tombs were usually arranged along the edges of major highways in order to capitalise on the high levels of visibility and opportunities for communication and display that they offered; each structure was built within its own individually owned burial plot. In essence, the cemeteries of the late Republic were composed of a series of individual blocks placed side by side with strict regulations against the burial of remains in land belonging to another individual. There was possibly, therefore, little opportunity for modest burials of the lower classes and the rest of the population to be made directly alongside these monumental tombs. As monument typologies began to change during the Augustan period concentrated nuclei of *columbarium*-type mausolea began to emerge, such as those of the Porta Romana and Via Laurentina at Ostia, and later at Isola Sacra. Although laws concerning plot ownership remained the same, these new cemeteries provided an officially recognised cemetery *space* in which burial could occur on a more modest scale. Simple burials of the lower classes could be accommodated more easily within the confines of a cemetery such as this, which now existed as a concentrated entity rather than a linear arrangement of individual tombs or plots.

The ideological nature of the cemetery space had also changed; tombs were now the focus for social interaction and frequent post-funerary activities. These concerns no doubt also influenced the lower classes and may have heightened the desire of poorer members of the community to be seen to be associated with such occasions and actively partaking in certain traditions and rituals (Graham, 2005b). The provision of facilities for libations and religious rituals also began to increase in importance and prevalence at all socio-economic levels at this time and, as noted above, these devices are commonly found in association with humble burials. The increased importance of returning to the site of burial in order to provide offerings to the deceased and partake in commemorative ritual activities may also have affected the typology of the graves, with greater emphasis being placed on the physical protection of the remains in order to ensure that libations and offerings reached them.

That these modest burials began to appear in large numbers during the late first and early second century AD, some time after the initial change in tomb typology and cemetery topography, may also perhaps be attributed to emulative delay. Both Cannon (1989) and Miller (1985) have examined processes of emulation within archaeological contexts and have emphasised the importance of the presence of an established social hierarchy to the processes involved – something that has been well established for the ancient Roman urban community. There is also clear evidence within Roman funerary and commemorative practices for what Cannon

---

[136] Although, as before, the performance of these cannot be entirely ruled out – perhaps they simply left no recoverable trace.

(1989: 447) describes as the "cycles of mortuary elaboration and restraint" that signal emulative practices. The emergence of cappuccina, amphora burials and other modest grave types that were provided with devices to aid continued ritual activities may be part of this process. Emulation of the customs or material culture of social or economic superiors is not, however, a particularly rapid process; these elements must first become established as socially desirable norms. This delay may explain the slightly later appearance of humble lower class burials that were provided with protective covers and libation devices within urban cemeteries. It may also provide an explanation for the absence of these features at Pompeii which was destroyed before the emulative cycle could be completed and the lower classes could come to the fore in the cemetery environment.

* * * * *

These tentative suggestions for explaining the comparatively late appearance of recognisable lower class burial are purely speculative and many questions remain to be asked. Where and how, for example, were these individuals – most probably the vast majority of the population of any urban centre – buried during the late Republic when urban cemeteries were less concentrated and social competition amongst the wealthy was at its peak? Regardless of whether or not they erected funerary monuments of any type, or engaged in commemorative ritual practices, their remains still required some form of disposal Did the graves of earlier periods make use of similar materials within their structure and if so why have so few been archaeologically identified? These questions, and the absence of definitive archaeological evidence for the burial practices of the lower classes at this time, form another study but, in the context of this one, they go some way to explaining the emphasis that has been placed on the *puticuli* as a mechanism of disposal for the corpses of the poor. Since there is little evidence for these people in the cemeteries of urban areas, their remains must have been disposed of elsewhere and the *puticuli* have always provided a convenient solution. However, it has now been established that the *puticuli* were *not* used in this capacity and we must therefore now begin to look for the urban poor elsewhere in the archaeological record and recognise that their responses to death were not unlike the rest of society's.

All members of Roman urban society, rich or poor, were clearly influenced by the same social pressures, religious beliefs and fears, legal restrictions and the immense weight of tradition, in relation to funerary behaviour. Although substantially less material evidence exists for the responses of the poor to these demands, this section of the urban community should not be disregarded in discussions of funerary practice or society as a whole. The perpetuation of Lanciani's interpretation of the *puticuli* is a symptom of modern perceptions of the Roman urban free poor as a differentiated and anomalous social group who were somehow detached from the rest of the community and consequently immune to the forces at work within it. The poor were certainly economically distinguishable but, equally, they belonged to a society in which individuals and groups were eager to display, negotiate and legitimise their existence whilst strictly observing religious traditions and expressing their varied identities. Recognising that these individuals were influenced by the same concerns as the more privileged members of the community of which they were a part, allows us to begin our search for them in earnest and understand more thoroughly what it meant to live and die in ancient Rome.

BIBLIOGRAPHY

Primary sources

Ausonius (Translated by H. G. E. White 1919). *Ausonius in Two Volumes*. London: William Heinemann.

Cassius Dio (Translated by E. Cary 1969). *Dio's Roman History in Nine Volumes*. London: William Heinemann.

Cicero, De Legibus (Translated by C. W. Keyes 1966). *Cicero in Twenty Eight Volumes, vol. 16: De Re Publica; De Legibus*. London: William Heinemann.

Cicero, De Officiis (Translated by W. Miller 1913). *Cicero in Twenty Eight Volumes, vol. 21: De Officiis*. London: William Heinemann.

Cicero, In Pis. (Translated by N. H. Watts 1953). *Cicero in Twenty Eight Volumes, vol. 14: Pro T. Annio Milone; In L. Calpurnium Pisonem; Pro M. Aemilio Scauro; Pro M. Fonteio; Pro C. Rabirio Postumo; Pro M. Marcello; Pro Q. Ligario; Pro Rege Deiotaro*. London: William Heinemann.

Cicero, Q. Rosc (Translated by J. H. Freese 1930). *Cicero in Twenty Eight Volumes, vol. 6: Pro Publio Quinctio Roscio Comoedo; De Lege Agraria I, II, III*. London: William Heinemann.

Cicero, Tusculan Disputations (Translated by J. E. King 1945). *Cicero in Twenty Eight Volumes, vol. 18: Tusculan Disputations*. London: William Heinemann.

Digest (Translated by A. Watson 1985). *The Digest of Justinian. 4 Volumes*. Philadelphia: University of Pennsylvania Press.

Festus, (Translated by W. M. Lindsay 1913). *Sexti Pompei Festi, De verborum signifiatu quae supersunt cum Pauli Epitome*. Lipsiae: B. G. Teubrieri.

Fronto, (Translated by C. R. Haines 1919). *The Correspondence of Marcus Cornelius Fronto with Marcus Aurelius Antoninus, Lucius Verus, Antoninus Pius, and Various Friends*. London: William Heinemann.

Horace, Odes (Translated by C. E. Bennett 1927). *Horace, The Odes and Epodes*. London: William Heinemann.

Horace, Satires (translated by H. Rushton Fairclough 1929). *Horace, Satires, Epistles and Ars Poetica*. London: William Heinemann.

Instiues of Gaius (Translated by W. M. Gordon and O. F. Robinson 1988). *The Institutes of Gaius*. London: Duckworth.

Justinian's Institues (Translated by P. Birks and G. McLeod 1987). *Justinian's Institutes*. London: Duckworth.

Juvenal (Translated by G. G. Ramsay 1918). *Juvenal and Persius*. London: William Heinemann.

Livy (Translated by B. O. Foster 1922). *Livy in Thirteen Volumes, vol. 2: Books III and IV*. London: William Heinemann.

Lucretius (Translated by W. H. D. Rouse 1975). *De Rerum Natura*. London: William Heinemann.

Martial (Translated by D.R. Shackleton Bailey 1993). *Epigrams*. London: William Heinemann.

Ovid (Translated by J. G. Frazer 1989). *Ovid in Six Volumes, vol. 5: Fasti*. London: William Heinemann.

Petronius, Satyricon (Translated by W. H. D. Rouse and M. Heseltine 1969). *Petronius. Apocolocyntosis. Seneca*. London: William Heinemann.

Plautus, (Translated by P. Nixon 1916 – 1938). *Plautus in Five Volumes*. London: William Heinemann.

Pliny the Elder, Natural History (Translated by H. Rackham 1942). *Pliny, Natural History in Ten Volumes*. London: William Heinemann.

Pliny the Younger, Epistles (Translated by B. Radice 1969). *Pliny, Letters and Panegyrics*. London: William Heinemann.

Plutarch, Moralia (Translated by W. C. Helmbold 1939). *Plutarch's Moralia, vol. 6: 439a-523b*. London: William Heinemann.

Plutarch, Quaest. (Translated by F. C. Babbitt 1936). *Plutarch's Moralia, vol. 4: Roman Questions*. London: William Heinemann.

Plutarch, Rom. (Translated by B. Perrin 1914). *Plutarch's Lives in Eleven Volumes, vol. 1: Theseus and Romulus, Lycurgus and Numa, Solon and Publicola*. London: William Heinemann.

Polybius (Translated by W. R. Paton 1922). *Polybius, The Histories in Two Volumes.* London: William Heinemann.

Procopius, De Bello Gothico (Translated by H. B. Dewing 1914). *Procopius in Seven Volumes, vol. 1: History of the Wars, Books I and II.* London: William Heinemann.

Propertius (Translated by G. P. Goold 1990). *Propertius, Elegies.* London: Harvard University Press.

Sallust (Translated by J. C. Rolfe 1931). *Sallust.* London: William Heinemann.

Seneca (Translated by T. H. Corcoran 1972). *Seneca in Ten Volumes, vol. 10: Naturales Quaestiones.* London: William Heinemann.

Seneca, Ad. Helv. (Translated by J. W. Basore 1932). *Seneca in Ten Volumes, vol. 2: Moral Essays.* London: William Heinemann.

Seneca, Ep. (Translated by R. M. Gummere 1917 – 1925). *Seneca in Ten Volumes, vols. 4, 5 and 6: Ad Lucilium Epistulae Morales.* London: William Heinemann.

Suetonius (Translated by J. C. Rolfe 1951). *Suetonius in Two Volumes.* London: William Heinemann.

Tacitus, Annals (Translated by J. Jackson 1937). *Tacitus in Five Volumes, vol. 5: The Annals, books 13 – 16.* London: William Heinemann.

Twelve Tables (Translated by E. H. Warmington 1967). *Remains of Old Latin Part 3: Lucilius; The Twelve Tables.* London: Heinemann.

Varro, De Lingua Latina (Translated by R. G. Kent 1938). *Varro, On the Latin Language.* London: William Heinemann.

Vitruvius (Translated by F. Granger 1931). *Vitruvius, On Architecture.* London: William Heinemann.

Modern sources

Albertoni, M. 1983. 'La necropoli Esquilina arcaica e repubblicana.' In *Roma Capitale 1870 – 1911: L'archeologia in Roma Capitale tra sterro e scavo.* Venice: Marsilio Editori: 140 -155.

Alcock, J. P. 1980. 'Classical Religious Belief and Burial Practice in Roman Britain.' *Archaeological Journal* 137: 50 – 85.

André, J-M. 1980. 'La notion de *Pestilentia* à Rome: du tabou religieux à l'interprtrétation préscientifique.' *Latomus* 39: 3 – 16.

Angelucci, S., Baldassarre, I., Bragantini, I., Lauro, M. G., Mannucci, V., Mazzoleni, A., Morselli, C., and Taglietti, F. 1990. 'Sepolture e riti nella necropolis dell'Isola Sacra.' *Bollettino di Archeologia* 5-6: 49 – 113.

Arie, S. 2003. 'Necropolis proves headache for Vatican car park builders.' *The Guardian* Tuesday March 11th 2003.

Ariès, P. 1981. *The Hour of Our Death.* (Trans. H. Weaver).Middlesex: Penguin Books.

Ashby, T. 1910. 'The Columbarium of Pomponius Hylas. With drawings by F. G. Newton.' *Papers of the British School* 5: 463 – 471.

Astolfi, F. 1998. *I Colombari di Vigna Codini.* Collana archeologica supplemento di Forma Urbis 3. Rome: Sydaco Editrice.

Baldassarre, I., Bragantini, I., Dolciotti, A. M., Morselli, C., Taglietti, F., and Taloni, M. 1985. 'La necropolis dell'Isola Sacra. Campagne di scavo 1976 – 1979.' *Quaderni de 'La Ricerca Scientifica.'* 112: 261 – 302.

Baldassare, I. 1987. 'La Necropoli dell'Isola Sacra (Porto).' In H. von Hesberg and P. Zanker (eds.). *Römische Gräberstraßen. Selbstdarstellung – Status – Standard.* Munich: Bayerische Akademie der Wissenschaften: 125 – 138.

Baldassarre, I., Bragantini, I., Morselli, C., and Taglietti, F. 1996. *Necropoli di Porto. Isola Sacra.* Rome: Istituto Poligrafico E Zecca Dello Stato, Libreria Dello Stato.

Balsdon, J. P. V. D. 1969. *Life and Leisure in Ancient Rome.* London: The Bodley Head.

Barrett, J. C. 1993. 'Chronologies of remembrance: the interpretation of some Roman inscriptions.' *World Archaeology* 25 (2): 236 – 247.

Bassett, S., Dyer, C. and Holt, R. 1992. 'Introduction.' In S. Bassett (ed.). *Death in Towns – Urban Responses to the Dying and the Dead, 100 – 1600.* Leicester: Leicester University Press: 1 – 7.

Basso, M. 1986. *Guida della Necropoli Vaticana.* Rome: Fabbrica di S. Pietro in Vaticano.

Bellen, H. 1981. *Die Germanische Liebwache der Römischen Kaiser des Julisch-Klaudischen Hauses.* Wiesbaden: Franz Steiner Verlag.

Berger, A. 1953. *Encyclopedic Dictionary of Roman Law.* Philadelphia: The American Philological Society.

Bodel, J. 1994. 'Graveyards and Groves: A study of the *Lex Lucerina.' American Journal of Ancient History* 7: 1 – 133.

Bodel, J. 1999. 'Death on Display: Looking at Roman Funerals.' In B. Bergmann and C. Kondoleon (eds.). *The

Art of Ancient Spectacle. Studies in the History of Art 56, Washington DC: The National Gallery of Art: 258 – 81.

Bodel, J. 2000. 'Dealing with the dead: undertakers, executioners and potter's fields in ancient Rome.' In V. M. Hope and E. Marshall (eds.). *Death and Disease in the Ancient City*. London: Routledge: 104 – 127.

Bodel, J. 2004. 'The organisation of the funerary trade at Puteoli and Cumae.' *Libitina e dintorni : Libitina e i luci sepolcrali, le leges libitinariae campane, iura sepulcrorum: vecchie e nuove iscrizioni*. Atti dell'XI Rencontre franco-italienne sur l'épigraphie. Rome: Edizioni Quasar: 147 – 172.

Bonanno, A. 1983. 'Sculpture.' In M. Henig (ed.). *A Handbook of Roman Art. A Survey of the Visual Arts of the Roman World*. London: Phaidon: 66 – 96.

Bradley, K. R. 1991. *Discovering the Roman Family. Studies in Roman Social History*. Oxford: Oxford University Press.

Brandt, O. 1993. 'Recent research on the tomb of Eurysaces.' *Opuscula Romana* XIX.2: 13 – 17.

Braun, E. 1852. 'Colombario di vigna Codini.' *Bullettino dell'Istituto di Corrispondenza Archeologica* 1852: 81 – 83.

Brilliant, R. 1974. *Roman Art from the Republic to Constantine*. London: Phaidon.

Brion, M. 1960. *Pompeii and Herculaneum: The Glory and the Grief*. London: Elek Books Limited.

Brunt, P. A. 1966. 'The Roman Mob,' *Past and Present* 35: 3 – 27.

Brunt, P. A. 1980. 'Free labour and public works at Rome.' *Journal of Roman Studies* 70: 81 – 100.

Brunt, P. A. 1987*a*. *Italian Manpower 225BC – AD 14*. Oxford: Clarendon Press.

Brunt, P. A. 1987*b* 'Labour,' in J. Wacher (ed.). *The Roman World, Volume II*. London and New York: Routledge and Kegan Paul: 701 – 716.

Callender, M. H. 1965. *Roman Amphorae*. London: Oxford University Press.

Carbonara, A., Pellegrino, A., and Zaccagnini, R. 2001. 'Necropoli di Pianabella: vecchi e nuovi ritrovamenti.' In M. Heinzelmann, J. Ortalli, P. Fasold, and M. Witteyer (eds.). *Römischer Bestattungsbrauch und Beigabensitten in Rom, Norditalien und den Nordwestprovinzen von der späten Republik bis in die Kaiserzeit* (Culto dei morti e costume funerari romani. Roma, Italia settentrionale e province nord-occidentali dalla tarda Repubblica all'età imperiale). Rome: Deutches Archäologisches Institut Rom: 139 – 148.

Calza, G. 1940. La *Necropoli Del Porto Di Roma Nell' Isola Sacra*. Rome: La Libreria Dello Stato.

Cannon, A. 1989. 'The Historical Dimension in Mortuary Expressions of Status and Sentiment.' *Current Anthropology* 30 (4): 437 – 458.

Carcopino, J. 1964. *Daily Life in Ancient Rome: The People and the City at the Height of the Empire*. London: Penguin Books.

Carroll, M. 2001. *Romans, Celts and Germans: The German Provinces of Rome*. Stroud: Tempus.

Carroll, M. 2006. *Spirits of the Dead: Roman Funerary Commemoration in Western Europe*. Oxford: Oxford University Press.

Champlin, E. 1982. 'The *suburbium* of Rome,' *American Journal of Ancient History* 7: 97 – 117.

Cipollone, M. 2002. 'Gubbio (Perugia). Necropoli in loc. Vittorina. Campagne di scavo 1980 – 1982 (1). *Notizie degli Scavi di Antichità*. Serie IX, Volume XI-XII: 5 – 371.

Coarelli, F and Monti, P. G. (eds). 1998. *Fregellae 1: Le fonti, la storia, il territorio*. Rome: Quasar.

Coarelli, F. 1999. 'Puticuli.' In E. M. Steinby (ed). *Lexicon Topographicum Urbis Romae* 4. Rome: Edizioni Quasar: 173 – 174.

Coates-Stephens, R. 2004. *Porta Maggiore: Monument and Landscape. Archaeology and topography of the southern Esquiline from the Late Republican period to the present*. Bullettino della Commissione Archeologica Comunale di Roma, Supplementi 12. Rome: "L'Erma" Bretschneider.

Connerton, P. 1989. *How Societies Remember*. Cambridge: Cambridge University Press.

Cooley, A. 2000. 'The Life-cycle of Inscriptions.' In A. Cooley (ed.). *The Afterlife of Inscriptions: Revising, Rediscovering, Reinventing and Revitalising Ancient Inscriptions*. London: Institute of Classical Studies School of Advanced Study: 1 – 5.

Cowell, F. R. 1961. *Everyday Life in Ancient Rome*. London: B.T. Batsford Ltd.

Crawford, M. H. (ed.). 1996. *Roman Statutes (Volume 1 and 2)*. London: Institute of Classical Studies School of Advanced Study University of London.

Crook, J. A. 1967. *Law and Life of Rome*. London: Thames and Hudson.

Cumont, F. 1922. *After Life in Roman Paganism*. New York: Dover Publications, Inc.

D'Ambra, E. 1993. 'Introduction.' In E. D'Ambra (ed.). *Roman Art in Context. An Anthology*. New Jersey: Prentice Hall: 1 – 9.

D'Ambra, E. 2002. 'Acquiring an Ancestor: the Importance of Funerary Statuary among the Non-Elite Orders of Rome.' In J. M. Højte (ed.). *Images of Ancestors*. Denmark: Aarhus University Press: 223 – 246.

D'Ambrosio, A. and De Caro, S. 1987. 'La Necropoli Di Porta Nocera. Campagna di Scavo 1983.' In H. von Hesberg and P. Zanker (eds.). *Römische Gräberstraßen. Selbstdarstellung – Status – Standard*. Munich: Bayerische Akademie der Wissenschaften: 199 – 228.

Davies, G. 1977. 'Burial in Italy up to Augustus.' In R. Reece (ed.). *Burial in the Roman World*. London: CBA Research Report 22: 13 – 19.

De Filippis, M. 2001. 'Ricerche in sepolcreti suburbani tra Salaria e Nomentana.' In M. Heinzelmann, J. Ortalli, P. Fasold, and M. Witteyer (eds.). *Römischer Bestattungsbrauch und Beigabensitten in Rom, Norditalien und den Nordwestprovinzen von der späten Republik bis in die Kaiserzeit* (Culto dei morti e costume funerari romani. Roma, Italia settentrionale e province nord-occidentali dalla tarda Repubblica all'età imperiale). Rome: Deutches Archäologisches Institut Rom: 55 – 61.

De Spagnolis, M. 2001. 'Costumi funerari romani nello necropolis monumentale romana di Pizzone a Nocera Superiore.' In M. Heinzelmann, J. Ortalli, P. Fasold, and M. Witteyer (eds.). *Römischer Bestattungsbrauch und Beigabensitten in Rom, Norditalien und den Nordwestprovinzen von der späten Republik bis in die Kaiserzeit* (Culto dei morti e costume funerari romani. Roma, Italia settentrionale e province nord-occidentali dalla tarda Repubblica all'età imperiale). Rome: Deutches Archäologisches Institut Rom: 169 – 177.

DeLaine, J. 2000. 'Building the Eternal City: the construction industry of imperial Rome.' In J. Coulston and H. Dodge (eds.). *Ancient Rome: The Archaeology of the Eternal City*. Oxford: Oxford University School of Archaeology Monograph 54: 119 – 41.

Dixon, S. 1991. 'The Sentimental Ideal of the Roman Family.' In B. Rawson (ed.). *Marriage, Divorce, and Children in Ancient Rome*. Oxford: Clarendon Press: 99 – 113.

Dixon, S. 1992. *The Roman Family*. Baltimore and London: The Johns Hopkins University Press.

Dixon, S. 2001. The 'other' Romans and their family values.' In S. Dixon (ed.). *Childhood, Class and Kin in the Roman World*. London and New York: Routledge: 1 – 17.

Duncan-Jones, R. 1965. 'An Epigraphic Survey of Costs in Roman Italy.' *Papers of the British School at Rome* 20: 139 – 306.

Duncan-Jones, R. 1982. *The Economy of the Roman Empire – Quantitative Studies*. Cambridge: Cambridge University Press.

Duncan-Jones, R. P. 1996. 'The impact of the Antonine plague.' *Journal of Roman Archaeology* 9: 108 – 36.

Dupont, F. 1992. *Daily Life in Ancient Rome*. Translated by C. Woodall. Oxford: Blackwell Publishers.

Dyer, T. H. 1875. *Pompeii. Its History, Buildings, and Antiquities*. London: George Bell and Sons.

Dyson, S. L. 1992. *Community and Society in Roman Italy*. London: The Johns Hopkins University Press.

Eck, W. 1987. 'Römische Grabinschriften. Aussageabsicht und Aussagefähigkeit im funerären Kontext.' In H. von Hesberg and P. Zanker (eds.). *Römische Gräberstraßen. Selbstdarstellung – Status – Standard*. Munich: Bayerische Akademie der Wissenschaften: 61 – 83.

Eck, W. 2001. 'Grabgröße und sozialer Status.' In M. Heinzelmann, J. Ortalli, P. Fasold, and M. Witteyer (eds.). *Römischer Bestattungsbrauch und Beigabensitten in Rom, Norditalien und den Nordwestprovinzen von der späten Republik bis in die Kaiserzeit* (Culto dei morti e costume funerari romani. Roma, Italia settentrionale e province nord-occidentali dalla tarda Repubblica all'età imperiale). Rome: Deutches Archäologisches Institut Rom: 197 – 201.

Elsner, J. 1998. *Imperial Rome and Christian Triumph. The Art of the Roman Empire AD 100 – 450*. Oxford: Oxford University Press.

Falzone, S., Olivanti, P., and Pellegrino, A. 2001. 'La necropolis di Fralana (Acilia).' In M. Heinzelmann, J. Ortalli, P. Fasold, and M. Witteyer (eds.). *Römischer Bestattungsbrauch und Beigabensitten in Rom, Norditalien und den Nordwestprovinzen von der späten Republik bis in die Kaiserzeit* (Culto dei morti e costume funerari romani. Roma, Italia settentrionale e province nord-occidentali dalla tarda Repubblica all'età imperiale). Rome: Deutches Archäologisches Institut Rom: 127 - 137.

Finley, M. I. 1981. 'The Elderly in Classical Antiquity.' *Greece and Rome* 28: 156 – 171.

Floriani Squarciapino, M. F. 1958. *Scavi di Ostia III. Le Necropoli*. Rome: Istituto Poligrafic Dello Stato, Libreria Dello Stato.

Flower, H. I. 1996. *Ancestor Masks and Aristocratic Power in Roman Culture*. Oxford: Clarendon Press.

Flower, H. 2002. Were Women ever "Ancestors" in Republican Rome? In J. M. Højte (ed.). *Images of Ancestors*. Denmark: Aarhus University Press: 159 – 184.

Friedländer, L. 1909. *Roman Life and Manners under the Early Empire – Volumes II and III*. London: George Routledge and Sons Ltd.

Frier, B. W. 1977. 'The rental market in early Imperial Rome.' *Journal of Roman Studies* 67: 27 – 37.

Friggeri, R. 2001. *The Epigraphic Collection of the Museo Nazionale Romano at the Baths of Diocletian.* Milan: Electa.

Garnsey, P. 1983. 'Famine in Rome.' In P. Garnsey and C. R. Whittaker (eds.). *Trade and Famine in Classical Antiquity*. Cambridge: Cambridge Philological Society Supplementary volume no. 8: 56 – 65.

Garnsey, P. and Rathbone, D. 1985. 'The background to the grain law of Gaius Gracchus.' *Journal of Roman Studies* 75: 20 – 25.

Garnsey, P. and Saller, R. 1987. *The Roman Empire – Economy, Society and Culture*. London: Duckworth.

Garnsey, P. 1988. *Famine and Food Supply in the Graeco-Roman World.* Cambridge: Cambridge University Press.

Garnsey, P. 1998. *Cities, Peasants and Food in Classical Antiquity – Essays in Social and Economic History.* Cambridge: Cambridge University Press.

Garnsey, P. 1999. *Food and Society in Classical Antiquity*. Cambridge: Cambridge University Press.

George, M. 2005. Family Imagery and Family Values in Roman Italy. In M. George (ed.). *The Roman Family in the Empire. Rome, Italy, and Beyond*. Oxford: Oxford University Press: 37 – 66.

Gittings, C. 1984. *Death, Burial and the Individual in Early Modern England.* London: Croom Helm.

Golden, M. 1988. 'Did the ancients care when the children died?' *Greece and Rome* 35 (2): 152 – 163.

Graham, E-J. 2005a. 'Dining *al fresco* with the living and the dead in Roman Italy.' In M. Carroll, D. Hadley and H. Willmott (eds.). *Consuming Passions: Dining from Antiquity to the Eighteenth Century.* Stroud: Tempus: 49-65.

Graham, E-J. 2005b. 'The Quick and the Dead in the extra-urban landscape: the Roman cemetery at Ostia/Portus as a lived environment.' In B. Croxford et al. (eds.). *TRAC 2004. Proceedings of the Fourteenth Annual Theoretical Roman Archaeology Conference. Durham 2004*. Oxford: Oxbow Books: 133-143.

Graham, E-J. 2006. 'Discarding the destitute: Ancient and modern attitudes towards burial practices and memory preservation amongst the lower classes of Rome.' In B. Croxford *et al.* (eds). *TRAC 2005.*

Proceedings of the Fifteenth Annual Theoretical Roman Archaeology Conference. Birmingham 2005. Oxford: Oxbow Books: 57-72.

Graham, E-J. (forthcoming a). 'Fragments of the departed: Re-assessing *os resectum* and its role within funerary ritual practices in Republican Rome.'

Graham, E-J. (forthcoming b). 'From fragments to ancestors: re-defining *os resectum* and its role in rituals of purification and commemoration in Republican Rome.' In M. Carroll and D. Hadley (eds.) *Living through the dead: The material culture and social context of commemoration of the dead from Antiquity to the eighteenth century.*

Hands, A. R. 1968. *Charities and Social Aid in Greece and Rome*. London: Thames and Hudson.

Hanson, A. E. 1991. 'Ancient illiteracy.' In J. H. Humphrey (ed.). *Literacy in the Roman World.* Ann Arbor: Journal of Roman Archaeology, Supplementary Series no. 3: 159 – 198.

Harlow, M. and Laurence, R. 2002. *Growing Up and Growing Old in Ancient Rome. A Life Course Approach.* London: Routledge.

Harris, W. V. 1994. 'Child-Exposure in the Roman Empire.' *Journal of Roman Studies* 84: 1 – 22.

Harrison, J. F. C. 1990. *Late Victorian Britain 1875 – 1901*. London: Fontana Press.

Hasegawa, K. 2005. *The 'Familia Urbana' during the Early Empire*. Oxford: BAR International Series 1440.

Hawkins, D. 1990. 'The Black Death and the new London cemeteries of 1348.' *Antiquity* 64: 637 – 42.

Heinzelmann, M. 2001. 'Grabarchitektur, Bestattungsbrauch und Sozialstruktur – Zur Rolle der *familia.*' In M. Heinzelmann, J. Ortalli, P. Fasold, and M. Witteyer (eds.). *Römischer Bestattungsbrauch und Beigabensitten in Rom, Norditalien und den Nordwestprovinzen von der späten Republik bis in die Kaiserzeit* (Culto dei morti e costume funerari romani. Roma, Italia settentrionale e province nord-occidentali dalla tarda Repubblica all'età imperiale). Rome: Deutches Archäologisches Institut Rom: 179 – 191.

Hermansen, G. 1978. 'The population of Imperial Rome: The Regionaries.' *Historia* 27: 129 – 68.

Hope, V. 1997. 'A roof over the dead: communal tombs and family structure.' In R. Laurence and A. Wallace-Hadrill (eds.). *Domestic Space in the Roman World: Pompeii and Beyond*. Journal of Roman Archaeology Supplementary Series Number 22: 69 – 88.

Hope, V. M. 1998. 'Negotiating identity and status. The gladiators of Roman Nîmes.' In R. Laurence and J. Berry (eds.). *Cultural Identity in the Roman Empire*. London: Routledge: 179 – 195.

Hope, V. M. and Marshall, E. 2000. 'Introduction.' In V. M. Hope and E. Marshall (eds.). *Death and Disease in the Ancient City*. London: Routledge: 1 – 7.

Hope, V. M. 2000*a*. 'Contempt and respect: the treatment of the corpse in ancient Rome.' In V. M. Hope and E. Marshall (eds.). *Death and Disease in the Ancient City*. London: Routledge: 104 – 127.

Hope, V. 2000*b*. 'Inscription and Sculpture: the Construction of Identity in the Military Tombstones of Roman Mainz.' In G. J. Oliver (ed.). *The Epigraphy of Death. Studies in the History and Society of Greece and Rome*. Liverpool: Liverpool University Press: 155 – 185.

Hope, V. 2001. *Constructing Identity: The Roman Funerary Monuments of Aquileia, Mainz and Nimes*. Oxford: BAR International Series 960 (2001).

Hope, V. 2003. 'Remembering Rome: Memory, funerary monuments and the Roman soldier.' In H. Williams (ed.). *Archaeologies of Remembrance. Death and Memory in Past Societies*. New York: Kluwer Academic/Plenum Publishers: 113 – 140.

Hopkins, K. 1978. *Conquerors and Slaves – Sociological Studies in Roman History, Volume I*. Cambridge: Cambridge University Press.

Hopkins, K. 1983. *Death and Renewal – Sociological Studies in Roman History, Volume 2*. Cambridge: Cambridge University Press.

Hopkins, K. 1987. 'Graveyards for historians.' In F. Hinard (ed.). *La mort, les morts et l'au-dela dans le monde Romain*. Caen: Université de Caen: 113 – 126.

Horsfall, N. 2003. *The Culture of the Roman Plebs*. London: Duckworth.

Ireland, R. 1983. 'Epigraphy.' In M. Henig (ed.). *A Handbook of Roman Art. A Survey of the Visual Arts of the Roman World*. London: Phaidon: 220 – 233.

Jacobelli, L. 2003. *Gladiators at Pompeii*. Rome: "L'Erma" di Bretschneider.

Jackson, R. 1988. *Doctors and Diseases in the Roman Empire*. London: British Museum Publications.

Jackson Knight, W. F. 1970. *Elysion – On Ancient Greek and Roman Beliefs Concerning a Life after Death*. London: Rider and Company.

Jones, A. H. M. 1968. 'Slavery in the Ancient World,' in M. I. Finley (ed.). *Slavery in Classical Antiquity – Views and Controversies*. Cambridge: Heffer: 1 – 15.

Jongman, W. 2003. 'Slavery and the Growth of Rome. The transformation of Italy in the second and first centuries BCE.' In C. Edwards and G. Woolf (eds.). *Rome the Cosmopolis*. Cambridge: Cambridge University Press: 100 – 122.

Joshel, S. R. 1992. *Work, Identity and Legal Status at Rome. A Study of the Occupational Inscriptions*. Norman and London: University of Oklahoma Press.

Kampen, N. B. 1981. 'Biographical Narration and Roman Funerary Art.' *American Journal of Archaeology* 85: 47 – 58.

Kaser, M. 1965. *Roman Private Law*. Durban: Butterworths.

Keppie, L. 1991. *Understanding Roman Inscriptions*. London: B.T. Batsford Ltd.

King, M. 2000. 'Commemoration of Infants on Roman Funerary Inscriptions.' In G. J. Oliver (ed.). *The Epigraphy of Death. Studies in the History and Society of Greece and Rome*. Liverpool: Liverpool University Press: 117 – 154.

Kleiner, D. E. E. 1977. *Roman Group Portraiture: The Funerary Reliefs of the late Republic and early Empire*. New York: Garland Publishers.

Kleiner, D. E. E. 1987a. *Roman Imperial Funerary Altars with Portraits*. Rome: Giorgio Bretschneider Editore.

Kleiner, D. E. E. 1987b. 'Women and Family Life on Roman Imperial Funerary Altars.' *Latomus* 46: 545 – 554.

Kockel, V. 1983. *Die Grabbauten vor dem Herkulaner Tor in Pompeji*. Mainz.
Kockel, V. 1993. *Porträtreliefs Stadtrömischer Grabbauten*. Mainz: Zabern.

Koortbojian, M. 1996. '*In commemorationem mortuorum*: text and image along the 'streets of tombs'.' In J. Elsner (ed.). *Art and Text in Roman Culture*. Cambridge: Cambridge University Press: 210 – 233.

Kyle, D. G. 1998. *Spectacles of Death in Ancient Rome*. London: Routledge.

Lanciani, R. 1874. '*Puticoli*.' *Bullettino Della Commissione Archeologica Comunale Roma* 2: 42 – 53.

Lanciani, R. 1875. 'Le antichissime sepolture Esquiline.' *Bullettino della Commissione Archeologica Comunale Roma* 3: 41 – 55.

Lanciani, R. 1891. *Ancient Rome in the Light of Recent Discoveries*. London: Macmillan and Company.

Lanciani, R. 1892. *Pagan and Christian Rome*. Boston and New York: Houghton, Mifflin and Company.

Lanciani, R. 1893 – 1901 (1988). *Forma Urbis Romae.* Italy: Edizioni Quasar.

Lanciani, R. 1897/1967 *The Ruins and Excavations of Ancient Rome*. New York: Bell Publishing Company.

Lanciani, R. 1988. *Notes from Rome*. Edited by Anthony L. Cubberley. Rome: British School at Rome.

Lattimore, R. 1942. *Themes in Greek and Latin Epitaphs*. Urbana: The University of Illinois Press.

Lazer, E. 1997. 'Pompeii AD 79: A Population in Flux?' In S. E. Bon and R. Jones (eds.). *Sequence and Space in Pompeii*. Oxbow Monograph 77. Oxford: Oxbow Books: 102 – 120.

Le Gall, J. 1980-81. 'La sépulture des pauvres à Rome.' *Bulletin De La Société Rationale des Antiquaires de France* 1980 – 81: 148 – 152.

Lewis, N. and Reinhold, M. 1966*b*. *Roman Civilization: Sourcebook II: The Empire*. New York: Harper and Row.

Lindsay, H. 2000. 'Death-pollution and funerals in the city of Rome.' In V. M. Hope and E. Marshall (eds.). *Death and Disease in the Ancient City*. London: Routledge: 152 – 73.

Littman, R. J. and Littman, M. L. 1973. 'Galen and the Antonine Plague.' *American Journal of Philology* 94: 243 – 53.

Lo Cascio, E. 1994. 'The size of the Roman population: Beloch and the meaning of the Augustan census figures.' *Journal of Roman Studies* 84: 23 – 40.

Lord Amulree. 1973. 'Hygienic conditions in Ancient Rome and Modern London,' *Medical History* 17: 244 – 55.

Lorenzini, C. 2004. 'L'Esquilino.' In F. Coarelli (ed.). *Lexicon Topographicum Urbis Romae, Supplementum II.1: Gli Scavi di Roma 1878 – 1921.* Rome: Edizioni Quasar: 25 – 46.

McDonnell, M. 1999. 'Un ballo in maschera: processions, portraits, and emotions.' *Journal of Roman Archaeology* 12: 541 - 552.

McKinley, J. 1989. 'Cremations: expectations, methodologies and realities.' In C. A. Roberts, F. Lee, and J. Bintliff (eds.). *Burial Archaeology. Current Research, Methods and Developments*. Oxford: BAR British Series 211: 65 – 76.

McKinley, J. I. 2000. 'Phoenix rising; aspects of cremation in Roman Britain.' In J. Pearce, M. Millett, and M. Struck (eds.). *Burial. Society and Context in the Roman World.* Oxford: Oxbow Books: 38 – 44.

McWilliam, J. 2001. Children among the dead: the influence of urban life on the commemoration of children on tombstone inscriptions. In S. Dixon (ed.). *Childhood, Class and Kin in the Roman World*. London and New York: Routledge: 74 – 98.

MacMullen, R. 1974. *Roman Social Relations 50 BC to AD 284*. New Haven and London: Yale University Press.

Magalhaes, M. M. 1999. 'Le iscrizioni e l'area funeraria dei *Q*. e *C. Poppaei* a *Stabiae* (loc. Calcarella di Privati).' *Rivista di Studi Pompeiana* X: 224 – 235.

Maiuri, A. 1929. *Pompeii*. Rome: Istituto Geografico De Agostini.

Mancioli, D. 1997. *Il Sepolcro degli Scipioni*. Collana archeologica supplemento di Forma Urbis 12. Rome: Syndaco Editrice.

Mattingly, D. J. and Aldrete, G. S. 2000. 'The Feeding of Imperial Rome: The Mechanics of the Food Supply System.' In J. Coulston and H. Dodge (eds.). *Ancient Rome: The Archaeology of the Eternal City*. Oxford: Oxford University School of Archaeology Monograph 54: 142 – 65.

Mau, A. 1899. *Pompeii: Its Life and Art*. London and New York: The MacMillan Company.

Meiggs, R. 1973. *Roman Ostia*. Oxford: Clarendon Press.

Meiggs, R. 1982. *Trees and Timber in the Ancient Mediterranean World*. Oxford: Clarendon Press.

Messineo, G. 1995. Nuovi dati dalla necropoli tra Via Salaria e Via Pinciana. *Archeologia Laziale* XII, 1: 257 – 266.

Messineo, G. 1999. Dalle necropoli del suburbio settentrionale di Roma. In A. Pellegrino (ed). *Dalle Necropoli di Ostia. Riti ed Usi Funerari*. Rome: Soprintendenza Archeologica di Ostia: 110 – 127.

Messineo, G. 2001. 'Dalle necropolis del suburbia settentrionale di Roma.' In M. Heinzelmann, J. Ortalli, P. Fasold, and M. Witteyer (eds.). *Römischer Bestattungsbrauch und Beigabensitten in Rom, Norditalien und den Nordwestprovinzen von der späten Republik bis in die Kaiserzeit* (Culto dei morti e costume funerari romani. Roma, Italia settentrionale e province nord-occidentali dalla tarda Repubblica all'età imperiale). Rome: Deutches Archäologisches Institut Rom: 35 – 45.

Meyer, E. A. 1990. 'Explaining the Epigraphic Habit in the Roman Empire: The Evidence of Epitaphs.' *Journal of Roman Studies* 80: 74 – 96.

Middleton, J. H. 1892. *The Remains of Ancient Rome, vol II*. London and Edinburgh: Adam and Charles Black.

Miller, D. 1985. *Artefacts as categories: a study of ceramic variability in central India.* Cambridge: Cambridge University Press.

Millett, M. 1999. 'Wages.' In S. Hornblower and A. Spawforth (eds.). *The Oxford Classical Dictionary.* (Third Edition). Oxford: Oxford University Press: 1615.

Morley, N. 2005. The salubriousness of the Roman city. In H. King (ed.). *Health in Antiquity.* London: Routledge: 192 – 204.

Morris, I. 1992. *Death Ritual and Social Structure in Classical Antiquity.* Cambridge: Cambridge University Press.

Mossé, C. 1969. *The Ancient World at Work.* London: Chatto and Windus.

Nielsen, H. S. 1997. 'Interpreting Epithets in Roman Epitaphs.' In B. Rawson and P. Weaver (eds.). *The Roman Family in Italy – Status, Sentiment, Space.* Oxford: Oxford University Press: 169 – 204.

Nock, A. D. 1972. 'Cremation and burial in the Roman Empire.' In Z. Stewart (ed.). *A. D. Nock, Essays on Religion and the Ancient World (vol. I).* Oxford: Clarendon Press: 277 – 307.

Noy, D. 2000a. *Foreigners at Rome: Citizens and Strangers.* Swansea: Classical Press of Wales.

Noy, D. 2000b. '*Half-burnt on an emergency pyre*: Roman cremations which went wrong.' *Greece and Rome* 47 (2): 186 – 96.

Noy, D. 2000c. Building a Roman funerary pyre. *Antichthon* 34: 30 – 45.

Oates, W. J. 1934. 'The Population of Rome,' *Classical Philology* 29: 101 – 116.

Oliver, G. 2000. 'An Introduction to the Epigraphy of Death: Funerary Inscriptions as Evidence.' In G. J. Oliver (ed.). *The Epigraphy of Death. Studies in the History and Society of Greece and Rome.* Liverpool: Liverpool University Press: 1 – 23.

Ortalli, J. 1987. 'La via dei sepolcri di Sarsina. Aspetti funzionali, formali e sociali.' In H. von Hesberg and P. Zanker (eds.). *Römische Gräberstraßen. Selbstdarstellung – Status – Standard.* Munich: Bayerische Akademie der Wissenschaften: 155 – 184.

Ortalli, J. 2001. 'Il funerario della Cispadana romana. Rappresentazione e interiorità.' In M. Heinzelmann, J. Ortalli, P. Fasold, and M. Witteyer (eds.). *Römischer Bestattungsbrauch und Beigabensitten in Rom, Norditalien und den Nordwestprovinzen von der späten Republik bis in die Kaiserzeit* (Culto dei morti e costume funerari romani. Roma, Italia settentrionale e province nord-occidentali dalla tarda Repubblica all'età imperiale).

Rome: Deutches Archäologisches Institut Rom: 215 – 241.

Paoli, U. G. 1963. *Rome – Its People, Life and Customs.* London: Longmans. (Translated by R. D. Macnaghten).

Parker Pearson, M. 1999. *The Archaeology of Death and Burial.* Stroud: Sutton Publishing.

Patterson, J. R. 1992. 'Patronage, *collegia* and burial in Imperial Rome.' In S. Bassett (ed.). *Death in Towns – Urban Responses to the Dying and the Dead, 100 – 1600.* Leicester: Leicester University Press: 15 – 27.

Patterson, J. R. 2000a. 'Living and Dying in the City of Rome: houses and tombs.' In J. Coulston and H. Dodge (eds.). *Ancient Rome: The Archaeology of the Eternal City.* Oxford: Oxford University School of Archaeology Monograph 54: 257 – 89.

Patterson, J. R. 2000b. 'On the margins of the city of Rome.' In V. M. Hope and E. Marshall (eds.). *Death and Disease in the Ancient City.* London: Routledge: 85 – 103.

Pavia, C. 1996. *Il Colombario di Pomponius Hylas.* Collana archeologica supplemento di Forma Urbis 6. Rome: Sydaco Editrice.

Pellegrino, A. 1999. 'I riti funerari ed il culto dei morti.' In A. Pellegrino (ed.). *Dalle Necropoli di Ostia. Riti e Usi Funerari.* Rome: Soprintendenza Archeologica di Ostia: 7 – 25.

Polfer, M. 2000. 'Reconstructing funerary rituals: the evidence of *ustrina* and related archaeological structure.' In J. Pearce, M. Millett and M. Struck (eds.). *Burial, Society and Context in the Roman World.* Oxford: Oxbow Books: 30 – 37.

Prowse, T., Schwarcz, H. P., Saunders, S., Macchiarelli, R., and Bondioli, L. 2004. 'Isotopic paleodiet studies of skeletons from the Imperial Roman-age cemetery of Isola Sacra, Rome, Italy.' *Journal of Archaeological Science* 31: 259 – 272.

Price, S. 2000. 'Religions of Rome.' In J. Coulston and H. Dodge (eds.). *Ancient Rome: The Archaeology of the Eternal City.* Oxford: Oxford University School of Archaeology Monograph 54: 290 – 305.

Purcell, N. 1987. 'Tomb and Suburb.' In H. von Hesberg and P. Zanker (eds.). *Römische Gräberstraßen. Selbstdarstellung – Status – Standard.* Munich: Bayerische Akademie der Wissenschaften: 25 – 41.

Purcell, N. 1994. 'The City of Rome and the *Plebs Urbana* in the Late Republic.' In J.A. Crook, A. Lintott and E. Rawson (eds.). *The Cambridge Ancient History – Volume IX: The Last Age of the Roman Republic 146 – 43BC* (2nd Edition). Cambridge: Cambridge University Press: 644 – 88.

Purcell, N. 1996. 'The Roman Garden as a Domestic Building.' In I. M. Barton (ed.). *Roman Domestic Buildings*. Exeter: University of Exeter Press: 121 – 151.

Rawson, B. 1966. 'Family Life among the Lower Classes at Rome in the first two centuries of the Empire,' *Classical Philology* 61: 71 – 83.

Rawson, B. (ed.). 1992. *The Family in Ancient Rome – New Perspectives*. London: Routledge.

Richardson, L. 1992. *A New Topographical Dictionary of Ancient Rome*. Baltimore: The Johns Hopkins Press.

Robinson, D. J. 1997. 'The Social Texture of Pompeii.' In S. E. Bon and R. Jones (eds.). *Sequence and Space in Pompeii*. Oxbow Monograph 77. Oxford: Oxbow Books: 135 – 144.

Robinson, O. 1975. 'The Roman Laws on Burials and Burial Grounds.' *The Irish Jurist* 10: 175 – 186.

Robinson, O. F. 1992. *Ancient Rome – City Planning and Administration*. London: Routledge.

Rose, H. J. 1923. 'Nocturnal Funerals in Rome.' *The Classical Quarterly* XVII: 191 – 94.

Ross Taylor, L. 1961. 'Freedmen and freeborn in the epitaphs of Imperial Rome.' *American Journal of Philology* 82(2): 113 – 132.

Rushforth, G. 1915. 'Funeral lights in Roman sepulchral monuments.' *Journal of Roman Studies* 5: 149 – 64.

Ryberg, I. S. 1940. *An Archaeological Record of Rome from the Seventh to the Second Century BC*. London: Christophers.

Salmon, E. T. 1974. *A History of the Roman World - 30 BC to AD 138*. London: Methuen and Co. Ltd.

Saller, R. 1997. 'Roman Kinship: Structure and Sentiment.' In B. Rawson and P. Weaver (eds.). *The Roman Family in Italy – Status, Sentiment, Space*. Oxford: Oxford University Press: 7 – 34.

Saller, R. P. and Shaw, B. D. 1984. 'Tombstones and Roman Family Relations in the Principate: Civilians, Soldiers and Slaves.' *Journal of Roman Studies* 74: 124 – 56.

Sartorio, G. P. 1983. 'L'Esquilino nell'antichità.' In *Roma Capitale 1870 – 1911: L'archeologia in Roma Capitale tra sterro e scavo*. Venice: Marsilio Editori: 101 – 105.

Scheidel, W. 2003. 'Germs for Rome.' In C. Edwards and G. Woolf (eds.). *Rome the Cosmopolis*. Cambridge: Cambridge University Press: 158 – 176.

Schoen, R. P. 2000. *Pro Facultatibus vel Dignitate Defuncti. Uitvaartritueel, Sociale Status en Regelgeving in Rome (100 v.Chr-300 n. Chr)*. Germany: Walburg Press.

Scobie, A. 1986. 'Slums, Sanitation, and Mortality in the Roman World.' *Klio* 68 (2): 399 – 433.

Scullard, H. H. 1981. *Festivals and Ceremonies of the Roman Republic*. London: Thames and Hudson.

Sertà, C.A. 2001-2002. 'La ordination epigrafica sulle stele pompeiane di T. Suedius Clemens fuori Porta Nocera e fuori Porta Marina.' *Rivista di Studi Pompeiani* XII-XIII: 228 – 237.

Shaw, B. D. 1996. 'Seasons of Death: Aspects of Mortality in Imperial Rome.' *Journal of Roman Studies* 86: 100 – 38.

Shelton, J. 1988. *As the Romans Did: A Source Book in Roman Social History*. Oxford: Oxford University Press.

Simon-Hiernard, D. 1987. 'Remarques sur le rite de l'*os resectum*.' *Nécropoles à incineration du Haut-Empire*. Table ronde de Lyon 1986. Rapports archéologiques préliminaires de la région Rhone-Alpes: 93 – 95.

Spera, L. and Mineo, S. 2004. *Via Appia I. Da Roma a 'Bovillae'*. Rome: Istituto Poligrafico e Zecca dello Stato.

Stambaugh, J. E. 1988. *The Ancient Roman City*. Baltimore and London: The Johns Hopkins University Press.

Steinby, E. M. 1987. 'La necropolis della Via Triumphalis pianificazione generale e tipologia dei monumenti funerari.' In H. von Hesberg and P. Zanker (eds.). *Römische Gräberstraßen. Selbstdarstellung – Status – Standard*. Munich: Bayerische Akademie der Wissenschaften: 85 – 110.

Storey, G. R. 1997. 'The population of ancient Rome.' *Antiquity* 71: 966 – 78.

Taglietti, F. 2001. 'Ancora su incinerazione e inhumazione: la necropolis dell'Isola Sacra.' In M. Heinzelmann, J. Ortalli, P. Fasold, and M. Witteyer (eds.). *Römischer Bestattungsbrauch und Beigabensitten in Rom, Norditalien und den Nordwestprovinzen von der späten Republik bis in die Kaiserzeit* (Culto dei morti e costume funerari romani. Roma, Italia settentrionale e province nord-occidentali dalla tarda Repubblica all'età imperiale). Rome: Deutches Archäologisches Institut Rom: 149 – 158.

Taloni, M. 1973. 'La necropoli dell'Esquilino.' In *Roma Medio Repubblicana. Aspetti culturali di Roma e del Lazio nei secoli IV e III A.C.* Rome: 188 – 196.

Tarlow, S. 1999. *Bereavement and Commemoration. An Archaeology of Mortality*. Oxford: Blackwell Publishers.

Tarlow, S. 2000. 'Emotion in Archaeology.' *Current Anthropology* 41: 713 – 746.

Thomas, E. 1899. *Roman Life Under the Caesars.* London: T. Fisher Unwin.

Thylander, H. 1952. *Inscriptions du Port d'Ostie (1): Texte.* Lund: C. W. K. Gleerup.

Toynbee, J. and Ward Perkins, J. 1956. *The Shrine of St. Peter and the Vatican Excavations.* London: Longmans, Green and Co.

Toynbee, J. M. C. 1971. *Death and Burial in the Roman World.* London: Thames and Hudson.

Treggiari, S. 1969. *Roman Freedmen During the Late Republic.* Oxford: Clarendon Press.

Treggiari, S. 1996. 'Social status and social legislation,' in A. K. Bowman, E. Champlin and A. Lintott (eds.). *The Cambridge Ancient History, Volume X: The Augustan Empire, 43 BC – AD 69.* Cambridge: Cambridge University Press: 873 – 904.

Tupman, C. M. L. 2002. *An Archaeological and Historical Study of the 'Columbaria' of Rome.* Unpublished MA Dissertation. Department of Classics, Kings College London.

Tupman, C. 2005. 'The *cupae* of Iberia in their monumental contexts: a study of the relationship between social status and commemoration with barrel-shaped and semi-cylindrical tombstones.' In B. Croxford et al. (eds.). *TRAC 2004. Proceedings of the Fourteenth Annual Theoretical Roman Archaeology Conference. Durham 2004.* Oxford: Oxbow Books: 119 – 132.

Veyne, P. 1987. 'The Roman Empire.' In P. Veyne (ed.). *A History of Private Life. 1. From Pagan Rome to Byzantium.* (Translated by Arthur Goldhammer). Massachusetts and London: The Bellknap Press of Harvard University Press: 5 – 233.

Veyne, P. 1990. *Bread and Circuses – Historical Sociology and Political Pluralism.* London: Penguin Books.

Vlahogiannis, N. 1998. Disabling Bodies. In D. Montserrat (ed.). *Changing Bodies, Changing Meanings. Studies on the Human Body in Antiquity.* London and New York: Routledge: 13 – 36.

Vout, C. 2003. 'Embracing Egypt.' In C. Edwards and G. Woolf (eds.). *Rome the Cosmopolis.* Cambridge: Cambridge University Press: 177 – 202.

Walker, S. 1985. *Memorials to the Roman Dead.* London: British Museum Publications Ltd.

Warde Fowler, W. 1908. *Social Life at Rome in the Age of Cicero.* London: MacMillan and Co. Ltd.

Weaver, P. 2001. Reconstructing lower-class Roman families.' In S. Dixon (ed.). *Childhood, Class and Kin in the Roman World.* London and New York: Routledge: 101 – 114.

Wells, C. 1960. 'A study of cremation.' *Antiquity* 34: 29 – 37.

Whaley, J. 1981. 'Symbolism for the Survivors: The Disposal of the Dead in Hamburg in the Late Seventeenth and Eighteenth Centuries.' In J. Whaley (ed.). *Mirrors of Mortality. Studies in the Social History of Death.* London: Europa Publications Limited: 80 – 105.

Whittaker, C. R. 1993. 'The poor in the city of Rome.' In C. R. Whittaker, *Land, City and Trade in the Roman Empire (Vol. VII).* Aldershot: 1 – 25.

Wilkinson, L. P. 1975. *The Roman Experience.* London: Paul Elek.

Williams, H. 2003. 'Introduction: The Archaeology of Death, Memory and Material Culture.' In H. Williams (ed.). *Archaeologies of Remembrance. Death and Memory in Past Societies.* New York: Kluwer Academic/Plenum Publishers: 1 – 24.

Williams, H. 2004. 'Ephemeral monuments and social memory in early Roman Britain.' In B. Croxford, H. Eckardt, J. Meade, and J. Weekes (eds.). *TRAC 2003. Proceedings of the Thirteenth Annual Theoretical Roman Archaeology Conference. Leicester 2003.* Oxford: Oxbow Books: 51 – 61.

Wiseman, T. P. 1998. 'A Stroll on the Rampart.' *Horti Romani. Atti del Convegno Internazionale BCAR Supplement* 6: 13 – 22.

Wolff, H. J. 1951. *Roman Law – An Historical Introduction.* Norman: University of Oklahoma Press.

Woolf, G. 1996. 'Monumental writing and the expansion of Roman society in the Early Empire.' *Journal of Roman Studies* 86: 22 – 39.

Yavetz, Z. 1958. 'The Living Conditions of the Urban Plebs in Republican Rome.' *Latomus* 17: 200 – 517.

Zander, P. 2003. *The Vatican Necropolis. Roma Sacra. Soprintendenza per i Beni Artistici e Storici di Roma. Guide to the Churches in the Eternal City.* Itinerary 25 (April 2003). Rome: Elio de Rosa Editore.

Zanker, P. 1975. 'Grabreliefs römischer Freigelassener.' *Jahrbuch des Deutschen Archäologischen Instituts* 90: 267 – 315.

www.ingramcontent.com/pod-product-compliance
Lightning Source LLC
Chambersburg PA
CBHW061000030426

42334CB00033B/3305